# CAMBRIDGE
## UNIVERSITY PRESS

# Business

## for Cambridge International AS & A Level

### EXAM PREPARATION AND PRACTICE

Kelly Chalk & Mark Johnson

# Contents

Digital questions for all chapters can be found online at Cambridge GO. For more information on how to access and use your digital resource, please see inside the front cover.

# > How to use this series

This suite of resources supports students and teachers following the Cambridge International AS & A Level Business syllabus (9609). All of the components in the series are designed to work together and help students develop the necessary knowledge and skills for this subject. With clear language and style, they are designed for international students.

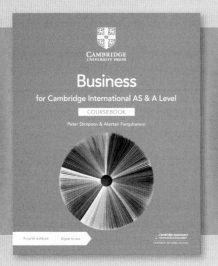

The coursebook is designed for students to use in class with guidance from the teacher. It offers complete coverage of the Cambridge International AS & A Level Business syllabus (9609). Each chapter contains an in-depth explanation of Business concepts with a variety of activities, case studies and images to engage students, help them make real-world connections and develop their analysis and evaluation skills.

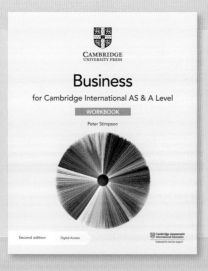

The workbook provides further practice of all the skills presented in the coursebook and is ideal for use in class or as homework. It provides engaging exercises, worked examples and opportunities for students to evaluate sample answers so they can put into practice what they have learnt.

The teacher's resource is the foundation of this series because it offers inspiring ideas about how to teach this course. You'll find everything you need to deliver the course in here, including teaching guidance, lesson plans, suggestions for differentiation, assessment and language support, answers and extra materials, including downloadable worksheets and PPTs.

The Exam Preparation and Practice provides dedicated support for students in preparing for their final assessments. Hundreds of questions in the book and accompanying digital resource will help students to check that they understand, and can recall, syllabus concepts. To help students to show what they know in an exam context, a specially developed checklist of exam skills with corresponding questions, and past paper question practice, is also included. Self-assessment and reflection features support students to identify any areas that need further practice. This resource should be used alongside the coursebook, throughout the course of study, so students can most effectively increase their confidence and readiness for their exams.

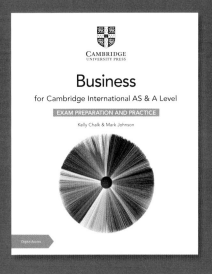

# > How to use this book

This book will help you to check that you **know** the content of the syllabus and practise how to **show** this understanding in an exam. It will also help you be cognitively prepared and in the **flow**, ready for your exam. Research has shown that it is important that you do all three of these things, so we have designed the Know, Show, Flow approach to help you prepare effectively for exams.

| Know | You will need to consolidate and then recall a lot of syllabus content. |

| Show | You should demonstrate your knowledge in the context of a Cambridge exam. |

| Flow | You should be cognitively engaged and ready to learn. This means reducing test anxiety. |

## Exam skills checklist

| Category | Exam skill |
|---|---|
| Understanding the question | Recognise different question types |
| | Understand command words |
| | Mark scheme awareness |
| Providing an appropriate response | Understand connections between concepts |
| | Keep to time |
| | Know what a good answer looks like |
| Developing supportive behaviours | Reflect on progress |
| | Manage test anxiety |

This **Exam skills checklist** helps you to develop the awareness, behaviours and habits that will support you when revising and preparing for your exams. For more exam skills advice, including understanding command words and managing your time effectively, please go to the **Exam skills chapter**.

# Know

The full syllabus content of your *Cambridge International AS & A Level Business* course is covered in your Cambridge coursebook. This book will provide you with different types of questions to support you as you prepare for your exams. You will answer **Knowledge recall questions** that are designed to make sure you understand a topic, and **Recall and connect questions** to help you recall past learning and connect different concepts.

## KNOWLEDGE FOCUS

Knowledge Focus boxes summarise the topics that you will answer questions on in each chapter of this book. You can refer back to your Cambridge coursebook to remind yourself of the full detail of the syllabus content.

You will find **Knowledge recall questions** to make sure you understand a topic, and **Recall and connect questions** to help you recall past learning and connect different concepts. It is recommended that you answer the Knowledge recall questions just after you have covered the relevant topic in class, and then return to them at a later point to check you have properly understood the content.

### Knowledge recall question

Testing yourself is a good way to check that your understanding is secure. These questions will help you to recall the core knowledge you have acquired during your course, and highlight any areas where you may need more practice. They are indicated with a blue bar with a gap, at the side of the page. We recommend that you answer the Knowledge recall questions just after you have covered the relevant topic in class, and then return to them at a later point to check you have properly understood the content.

## « RECALL AND CONNECT «

To consolidate your learning, you need to test your memory frequently. These questions will test that you remember what you learned in previous chapters, in addition to what you are practising in the current chapter.

## UNDERSTAND THESE TERMS

These list the important vocabulary that you should understand for each chapter. Definitions are provided in the glossary of your Cambridge coursebook.

## Show

Exam questions test specific knowledge, skills and understanding. You need to be prepared so that you have the best opportunity to show what you know in the time you have during the exam. In addition to practising recall of the syllabus content, it is important to build your exam skills throughout the year.

### EXAM SKILLS FOCUS

This feature outlines the exam skills you will practise in each chapter, alongside the Knowledge focus. They are drawn from the core set of eight exam skills, listed in the exam skills checklist. You will practise specific exam skills, such as understanding command words, within each chapter. More general exam skills, such as managing text anxiety, are covered in the Exam skills chapter.

### Exam skills question

These questions will help you to develop your exam skills and demonstrate your understanding. To help you become familiar with exam-style questioning, many of these questions follow the style and use the language of real exam questions, and have allocated marks. They are indicated with a solid red bar at the side of the page.

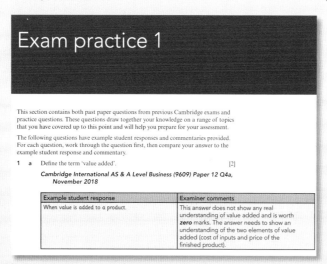

Looking at sample answers to past paper questions helps you to understand what to aim for.

The **Exam practice** sections in this resource contain example student responses and examiner-style commentary showing how the answer could be improved (both written by the authors).

# Flow

Preparing for exams can be stressful. One of the approaches recommended by educational psychologists to help with this stress is to improve behaviours around exam preparation. This involves testing yourself in manageable chunks, accompanied by self-evaluation. You should avoid cramming and build in more preparation time. This book is structured to help you do this.

Increasing your ability to recognise the signs of exam-related stress and working through some techniques for how to cope with it will help to make your exam preparation manageable.

## REFLECTION

This feature asks you to think about the approach that you take to your exam preparation, and how you might improve this in the future. Reflecting on how you plan, monitor and evaluate your revision and preparation will help you to do your best in your exams.

## SELF-ASSESSMENT CHECKLIST

These checklists return to the Learning intentions from your coursebook, as well as the Exam skills focus boxes from each chapter. Checking in on how confident you feel in each of these areas will help you to focus your exam preparation. The 'Show it' prompts will allow you to test your rating. You should revisit any areas that you rate 'Needs more work' or 'Almost there'.

| Now I can | Show it | Needs more work | Almost there | Confident to move on |
|-----------|---------|-----------------|--------------|----------------------|
|           |         |                 |              |                      |

Increasing your ability to recognise the signs of exam-related stress and working through some techniques for how to cope with it will help to make your exam preparation manageable. The **Exam skills chapter** will support you with this.

## Digital support

**Extra self-assessment knowledge questions** for all chapters can be found online at Cambridge GO. For more information on how to access and use your digital resource, please see inside the front cover.

You will find **Answers** for all of the questions in the book on the 'supporting resources' area of the Cambridge GO platform.

### Multiple choice questions

These ask you to select the correct answer to a question from four options. These are auto-marked and feedback is provided.

### Flip card questions

These present a question on one screen, and suggested answers on the reverse.

## Syllabus assessment objectives for *Cambridge International AS & A Level Business*

You should be familiar with the Assessment Objectives from the syllabus, as the examiner will be looking for evidence of these requirements in your responses and allocating marks accordingly.

The assessment objectives for this syllabus are:

| Assessment objective | AS Level weighting | A Level weighting |
|---|---|---|
| AO1: Knowledge and Understanding | 30% | 25% |
| AO2: Application | 30% | 25% |
| AO3: Analysis | 20% | 25% |
| AO4: Evaluation | 20% | 25% |

# Exam skills

by Lucy Parsons

## What's the point of this book?

Most students make one really basic mistake when they're preparing for exams. What is it? It's focusing far too much on learning 'stuff' – that's facts, figures, ideas, information – and not nearly enough time practising exam skills.

The students who work really, really hard but are disappointed with their results are nearly always students who focus on memorising stuff. They think to themselves, 'I'll do practice papers once I've revised everything.' The trouble is, they start doing practice papers too late to really develop and improve how they communicate what they know.

What could they do differently?

When your final exam script is assessed, it should contain specific language, information and thinking skills in your answers. If you read a question in an exam and you have no idea what you need to do to give a good answer, the likelihood is that your answer won't be as brilliant as it could be. That means your grade won't reflect the hard work you've put into revising for the exam.

There are different types of questions used in exams to assess different skills. You need to know how to recognise these question types and understand what you need to show in your answers.

So, how do you understand what to do in each question type?

That's what this book is all about. But first a little background.

### Meet Benjamin Bloom

The psychologist Benjamin Bloom developed a way of classifying and valuing different skills we use when we learn, such as analysis and recalling information. We call these thinking skills. It's known as Bloom's Taxonomy and it's what most exam questions are based around.

If you understand Bloom's Taxonomy, you can understand what any type of question requires you to do. So, what does it look like?

**Bloom's Taxonomy of thinking skills**

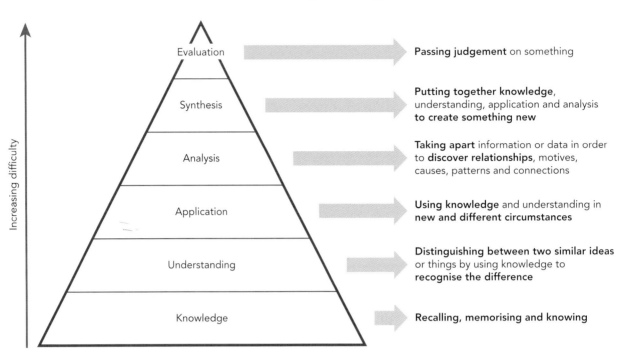

The key things to take away from this diagram are:

- Knowledge and understanding are known as lower-level thinking skills. They are less difficult than the other thinking skills. Exam questions that just test you on what you know are usually worth the lowest number of marks.

- All the other thinking skills are worth higher numbers of marks in exam questions. These questions need you to have some foundational knowledge and understanding but are far more about how you think than what you know. They involve:

  - Taking what you know and using it in unfamiliar situations (application).
  - Going deeper into information to discover relationships, motives, causes, patterns and connections (analysis).
  - Using what you know and think to create something new – whether that's an essay, long-answer exam question a solution to a maths problem, or a piece of art (synthesis).
  - Assessing the value of something, e.g. the reliability of the results of a scientific experiment (evaluation).

In this introductory chapter, you'll be shown how to develop the skills that enable you to communicate what you know and how you think. This will help you achieve to the best of your abilities. In the rest of the book, you'll have a chance to practise these exam skills by understanding how questions work and understanding what you need to show in your answers.

Every time you pick up this book and do a few questions, you're getting closer to achieving your dream results. So, let's get started!

# Exam preparation and revision skills

## What is revision?

If you think about it, the word 'revision' has two parts to it:

- re – which means 'again'
- vision – which is about seeing.

So, revision is literally about 'seeing again'. This means you're looking at something that you've already learned.

Typically, a teacher will teach you something in class. You may then do some questions on it, write about it in some way, or even do a presentation. You might then have an end-of-topic test sometime later. To prepare for this test, you need to 'look again' or revise what you were originally taught.

## Step 1: Making knowledge stick

Every time you come back to something you've learned or revised you're improving your understanding and memory of that particular piece of knowledge. This is called **spaced retrieval**. This is how human memory works. If you don't use a piece of knowledge by recalling it, you lose it.

Everything we learn has to be physically stored in our brains by creating neural connections – joining brain cells together. The more often we 'retrieve' or recall a particular piece of knowledge, the stronger the neural connection gets. It's like lifting weights – the more often you lift, the stronger you get.

However, if you don't use a piece of knowledge for a long time, your brain wants to recycle the brain cells and use them for another purpose. The neural connections get weaker until they finally break, and the memory has gone. This is why it's really important to return often to things that you've learned in the past.

Great ways of doing this in your revision include:

- Testing yourself using flip cards – use the ones available in the digital resources for this book.
- Testing yourself (or getting someone else to test you) using questions you've created about the topic.
- Checking your recall of previous topics by answering the Recall and connect questions in this book.
- Blurting – writing everything you can remember about a topic on a piece of paper in one colour. Then, checking what you missed out and filling it in with another colour. You can do this over and over again until you feel confident that you remember everything.
- Answering practice questions – use the ones in this book.
- Getting a good night's sleep to help consolidate your learning.

> **The importance of sleep and creating long-term memory**
>
> When you go to sleep at night, your brain goes through an important process of taking information from your short-term memory and storing it in your long-term memory.
>
> This means that getting a good night's sleep is a very important part of revision. If you don't get enough good quality sleep, you'll actually be making your revision much, much harder.

## Step 2: Developing your exam skills

We've already talked about the importance of exam skills, and how many students neglect them because they're worried about covering all the knowledge.

What actually works best is developing your exam skills at the same time as learning the knowledge.

What does this look like in your studies?

- Learning something at school and your teacher setting you questions from this book or from past papers. This tests your recall as well as developing your exam skills.

- Choosing a topic to revise, learning the content and then choosing some questions from this book to test yourself at the same time as developing your exam skills.

The reason why practising your exam skills is so important is that it helps you to get good at communicating what you know and what you think. The more often you do that, the more fluent you'll become in showing what you know in your answers.

## Step 3: Getting feedback

The final step is to get feedback on your work.

If you're testing yourself, the feedback is what you got wrong or what you forgot. This means you then need to go back to those things to remind yourself or improve your understanding. Then, you can test yourself again and get more feedback. You can also congratulate yourself for the things you got right – it's important to celebrate any success, big or small.

If you're doing past paper questions or the practice questions in this book, you will need to mark your work. Marking your work is one of the most important things you can do to improve. It's possible to make significant improvements in your marks in a very short space of time when you start marking your work.

Why is marking your own work so powerful? It's because it teaches you to identify the strengths and weaknesses of your own work. When you look at the mark scheme and see how it's structured, you will understand what is needed in your answers to get the results you want.

This doesn't just apply to the knowledge you demonstrate in your answers. It also applies to the language you use and whether it's appropriately subject-specific, the structure of your answer, how you present it on the page and many other factors. Understanding, practising and improving on these things are transformative for your results.

## The most important thing about revision

The most important way to make your revision successful is to make it active.

Sometimes, students say they're revising when they sit staring at their textbook or notes for hours at a time. However, this is a really ineffective way to revise because it's passive. In order to make knowledge and skills stick, you need to be doing something like the suggestions in the following diagram. That's why testing yourself and pushing yourself to answer questions that test higher-level thinking skills are so effective. At times, you might actually be able to feel the physical changes happening in your brain as you develop this new knowledge and these new skills. That doesn't come about without effort.

The important thing to remember is that while active revision feels much more like hard work than passive revision, you don't actually need to do nearly as much of it. That's because you remember knowledge and skills when you use active revision. When you use passive revision, it is much, much harder for the knowledge and skills to stick in your memory.

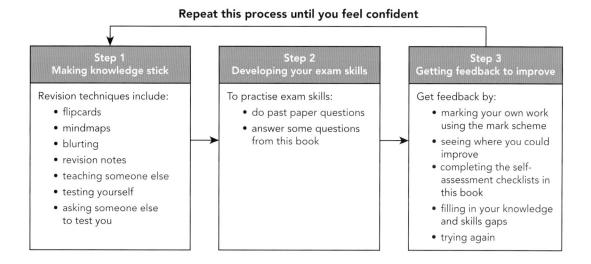

**Repeat this process until you feel confident**

| Step 1
Making knowledge stick | Step 2
Developing your exam skills | Step 3
Getting feedback to improve |
|---|---|---|
| Revision techniques include:<br>• flipcards<br>• mindmaps<br>• blurting<br>• revision notes<br>• teaching someone else<br>• testing yourself<br>• asking someone else to test you | To practise exam skills:<br>• do past paper questions<br>• answer some questions from this book | Get feedback by:<br>• marking your own work using the mark scheme<br>• seeing where you could improve<br>• completing the self-assessment checklists in this book<br>• filling in your knowledge and skills gaps<br>• trying again |

## How to improve your exam skills

This book helps you to improve in eight different areas of exam skills, which are divided across three categories. These skills are highlighted in this book in the Exam skills focus at the start of each chapter and developed throughout the book using targeted questions, advice and reflections.

1 **Understand the questions: what are you being asked to do?**

- Know your question types.

- Understand command words.

- Work with mark scheme awareness.

2 **How to answer questions brilliantly**

- Understand connections between concepts.

- Keep to time.

- Know what a good answer looks like.

3 **Give yourself the best chance of success**

- Reflection on progress.

- How to manage test anxiety.

## Understand the questions: what are you being asked to do?

### Know your question types

In any exam, there will be a range of different question types. These different question types will test different types of thinking skills from Bloom's Taxonomy.

It is very important that you learn to recognise different question types. If you do lots of past papers, over time you will begin to recognise the structure of the paper for each of your subjects. You will know which types of questions may come first and which ones are more likely to come at the end of the paper. You can also complete past paper questions in the Exam practice sections in this book for additional practice.

You will also recognise the differences between questions worth a lower number of marks and questions worth more marks. The key differences are:

- how much you will need to write in your answer

- how sophisticated your answer needs to be in terms of the detail you give and the depth of thinking you show.

### Types of questions

#### 1 Multiple-choice questions

Multiple-choice questions are generally worth smaller numbers of marks. You will be given several possible answers to the question, and you will have to work out which one is correct using your knowledge and skills.

There is a chance of you getting the right answer with multiple-choice questions even if you don't know the answer. This is why you must **always give an answer for multiple-choice questions** as it means there is a chance you will earn the mark.

Multiple-choice questions are often harder than they appear. The possible answers can be very similar to each other. This means you must be confident in how you work out answers or have a high level of understanding to tell the difference between the possible answers.

Being confident in your subject knowledge and doing lots of practice multiple-choice questions will set you up for success. Use the resources in this book and the accompanying online resources to build your confidence.

This example of a multiple-choice question is worth one mark. You can see that all the answers have one part in common with at least one other answer. For example, palisade cells is included in three of the possible answers. That's why you have to really know the detail of your content knowledge to do well with multiple-choice questions.

**Which two types of cells are found in plant leaves?**

- A   Palisade mesophyll and stomata
- B   Palisade mesophyll and root hair
- C   Stomata and chloroplast
- D   Chloroplast and palisade mesophyll

## 2 Questions requiring longer-form answers

Questions requiring longer-form answers need you to write out your answer yourself.

With these questions, take careful note of how many marks are available and how much space you've been given for your answer. These two things will give you a good idea about how much you should say and how much time you should spend on the question.

A rough rule to follow is to write one sentence, or make one point, for each mark that is available. You will get better and better at these longer form questions the more you practise them.

In this example of a history question, you can see it is worth four marks. It is not asking for an explanation, just for you to list Lloyd George's aims. Therefore, you need to make four correct points in order to get full marks.

What were Lloyd George's aims during negotiations leading to the
Treaty of Versailles?                                                                                    [4]

## 3 Essay questions

Essay questions are the longest questions you will be asked to answer in an exam. They examine the higher-order thinking skills from Bloom's Taxonomy such as analysis, synthesis and evaluation.

To do well in essay questions, you need to talk about what you know, giving your opinion, comparing one concept or example to another, and evaluating your own ideas or the ones you're discussing in your answer.

You also need to have a strong structure and logical argument that guides the reader through your thought process. This usually means having an introduction, some main body paragraphs that discuss one point at a time, and a conclusion.

Essay questions are usually level-marked. This means that you don't get one mark per point you make. Instead, you're given marks for the quality of the ideas you're sharing as well as how well you present those ideas through the subject-specific language you use and the structure of your essay.

Practising essays and becoming familiar with the mark scheme is the only way to get really good at them.

## Understand command words

### What are command words?

Command words are the most important words in every exam question. This is because command words tell you what you need to do in your answer. Do you remember Bloom's Taxonomy? Command words tell you which thinking skill you need to demonstrate in the answer to each question.

Two very common command words are **describe** and **explain**.

When you see the command word describe in a question, you're being asked to show lower-order thinking skills like knowledge and understanding. The question will either be worth fewer marks, or you will need to make more points if it is worth more marks.

The command word explain is asking you to show higher-order thinking skills. When you see the command word explain, you need to be able to say how or why something happens.

You need to understand all of the relevant command words for the subjects you are taking. Ask your teacher where to find them if you are not sure. It's best not to try to memorise the list of command words, but to become familiar with what command words are asking for by doing lots of practice questions and marking your own work.

## How to work with command words

When you first see an exam question, read it through once. Then, read it through again and identify the command word(s). Underline the command word(s) to make it clear to yourself which they are every time you refer back to the question.

You may also want to identify the **content** words in the question and underline them with a different colour. Content words tell you which area of knowledge you need to draw on to answer the question.

In this example, command words are shown in red and content words in blue:

**1  a**  Explain **four** reasons why governments might support business start-ups.  [8]

> *Adapted from Cambridge IGCSE Business Studies (0450)*
> *Q1a Paper 21 June 2022*

Marking your own work using the mark scheme will help you get even better at understanding command words and knowing how to give good answers for each.

## Work with mark scheme awareness

The most transformative thing that any student can do to improve their marks is to work with mark schemes. This means using mark schemes to mark your own work at every opportunity.

Many students are very nervous about marking their own work as they do not feel experienced or qualified enough. However, being brave enough to try to mark your own work and taking the time to get good at it will improve your marks hugely.

### Why marking your own work makes such a big difference

Marking your own work can help you to improve your answers in the following ways:

**1  Answering the question**

Having a deep and detailed understanding of what is required by the question enables you to answer the question more clearly and more accurately.

It can also help you to give the required information using fewer words and in less time, as you can avoid including unrelated points or topics in your answer.

**2  Using subject-specific vocabulary**

Every subject has subject-specific vocabulary. This includes technical terms for objects or concepts in a subject, such as mitosis and meiosis in biology. It also includes how you talk about the subject, using appropriate vocabulary that may differ from everyday language. For example, in any science subject you might be asked to describe the trend on a graph.

Your answer could say it 'goes up fast' or your answer could say it 'increases rapidly'. You would not get marks for saying 'it goes up fast', but you would for saying it 'increases rapidly'. This is the difference between everyday language and formal, scientific language.

When you answer lots of practice questions, you become fluent in the language specific to your subject.

## 3    Knowing how much to write

It's very common for students to either write too much or too little to answer questions. Becoming familiar with the mark schemes for many different questions will help you to gain a better understanding of how much you need to write in order to get a good mark.

## 4    Structuring your answer

There are often clues in questions about how to structure your answer. However, mark schemes give you an even stronger idea of the structure you should use in your answers.

For example, if a question says:

'Describe and explain two reasons why…'

You can give a clear answer by:

- Describing reason 1

- Explaining reason 1

- Describing reason 2

- Explaining reason 2

Having a very clear structure will also make it easier to identify where you have earned marks. This means that you're more likely to be awarded the number of marks you deserve.

## 5    Keeping to time

Answering the question, using subject-specific vocabulary, knowing how much to write and giving a clear structure to your answer will all help you to keep to time in an exam. You will not waste time by writing too much for any answer. Therefore, you will have sufficient time to give a good answer to every question.

# How to answer exam questions brilliantly

## Understand connections between concepts

One of the higher-level thinking skills in Bloom's Taxonomy is **synthesis**. Synthesis means making connections between different areas of knowledge. You may have heard about synoptic links. Making synoptic links is the same as showing the thinking skill of synthesis.

Exam questions that ask you to show your synthesis skills are usually worth the highest number of marks on an exam paper. To write good answers to these questions, you need to spend time thinking about the links between the topics you've studied **before** you arrive in your exam. A great way of doing this is using mind maps.

## How to create a mind map

To create a mind map:

1  Use a large piece of paper and several different coloured pens.

2  Write the name of your subject in the middle. Then, write the key topic areas evenly spaced around the edge, each with a different colour.

3  Then, around each topic area, start to write the detail of what you can remember. If you find something that is connected with something you studied in another topic, you can draw a line linking the two things together.

This is a good way of practising your retrieval of information as well as linking topics together.

## Answering synoptic exam questions

You will recognise questions that require you to make links between concepts because they have a higher number of marks. You will have practised them using this book and the accompanying resources.

To answer a synoptic exam question:

1  **Identify the command and content words.** You are more likely to find command words like **discuss** and **explain** in these questions. They might also have phrases like 'the connection between'.

2  **Make a plan for your answer.** It is worth taking a short amount of time to think about what you're going to write in your answer. Think carefully about what information you're going to put in, the links between the different pieces of information and how you're going to structure your answer to make your ideas clear.

3  **Use linking words and phrases in your answer.** For example, 'therefore', 'because', due to', 'since' or 'this means that'.

Here is an example of an English Literature exam question that requires you to make synoptic links in your answer.

1  Discuss Carol Ann Duffy's exploration of childhood in her poetry. Refer to two poems in your answer.                                    [25]

Content words are shown in blue; command words are shown in red.

This question is asking you to explore the theme of childhood in Duffy's poetry. You need to choose two of her poems to refer to in your answer. This means you need a good knowledge of her poetry, and to be familiar with her exploration of childhood, so that you can easily select two poems that will give you plenty to say in your answer.

## Keep to time

Managing your time in exams is really important. Some students do not achieve to the best of their abilities because they run out of time to answer all the questions. However, if you manage your time well, you will be able to attempt every question on the exam paper.

### Why is it important to attempt all the questions on an exam paper?

If you attempt every question on a paper, you have the best chance of achieving the highest mark you are capable of.

Students who manage their time poorly in exams will often spend far too long on some questions and not even attempt others. Most students are unlikely to get full marks on many questions, but you will get zero marks for the questions you don't answer. You can maximise your marks by giving an answer to every question.

### Minutes per mark

The most important way to keep to time is knowing how many minutes you can spend on each mark.

For example, if your exam paper has 90 marks available and you have 90 minutes, you know there is 1 mark per minute.

Therefore, if you have a 5 mark question, you should spend five minutes on it.

Sometimes, you can give a good answer in less time than you have budgeted using the minutes per mark technique. If this happens, you will have more time to spend on questions that use higher-order thinking skills, or more time on checking your work.

### How to get faster at answering exam questions

The best way to get faster at answering exam questions is to do lots of practice. You should practise each question type that will be in your exam, marking your own work, so that you know precisely how that question works and what is required by the question. Use the questions in this book to get better and better at answering each question type.

Use the 'Slow, Slow, Quick' technique to get faster.

Take your time answering questions when you first start practising them. You may answer them with the support of the textbook, your notes or the mark scheme. These things will support you with your content knowledge, the language you use in your answer and the structure of your answer.

Every time you practise this question type, you will get more confident and faster. You will become experienced with this question type, so that it is easy for you to recall the subject knowledge and write it down using the correct language and a good structure.

Calculating marks per minute

Use this calculation to work out how long you have for each mark:

Total time in the exam / Number of marks available = Minutes per mark

Calculate how long you have for a question worth more than one mark like this:

Minutes per mark × Marks available for this question = Number of minutes for this question

What about time to check your work?

It is a very good idea to check your work at the end of an exam. You need to work out if this is feasible with the minutes per mark available to you. If you're always rushing to finish the questions, you shouldn't budget checking time. However, if you usually have time to spare, then you can budget checking time.

To include checking time in your minutes per mark calculation:

(Total time in the exam – Checking time) / Number of marks available = Minutes per mark

## Know what a good answer looks like

It is much easier to give a good answer if you know what a good answer looks like.

Use these methods to know what a good answer looks like.

1  **Sample answers** – you can find sample answers in these places:

   - from your teacher

   - written by your friends or other members of your class

   - in this book.

2  **Look at mark schemes** – mark schemes are full of information about what you should include in your answers. Get familiar with mark schemes to gain a better understanding of the type of things a good answer would contain.

3  **Feedback from your teacher** – if you are finding it difficult to improve your exam skills for a particular type of question, ask your teacher for detailed feedback. You should also look at their comments on your work in detail.

# Give yourself the best chance of success

## Reflection on progress

As you prepare for your exam, it's important to reflect on your progress. Taking time to think about what you're doing well and what could be improved brings more focus to your revision. Reflecting on progress also helps you to continuously improve your knowledge and exam skills.

## How do you reflect on progress?

Use the 'reflection' feature in this book to help you reflect on your progress during your exam preparation. Then, at the end of each revision session, take a few minutes to think about the following:

| | What went well? What would you do the same next time? | What didn't go well? What would you do differently next time? |
|---|---|---|
| Your subject knowledge | | |
| How you revised your subject knowledge – did you use active retrieval techniques? | | |
| Your use of subject-specific and academic language | | |
| Understanding the question by identifying command words and content words | | |
| Giving a clear structure to your answer | | |
| Keeping to time | | |
| Marking your own work | | |

Remember to check for silly mistakes – things like missing the units out after you carefully calculated your answer.

Use the mark scheme to mark your own work. Every time you mark your own work, you will be recognising the good and bad aspects of your work, so that you can progressively give better answers over time.

### When do you need to come back to this topic or skill?

Earlier in this section of the book, we talked about revision skills and the importance of spaced retrieval. When you reflect on your progress, you need to think about how soon you need to return to the topic or skill you've just been focusing on.

For example, if you were really disappointed with your subject knowledge, it would be a good idea to do some more active retrieval and practice questions on this topic tomorrow. However, if you did really well you can feel confident you know this topic and come back to it again in three weeks' or a month's time.

The same goes for exam skills. If you were disappointed with how you answered the question, you should look at some sample answers and try this type of question again soon. However, if you did well, you can move on to other types of exam questions.

## Improving your memory of subject knowledge

Sometimes students slip back into using passive revision techniques, such as only reading the coursebook or their notes, rather than also using active revision techniques, like testing themselves using flip cards or blurting.

You can avoid this mistake by observing how well your learning is working as you revise. You should be thinking to yourself, 'Am I remembering this? Am I understanding this? Is this revision working?'

If the answer to any of those questions is 'no', then you need to change what you're doing to revise this particular topic. For example, if you don't understand, you could look up your topic in a different textbook in the school library to see if a different explanation helps. Or you could see if you can find a video online that brings the idea to life.

## You are in control

When you're studying for exams it's easy to think that your teachers are in charge. However, you have to remember that you are studying for your exams and the results you get will be yours and no one else's.

That means you have to take responsibility for all your exam preparation. You have the power to change how you're preparing if what you're doing isn't working. You also have control over what you revise and when: you can make sure you focus on your weaker topics and skills to improve your achievement in the subject.

This isn't always easy to do. Sometimes you have to find an inner ability that you have not used before. But, if you are determined enough to do well, you can find what it takes to focus, improve and keep going.

## What is test anxiety?

Do you get worried or anxious about exams? Does your worry or anxiety impact how well you do in tests and exams?

Test anxiety is part of your natural stress response.

The stress response evolved in animals and humans many thousands of years ago to help keep them alive. Let's look at an example.

## The stress response in the wild

Imagine an impala grazing in the grasslands of east Africa. It's happily and calmly eating grass in its herd in what we would call the parasympathetic state of rest and repair.

Then the impala sees a lion. The impala suddenly panics because its life is in danger. This state of panic is also known as the stressed or sympathetic state. The sympathetic state presents itself in three forms: flight, fight and freeze.

The impala starts to run away from the lion. Running away is known as the flight stress response.

The impala might not be fast enough to run away from the lion. The lion catches it but has a loose grip. The impala struggles to try to get away. This struggle is the fight stress response.

However, the lion gets an even stronger grip on the impala. Now the only chance of the impala surviving is playing dead. The impala goes limp, its heart rate and breathing slows. This is called the freeze stress response. The lion believes that it has killed the impala so it drops the impala to the ground. Now the impala can switch back into the flight response and run away.

The impala is now safe – the different stages of the stress response have saved its life.

## What has the impala got to do with your exams?

When you feel test anxiety, you have the same physiological stress responses as an impala being hunted by a lion. Unfortunately, the human nervous system cannot tell the difference between a life-threatening situation, such as being chased by a lion, and the stress of taking an exam.

If you understand how the stress response works in the human nervous system, you will be able to learn techniques to reduce test anxiety.

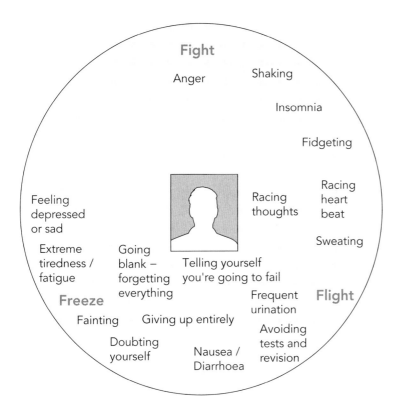

## The role of the vagus nerve in test anxiety

The vagus nerve is the part of your nervous system that determines your stress response. Vagus means 'wandering' in Latin, so the vagus nerve is also known as the 'wandering nerve'. The vagus nerve wanders from your brain, down each side of your body, to nearly all your organs, including your lungs, heart, kidneys, liver, digestive system and bladder.

If you are in a stressful situation, like an exam, your vagus nerve sends a message to all these different organs to activate their stress response. Here are some common examples:

- **Heart** beats faster.
- **Kidneys** produce more adrenaline so that you can run, making you fidgety and distracted.
- **Digestive system** and **bladder** want to eliminate all waste products so that energy can be used for fight or flight.

If you want to feel calmer about your revision and exams, you need to do two things to help you move into the parasympathetic, or rest and repair, state:

**1** Work with your vagus nerve to send messages of safety through your body.

**2** Change your perception of the test so that you see it as safe and not dangerous.

## How to cope with test anxiety

### 1 Be well prepared

Good preparation is the most important part of managing test anxiety. The better your preparation, the more confident you will be. If you are confident, you will not perceive the test or exam as dangerous, so the sympathetic nervous system responses of fight, flight and freeze are less likely to happen.

This book is all about helping you to be well prepared and building your confidence in your knowledge and ability to answer exam questions well. Working through the knowledge recall questions will help you to become more confident in your knowledge of the subject. The practice questions and exam skills questions will help you to become more confident in communicating your knowledge in an exam.

To be well prepared, look at the advice in the rest of this chapter and use it as you work through the questions in this book.

### 2 Work with your vagus nerve

The easiest way to work with your vagus nerve to tell it that you're in a safe situation is through your breathing. This means breathing deeply into the bottom of your lungs, so that your stomach expands, and then breathing out for longer than you breathed in. You can do this with counting.

Breathe in deeply, expanding your abdomen, for the count of four; breathe out drawing your navel back towards your spine for the count of five, six or seven. Repeat this at least three times. However, you can do it for as long as it takes for you to feel calm.

The important thing is that you breathe out for longer than you breathe in. This is because when you breathe in, your heart rate increases slightly, and when you breathe out, your heart rate decreases slightly. If you're spending more time breathing out overall, you will be decreasing your heart rate over time.

### 3 Feel it

Anxiety is an uncomfortable, difficult thing to feel. That means that many people try to run away from anxious feelings. However, this means the stress just gets stored in your body for you to feel later.

When you feel anxious, follow these four steps:

**1** Pause.

**2** Place one hand on your heart and one hand on your stomach.

**3** Notice what you're feeling.

**4** Stay with your feelings.

What you will find is that if you are willing to experience what you feel for a minute or two, the feeling of anxiety will usually pass very quickly.

4    Write or talk it out

If your thoughts are moving very quickly, it is often better to get them out of your mind and on to paper.

You could take a few minutes to write down everything that comes through your mind, then rip up your paper and throw it away. If you don't like writing, you can speak aloud alone or to someone you trust.

## Other ways to break the stress cycle

| Exercise and movement | Being friendly | Laughter |
|---|---|---|
| • Run or walk.<br>• Dance.<br>• Lift weights.<br>• Yoga.<br>Anything that involves moving your body is helpful. | • Chat to someone in your study break.<br>• Talk to the cashier when you buy your lunch. | • Watch or listen to a funny show on TV or online.<br>• Talk with someone who makes you laugh.<br>• Look at photos of fun times. |
| Have a hug | Releasing emotions | Creativity |
| • Hug a friend or relative.<br>• Cuddle a pet e.g. a cat.<br>Hug for 20 seconds or until you feel calm and relaxed. | It is healthy to release negative or sad emotions.<br><br>Crying is often a quick way to get rid of these difficult feelings so if you feel like you need to cry, allow it. | • Paint, draw or sketch.<br>• Sew, knit or crochet.<br>• Cook, build something. |

If you have long-term symptoms of anxiety, it is important to tell someone you trust and ask for help.

# Your perfect revision session

**1 Intention**

### What do you want to achieve in this revision session?
- Choose an area of knowledge or an exam skill that you want to focus on.
- Choose some questions from this book that focus on this knowledge area or skill.
- Gather any other resources you will need e.g. pen, paper, flashcards, coursebook.

**2 Focus**

### Set your focus for the session
- Remove distractions from your study area e.g. leave your phone in another room.
- Write down on a piece of paper or sticky note the knowledge area or skill you're intending to focus on.
- Close your eyes and take three deep breaths, with the exhale longer than the inhale.

**3 Revision**

### Revise your knowledge and understanding
- To improve your knowledge and understanding of the topic, use your coursebook, notes or flashcards, including active learning techniques.
- To improve your exam skills, look at previous answers, teacher feedback, mark schemes, sample answers or examiners' reports.

**4 Practice**

### Answer practice questions
- Use the questions in this book, or in the additional online resources, to practise your exam skills.
- If the exam is soon, do this in timed conditions without the support of the coursebook or your notes.
- If the exam is a long time away, you can use your notes and resources to help you.

**5 Feedback**

### Mark your answers
- Use mark schemes to mark your work.
- Reflect on what you've done well and what you could do to improve next time.

**6 Next steps**

### What have you learned about your progress from this revision session? What do you need to do next?
- What did you do well? Feel good about these things, and know it's safe to set these things aside for a while.
- What do you need to work on? How are you going to improve? Make a plan to get better at the things you didn't do well or didn't know.

**7 Rest**

### Take a break
- Do something completely different to rest: get up, move or do something creative or practical.
- Remember that rest is an important part of studying, as it gives your brain a chance to integrate your learning.

# 1 Enterprise

An important part of understanding exam questions is knowing what command words are and what they mean. Command words are particular words that tell you how to answer a specific exam question or complete an assessment task. Knowing how to identify command words, and recognising what they mean, will help you interpret what you are being asked to do and will give you clear guidance on how to answer the question to best show your knowledge.

In this chapter, you will be introduced to the command words 'define' and 'explain' and will start to gain an understanding of the skills required to answer these question types. To define means to give precise meaning. To explain means to set out purposes or reasons, to make the relationships between things evident or to provide the why and/or how of a matter and support it with relevant evidence.

# 1.1 The nature of business activity

## UNDERSTAND THESE TERMS

- entrepreneur
- factors of production

1  Businesses operate in a constantly changing world. The main purpose of business activity, however, remains the same. What do businesses do? You should try to use examples in your answer.

2  All businesses need resources to be able to operate and produce goods and services. Using examples, outline the **four** factors of production.

3
> ### Totally Totes (TT)
>
> Jin founded TT six years ago as a sole trader. She wanted to create a range of tote bags that could be personalised based on the needs of the customer.

The concept of adding value is an important one for firms.

a  Explain what is meant by the term 'adding value'.

b  Outline **three** ways Jin could add value to the tote bags she sells.

## UNDERSTAND THIS TERM

- opportunity cost

4  Businesses can fail for many reasons; some are within their control, others are not. Explain **two** reasons why a business might fail. Try and find some real-world reasons why businesses have failed to include in your answer.

# 1.2 The role of entrepreneurs and intrapreneurs

1  An entrepreneur is someone who takes a risk and sets up a business. Entrepreneurship is the activity of this person and their business. To set up a business is not an easy task. Outline **three** barriers to entrepreneurship.

2  If an entrepreneur can create and develop a successful business, this can have some significant benefits for the economy in which they are operating.

a  Explain **three** benefits to an economy from a successful business enterprise.

b  Which of the benefits you have mentioned in Question 2(a) do you think is the most important to an economy? Explain your answer.

It is vital to acknowledge the importance of the short-answer questions on an exam paper. These may not seem as though they matter much as they only contain a small number of marks, but they do provide an opportunity to demonstrate your knowledge of a topic. They may stem from a case study, but you may not always be required to make reference to the case study in your answer. If there is reference to the name of the business, a person or the product from the case study in the question, then you will need to use the case study in your answer.

**3**

> **Ridley's Cakes (RC)**
>
> Ridley has always been a keen baker. She works full-time as an accountant but also runs a small part-time business in which she is commissioned to make celebration cakes, which she has been doing for nearly a year. Ridley prefers to make wedding cakes, which can take anywhere from one to two days each. Ridley can be described as an entrepreneur who sells consumer products.

    **a**    Define the term 'consumer products'.                 [2]

For a question using the command word 'define', you are expected to give a precise meaning of the key term in the question. To approach this type of question you should ensure that your answer explains the meaning of the key term or concept clearly. You should try to include any key vocabulary that might be related to that particular concept, ensuring that the answer explains the meaning of the term clearly. As there are two marks available, you are expected to try to include two relevant aspects in your definition. In this case you would need to show an understanding of 'consumer' and of 'product'. For example:

> Consumer products are the *physical and tangible* goods that are sold to customers that are *not intended for resale*.

Try to answer the next question yourself.

    **b**    Define the term 'entrepreneur'.                     [2]

The next question uses the command word 'explain'. For a question using the command word 'explain', you are required to set out purposes or reasons / make the relationships between things evident / provide the why and/or how of a matter and support with relevant evidence. You should aim to give more detail than 'define' by, for example, applying your answer to the case study context. This may require you to provide more than one relevant point, or one relevant point and a contextual example. There are usually three marks available for an explain question, so you need to get used to answering these and understanding what they are asking you for.

Knowing when to use the case study in your answer is really important. The general rule is that if the name of the business appears in the question, then you should use some references to the case study in your answer. Question 3(c) has a mark allocation of [3], which means it needs a developed reason for the marks to be awarded. It also uses the name of the business in the question, so case study evidence needs to be used (this can be seen in bold in the answer), for example:

c    Explain **one** reason why new businesses such as Ridley Cakes may fail.    [3]

One reason why a new business such as Ridley Cakes may fail is because the owner **Ridley** *may not have the time to fully commit to the running of the business* as **she has a full-time job**, meaning that she *may not be able to manage her finances correctly and may become unable to pay her bills.*

Try to answer the next question yourself.

d    Explain **one** quality of a successful entrepreneur.    [3]

> **REFLECTION**
>
> How did you feel answering these questions? Did you understand how the marks were allocated? How can you improve your confidence with short-answer questions?

> **UNDERSTAND THIS TERM**
> * intrapreneur

# 1.3 Purpose and key elements of business plans

1

> **KM Clothing (KMC)**
>
> Kamala and Miya are two sisters with a passion for designer fashion for babies and young children. They set up their business as a partnership seven years ago, with each partner taking an equal role in the running of the business. They own one shop which has been making a profit over the years. They are considering developing their product range to include a collection of baby footwear and are currently creating a business plan for this idea.

Kamala and Miya are considering developing their product range to include a collection of baby footwear and are currently creating a business plan for this idea. What is the purpose of a business plan?

2    State and explain **four** elements that might be found in KMC's business plan for the new range of baby footwear.

> **REFLECTION**
>
> How confident are you that you understand the purpose of business activity? What can you do to improve your understanding of this concept?

> **UNDERSTAND THIS TERM**
> * business plan

## SELF-ASSESSMENT CHECKLIST

Let's revisit the Knowledge focus and Exam skills focus for this chapter.
Decide how confident you are with each statement.

| Now I can | Show it | Needs more work | Almost there | Confident to move on |
|---|---|---|---|---|
| analyse what business activity involves | Write a short report of no more than 300 words about a firm and explain how its business activity operates. | | | |
| recognise that the 'economic problem' requires choices to be made which always result in an opportunity cost | Give an example of an opportunity cost that might be faced by a firm. | | | |
| analyse the meaning and importance of adding value | Explain what would happen to a firm if it did not add value to its materials. | | | |
| recognise the key characteristics of successful entrepreneurs and intrapreneurs | Research a well-known entrepreneur and write a short report of no more than 300 words detailing the characteristics they display that have allowed them to be successful. | | | |
| evaluate the importance of enterprise, entrepreneurs and intrapreneurs to a country's economy | Outline the benefits and costs to a country of supporting entrepreneurs. | | | |
| analyse the meaning, purpose, benefits and limitations of business plans | Look at your answer to Question 1 in Section 1.3 and explain which of these elements is the most important in a business plan for a new firm. Justify your answer. | | | |
| be introduced to the command words 'define' and 'explain' | Explain the purpose of a short answer question. | | | |
| gain an awareness of the skills required to answer questions using the command words 'define' and 'explain' | Explain how the marks for a three-mark explain question are allocated. | | | |

# 2 Business structure

## KNOWLEDGE FOCUS

You will answer questions on:

**2.1** Economic sectors

**2.2** Business ownership

## EXAM SKILLS FOCUS

In this chapter you will:

- be introduced to the command word 'analyse' and gain an awareness of how to answer an 'analyse' question

- learn how to identify assessment objectives within an answer.

To analyse means 'to examine in detail, to show meaning, identify elements and the relationship between them'. The ability to analyse business issues is a vital skill not only on analysis questions, but on questions that require you to demonstrate your skills of evaluation: analysis is a skill that underpins evaluation.

When learning how to approach exam questions, you need to be able to understand what each of the assessment objectives looks like in an answer. In this chapter, to support your development of analysis skills, you will be given the opportunity to mark, answer and identify where you think the assessment objectives can be seen and awarded. This will allow you to develop your knowledge of what a good answer looks like.

# 2.1 Economic sectors

1 Economic sectors are ways of classifying business activity based on the type of product or service being produced. Using an example in every case, explain the purpose of each of the following economic sectors.

   a primary sector
   b secondary sector
   c tertiary sector
   d quaternary sector.

2 Outline the advantages and disadvantages of public-sector (government-run) organisations.

**UNDERSTAND THESE TERMS**

- public sector
- private sector

# 2.2 Business ownership

1 You need to be able to identify the different forms of legal structures of business, as well as have a knowledge of their advantages and disadvantages. Explain **three** benefits and **three** costs for each of the following business ownership forms.

   a sole trader
   b partnership
   c private limited company
   d public limited company
   e cooperative.

**UNDERSTAND THESE TERMS**

- unlimited liability
- limited liability
- share
- shareholder

2 Copy the following text. Fill in the gaps using words from this chapter and your own knowledge.

A s_____ t_____ is a type of business organisation that is owned and controlled by one person. The owners' personal possessions and property can be used to pay off the debts of the business. This is called u_____ l_____. In order to remain a sole trader, the owner must be dependent on their own savings, profits and loans for injections of c_____.
A p_____ is a business formed by two or more people to carry on a business together, with shared capital investment and, usually, shared r_____. It is usual with all partnerships, although not a legal requirement, to draw up a formal d_____ of partnership between all partners. This provides agreement on issues such as voting rights and the distribution of p_____.

When it comes to limited companies, there are three main differences between these and sole traders and partnerships (often referred to as u_____ business organisations). The three differences are to do with:

   1 l_____
   2 l_____ p_____
   3 c_____.

The ownership of companies is divided into small units called shares. People can buy these and become s_____: part owners of the business.

## ≪ RECALL AND CONNECT 1 ≪

How can the personal objectives of an entrepreneur affect the type of business ownership form they select when setting up their business?

3   Adam owns a coffee shop. He has been trading successfully for two years and has established a good reputation in the local area. He has decided that he wants to expand his business into other locations and is considering allowing others the legal right to use the name of his coffee shop, its logo and its trading systems as part of a franchise agreement as a method of doing this. Write a letter to Adam to advise him on whether or not this is the best way to grow his business. You should include the advantages and disadvantages of franchising in your response.

4

> ### SK Carpets (SK)
>
> SK sells carpets, rugs and other floor coverings. The business was started ten years ago by Silva Kamal, a sole trader. Silva had always worked in carpet and flooring shops as an employee, but he decided he no longer wanted to work for other people and wanted to be his own boss. He has been making enough profit during this time to provide himself with a good income and the business has gained a good reputation due to the excellent customer service that is provided by the three store employees.

Analyse **one** advantage and **one** disadvantage to Silva of being a sole trader.   [8]

To help you learn how to approach an analyse question, you need to know what skills need to be included in your answer. You will need to include the following:

*   AO1 Knowledge and understanding. Demonstrate knowledge and understanding of business concepts, terms and theories.

*   AO2 Application. Apply knowledge and understanding of business concepts, terms and theories to problems and issues in a variety of familiar and unfamiliar business situations and contexts.

*   AO3 Analysis. Analyse business problems, issues and situations by

    *   using appropriate methods and techniques to make sense of qualitative and quantitative business information

    *   searching for causes, impact and consequences

    *   distinguishing between factual evidence and opinion or value judgement

    *   drawing valid inferences and making valid generalisations.

Questions that contain the command word 'analyse' can be worth either five or eight marks and both require a similar approach. If an analyse question has five marks, it is likely to be asking you to analyse **one** business problem (or point). If an analyse question has eight marks, it is likely to be asking you to analyse **two** business problems (or points). Regardless of the marks awarded, an exam question that asks you to analyse will require you to show AO1, AO2 and AO3 skills. Copy the sample student answer below. Using highlighters of different colours for each of the assessment objectives, you should indicate where you think each assessment objective can be found in the answer below.

> One advantage to Silva of being a sole trader was that Silva was able to be his own boss. This means that he was able to make any decisions that he wanted to about his carpet shop when he opened it up ten years ago, such as what types of carpet to sell, who to employ and what hours the shop should open, giving him the freedom he did not have when he was working for someone else. This means that Silva was able to run his business in the way that he wanted, without having to discuss his ideas with others, which he would have had to if he had been in a partnership. As a result, Silva was able to give more of his time to running the business and focus on making sales, which would lead to his business potentially being more successful.
>
> One disadvantage to Silva of being a sole trader was that Silva may have found he had limited sources of finance. Sole traders often use their own savings to start up their business, and Silva may not have had much finance available when he set up his carpet shop and would struggle to access a loan from a bank as he was setting up a new business. This may have meant that he had to start with a smaller range of carpets to sell than if he had set up the business with other people who could have provided him with some capital. As a result, the growth of his business could have been slower in the early part than Silva would have liked, lowering the amount of income he was able to make for himself.

## ≪ RECALL AND CONNECT 2 ≪

What is meant by the term 'opportunity cost'? Why is this an important concept for someone when setting up a business?

### UNDERSTAND THESE TERMS

- cooperative
- franchise
- franchiser
- franchisee
- joint venture
- social enterprise

### REFLECTION

In Chapter 1, you were introduced to short-answer questions. What skills were these looking for? How does this differ from what you needed to do for the Exam skills question in this chapter? Imagine you were trying to explain this to someone who does not study AS and A Level Business; what would you say to them?

## SELF-ASSESSMENT CHECKLIST

Let's revisit the Knowledge focus and Exam skills focus for this chapter.
Decide how confident you are with each statement.

| Now I can | Show it | Needs more work | Almost there | Confident to move on |
|---|---|---|---|---|
| classify industries into levels of economic activity – primary, secondary, tertiary and quaternary – and analyse changes in their relative importance | Take a product and explain how it has been created using each of the four economic sectors. | | | |
| understand the differences between the private sector and public sector in your country | Explain the difference between businesses in the public and private sectors – use examples for this. | | | |
| identify the different forms of legal structures of business and evaluate the most appropriate one for different businesses | Create a mind map outlining the advantages and disadvantages of five different forms of business ownership. | | | |
| analyse the advantages and disadvantages of changing from one type of business ownership to another | Create a revision card to show the advantages and disadvantages for a business changing from a sole trader to a partnership, a sole trader to a private limited company and a private limited company to a public limited company. | | | |
| be introduced to the command word 'analyse' and gain an awareness of how to answer an 'analyse' question | Explain what is meant by the command word 'analyse' and outline the skills required for a question using this word. | | | |
| learn how to identify assessment objectives within an answer | Outline the three assessment skills needed in an exam question that is assessing the skill of analysis. | | | |

# 3 Size of business

## KNOWLEDGE FOCUS

You will answer questions on:

**3.1** Measurements of business size

**3.2** Significance of small businesses

**3.3** Business growth

## EXAM SKILLS FOCUS

In this chapter you will:

- learn how to use a 'brain tip' to help manage test anxiety

- begin to make links with knowledge in previous chapters.

Test anxiety can happen to anyone, and it can be very common for students to have this in exams. It is important to develop techniques throughout your learning to support you in reducing any potential test anxiety. In this chapter, you will be introduced to one technique called a 'brain tip' (and sometimes called a 'brain dump').

Another important skill is making links between your current knowledge and previous knowledge gained on your course. Business is a synoptic subject. This means that you need to show an understanding of the links between the different areas of this course. Making links between your current subject knowledge and your previous knowledge from earlier topics as you move through this course will support you in gaining a better understanding of how the topics work together.

## 3.1 Measurements of business size

1   Businesses can be measured in many ways. Explain how each of the following can be used as a measure of business size. Also provide **one** advantage and **one** disadvantage for each measure.

   a   number of employees

   b   revenue

   c   capital employed

   d   market share.

2   In addition to the methods of measuring size covered in Question 1, there are many other ways that size can be determined. Outline **three** other ways the size of a business can be measured. Try to use business examples (context) in your answers.

3   Explain **two** problems with attempting to measure business size.

| UNDERSTAND THESE TERMS |
| --- |
| • revenue |
| • market share |
| • capital employed |

## 3.2 Significance of small businesses

1   Small businesses are very important to all industries and the economies in which they operate. Explain **three** benefits small businesses can bring to an economy.

2

> **AK Designs**
>
> Aisha Kapoor is a very talented dressmaker. She has been running her tailoring business, AK Designs, for the last 20 years with her daughter Sita. Over the years, Aisha has been teaching Sita how to manage aspects of the business, such as the accounting documentation and managing customer records.

Analyse **one** benefit to Aisha of her choice to operate AK Designs as a family business.                                                                  [5]

How confident do you feel about answering this question? Give yourself a mark out of ten (one being not at all confident and ten being very confident). You will come back to this later as a reflection task.

You need to learn how to approach exam questions. The approach to answering any exam question starts before you even attempt to write your answer. Before you write an answer to a question that is assessing your AO3 Analysis and AO4 Evaluation skills, you could do a brain tip. This is a useful technique to help you identify the knowledge you have on a topic before you think about what to include in your answer. It is also a useful tool that allows you to take a moment to reflect before you answer a question. After doing this, you should feel prepared to approach the question as you have taken the time to consider the topic being assessed.

Complete a brain tip for Question 2 by following these steps.

- Step 1: select the area of business knowledge you are being assessed on (in this case, it is family businesses).

- Step 2: allow yourself one minute to write down anything you can think of to do with this area of business knowledge.

- Step 3: from the points you have written down, select the ones you think you know most about. Use these as the basis of your answer.

## REFLECTION

Think back to the confidence score you gave yourself before you completed the brain tip for Question 2. Now you have completed the brain tip, how confident do you feel about answering this question? Give yourself a mark out of ten (one being not at all confident and ten being very confident). Has your confidence score changed? If it has, explain why.

You should now try to write an answer to Question 2.

## ≪ RECALL AND CONNECT 1 ≪

Does the type of business structure affect how you can measure the size of a business? Try to find some examples of large and small businesses for each type of business structure using different ways of measuring business size.

# 3.3 Business growth

1   What is the difference between a merger and a takeover? You should research some real-world examples to use in your answer.

2   Speedy Cars (SC) designs and manufactures sports cars that are used exclusively for racing in competitions. SC can spend in excess of $200,000 on the research and development involved in the production of one model of sports car. However, it often depends on other small businesses to support it with complex computer systems and engine building within the cars. Explain how SC could grow through internal (organic) growth.

3   Why would a firm choose to grow through a strategic alliance?

4   Identify which type of external growth is shown in each of the following situations and outline a reason why the firm has decided to grow in this way.

   a   A car manufacturer merges with another car manufacturer.
   b   A supermarket merges with a dairy farm.
   c   An ice cream manufacturer takes over a hair salon.
   d   A cell phone producer takes over a chain of cell phone stores.

## UNDERSTAND THESE TERMS

- external growth
- horizontal integration
- vertical integration
- forward vertical integration
- backward vertical integration

## « RECALL AND CONNECT 2 «

In Chapter 2, you covered the concept of joint ventures. What is a joint venture, and how can it lead to growth for a firm? You should make notes on the impact of the joint venture in the short term and in the long term for the firms involved.

## REFLECTION

How much knowledge from Chapters 1 and 2 have you used when answering the questions in this chapter? Go back over your answers in Chapter 3 and try to identify where you could have made links with the knowledge you gained from previous chapters. It is important to keep reviewing your new knowledge by applying it to earlier knowledge.

### UNDERSTAND THIS TERM

- strategic alliance

## SELF-ASSESSMENT CHECKLIST

Let's revisit the Knowledge focus and Exam skills focus for this chapter.
Decide how confident you are with each statement.

| Now I can | Show it | Needs more work | Almost there | Confident to move on |
|---|---|---|---|---|
| identify several ways of measuring the size of businesses | List six different ways of measuring the size of businesses. | | | |
| analyse the benefits small businesses can have on industry and a country's economy | Create a leaflet to highlight the benefits of small businesses to the economy of your country. | | | |
| analyse the advantages and disadvantages of small businesses and family businesses | Create a revision card to explain the advantages and disadvantages of small and family businesses. | | | |
| explain the difference between internal and external growth | Write an explanation of the difference between internal and external growth for someone with no knowledge of business. | | | |
| identify and analyse different forms of external growth: mergers/takeovers, joint ventures and strategic alliances | Find real-world examples for each form of external growth. | | | |

**CONTINUED**

| | | | | |
|---|---|---|---|---|
| evaluate the impact of different forms of external growth on business stakeholders | Create a table to show the advantages and disadvantages of each form of business growth on four different stakeholders. | | | |
| analyse why a merger/takeover may not achieve its objectives | Find some examples of mergers/takeovers that failed and explain why this happened. | | | |
| learn how to use a 'brain tip' to help manage test anxiety | Look at the Chapter 3 questions in your coursebook and practise using a brain tip for all the 'analyse' questions that appear throughout the chapter. | | | |
| begin to make links with knowledge in previous chapters | Revisit the Reflection in Section 3.3. Create a mind map to show links between the topics covered in Chapters 1, 2 and 3. | | | |

# 4 Business objectives

## EXAM SKILLS FOCUS

In this chapter you will:

- be introduced to the command word 'identify'

- further explore the command word 'explain'.

In this chapter you will be introduced to the command word 'identify'. To identify means to name/state/recognise. In questions with this command word, you need to state a relevant point about a business term/concept, but you do not need to explain this in any depth. These questions may only require you to write a few words, but you need to make sure that the point you make in your answer is clearly relevant to the question set.

It is important to have a developed understanding of the different types of command words that you may be presented with in exams. The more practice you gain with different command words, the more confident you should become with these, which should help you reduce any level of exam anxiety you may feel. You were introduced to the command word 'explain' in Chapter 1. In this chapter you will gain more experience with Exam skills questions that use this command word.

# 4.1 The importance of business objectives

## UNDERSTAND THESE TERMS

- business objective
- SMART objectives
- mission statement
- business strategy
- tactic

**1** What is the difference between profit maximising and profit satisficing as business objectives?

**2** How do the objectives of a social enterprise differ from other businesses?

## ≪ RECALL AND CONNECT 1 ≪

What is the difference between an entrepreneur and an intrapreneur?

It is important to have a developed understanding of the different types of command words that you may be presented with in exams. In this section you will practise the different skills that are required to answer an 'identify' question compared with an 'explain' question.

A key point to consider with questions that carry fewer than four marks is to think about how these marks will be allocated and awarded in your answer. For example, if a question has one mark, then it is likely to require one rewardable point within the answer, compared with a question that has three marks, which is likely to require three rewardable points. This can be seen in the example answers for Questions 3(a) and (b).

**3**

### Mr Chips (MC)

MC is a fast-food restaurant in City A. It is owned and operated by Jack Marsh, who is a sole trader. The restaurant has won numerous awards for the quality of its food and is often referred to as 'the best place to eat in the city'. MC employs 16 members of staff, including cashiers, cooks and managers. When Jack set up the business 20 years ago his business objectives were very different from what they are today.

**a** Identify **one** objective for a business during its first year of trading. [1]

| Sample student answer | Commentary |
| --- | --- |
| Survival. [1] | This is a suitable objective to suggest and clearly answers the question. |

**b** Explain **one** objective MC would have had during its first year of trading. [3]

| Sample student answer | Commentary |
|---|---|
| One objective that MC would have had during its first year of trading is survival [1]. This is because it was opening a new restaurant [1] and needed to find its place within the fast-food market, which is very saturated, so that it could keep trading in the future [1]. | This type of question requires a more developed answer than an 'identify' question, which is provided here. There is some knowledge of an objective that MC would have had during its first year of trading. This is followed by a reference to the case study in the question, so context needs to be used in the answer. One mark is given for knowledge of the objective, another for a good use of the case study and a third mark for further explanation of why the objective was required in context. |

You should now answer the following questions yourself.

**c** Identify **one** reason a firm could change its business objectives. [1]

**d** Explain **one** reason MC could change its business objectives. [3]

**e** Identify **one** reason why a firm could have survival as an objective. [1]

**f** Explain **one** reason why MC could have survival as an objective. [3]

## ≪ RECALL AND CONNECT 2 ≪

What is meant by the term 'dynamic business environment'? How can the dynamic business environment affect a business's choice of objectives?

## UNDERSTAND THESE TERMS

- corporate social responsibility
- pressure group
- triple bottom line

**4** You should create a mind map to outline the main influences on business objectives. Figure 4.1 provides you with some examples to help you get started, but you should try to add more to this. You need to think about how each point impacts on business objectives. Can you find any real-world examples to add to your mind map?

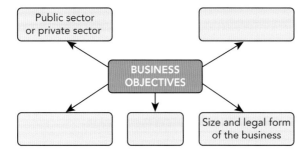

**Figure 4.1:** Influences on business objectives

# 4.2 Objectives and business decisions

1

> **Amit's Animals (AA)**
>
> Amit has a degree in zoology and has always been interested in animals.
> He has built up a small collection of reptiles that he wants to start taking into
> schools and use as part of an interactive workshop to educate young people
> about these creatures. As part of his initial business plan, Amit needs to make
> a number of decisions and create some business objectives.

Outline the **seven** stages Amit will need to go through to set clear objectives
and support his decision-making for his new business venture.

2   'Setting an objective to make a profit is more important than setting
an objective to be ethical for a business.' Do you agree with this statement?
Justify your decision.

**UNDERSTAND THESE TERMS**

- target
- budget

## ≪ RECALL AND CONNECT 3 ≪

What is the difference between the public and private sectors?
How do the objectives of firms in these two sectors differ?

## REFLECTION

When you answered Question 2 in Section 4.2, how did you decide which
option was more important for a business when setting its objectives? Was it
challenging to arrive at a conclusion, or did you find it easy? Ask the question
to another student and listen to their answer. Was this a different decision than
the one you made? Can you justify your own conclusions to them?

## SELF-ASSESSMENT CHECKLIST

Let's revisit the Knowledge focus and Exam skills focus for this chapter.
Decide how confident you are with each statement.

| Now I can | Show it | Needs more work | Almost there | Confident to move on |
|---|---|---|---|---|
| explain the importance to the business of setting objectives | List three reasons why setting objectives is important to a business. | | | |
| analyse the objectives for businesses – private sector, public sector and social enterprises | Explain how the objectives are different between private sector, public sector and social enterprises. | | | |

**CONTINUED**

| | | | | |
|---|---|---|---|---|
| analyse the importance of business objectives being SMART | Set yourself a SMART objective that you wish to achieve by the end of your course. | | | |
| discuss the importance of corporate social responsibility and the triple bottom line | Talk to another student for one minute and explain the role of the triple bottom line to them. | | | |
| analyse the links between mission statements, aims, objectives and strategy | Create a diagram to show the relationship between mission statements, aims, objectives and strategy. | | | |
| analyse the role of objectives in business decision-making | Write a revision card that outlines the hierarchy of objectives and explains the link between each level. | | | |
| consider the need for communication of objectives and their likely impact on the workforce | Explain what would happen if a business did not correctly communicate its objectives to its workforce. | | | |
| analyse why objectives might change over time | Using a real-world example, write a short article explaining why and how its objectives are likely to have changed at key points in its history. | | | |
| evaluate how ethics can influence business objectives and activities | Find three news articles that demonstrate how businesses have adapted to become more ethical in their business practices. | | | |
| be introduced to the command word 'identify' | Define what is meant by the command word 'identify'. | | | |
| further explore the command word 'explain' | Briefly outline how your approach to answering 'explain' questions should be different to answering 'identify' questions. | | | |

# 5 Stakeholders in a business

Metacognitive practice is an important skill to master when assessing your own progress. It helps you become aware of your strengths and weaknesses in all areas of your learning. There are many tasks that can support metacognitive practice, including planning, monitoring progress and self-evaluation. You will be introduced to some activities to support your metacognition in this chapter.

# 5.1 Business stakeholders

1   Stakeholders have many different roles, objectives, rights and responsibilities. For each of the following stakeholders, explain in no more than three sentences for each stakeholder what their roles, rights and responsibilities are.

    **a**   customers

    **b**   suppliers

    **c**   employees

    **d**   local community

    **e**   government

    **f**   owners/shareholders.

---

## UNDERSTAND THESE TERMS

- stakeholders
- external stakeholders
- internal stakeholders
- trade union

---

## ≪ RECALL AND CONNECT 1 ≪

The term 'stakeholder' is often confused with the term 'shareholder'.
Explain the difference between the terms 'stakeholder' and 'shareholder'.

---

You were introduced to the command word 'explain' in Chapter 1. Look back to remind yourself how to approach this type of question; then answer Question 2.

2

### QuickFly Airlines (QA)

QA is a large national airline. It has been operating for over 30 years but has been facing some financial difficulties recently due to the increase in competitors in the market. It has decided to cut 20 of its travel routes over the next year to save on costs. It has many internal and external stakeholders.

Explain the difference between internal stakeholders and external stakeholders at QuickFly Airlines.                                          [3]

The next question is a 12-mark question that uses the command word 'evaluate'. To help you learn how to approach this, you need to be aware of what skills need to be included in an answer to this type of question.

You will need to:

- demonstrate knowledge and understanding of business concepts, terms and theories (AO1 Knowledge and understanding)

- apply knowledge and understanding of business concepts, terms and theories to problems and issues in a variety of familiar and unfamiliar business situations and contexts (AO2 Application)

- analyse business problems, issues and situations by using appropriate methods and techniques to make sense of qualitative and quantitative business information, searching for causes, impacts and consequences, distinguishing between factual evidence and opinion or value judgement or drawing valid inferences and making valid generalisations (AO3 Analysis)

- evaluate evidence in order to make reasoned judgements, present substantiated conclusions and, where appropriate, make recommendations for action and implementation (AO4 Evaluation).

Copy the following sample student answer. Using highlighters of different colours for each of the assessment objectives, you should indicate where you think each assessment objective can be found in the answer.

3   a   Evaluate the impact on **one** stakeholder of QuickFly Airlines of the decision to cut 20 of its travel routes over the next year to save costs.        [12]

> One stakeholder that will be affected by the decision by QuickFly Airlines to cut 20 of its travel routes is its employees as they might lose their jobs. This is because if there are fewer flights taking place, then there is going to be less need for employees such as cabin crew or baggage handlers. As a result, some employees might find they have had their work hours cut, which could lead to a lower level of income. This is likely to mean that these workers will have a lower standard of living as they will not be able to afford to buy all the things that they want to buy.
>
> Another impact on the employees is that they may be placed on different flight routes to those they are used to working on. As QuickFly Airlines are removing 20 of its travel routes over the next year, the cabin crew and pilots may be moved to flights to different destinations. This may be a benefit to these employees as they will get to experience new places, as well as having a new challenge in their day-to-day working lives dealing with customers from different countries and cultures, which could be motivational.
>
> The greatest impact on employees is that they may lose their jobs entirely. This is because if there are fewer flights taking place, and if QuickFly Airlines continues with its cost-cutting measures, cabin crew and pilots might find that they lose their jobs altogether. This is a bigger impact than being moved to work on different travel routes as if the employees are moved to work on flights to different destinations, at least they will still have a job and some income. However, this may depend on the actions of the firm as it may decide to move employees like cabin crew and pilots over from the cut routes to other routes that are doing well, allowing employees to keep working and earning an income. There may not be this option, as all travel routes not being cut may already be fully staffed, meaning that QuickFly have no option other than to make a large number of employees redundant. This means it is more likely that employees will lose their jobs than keep them.

   b   You should now try to write your own answer to Question 3(a) using a different stakeholder that might be affected by QA's decision to cut twenty of its travel routes over the next year to save costs.        [12]

REFLECTION

How easy or difficult did you find the task in Question 3? How did you go about identifying all the skills that were needed? Were there any particular assessment objectives you found more challenging to identify than others?

# 5.2 Importance and influence of stakeholders on business activities

1  Business have accountability towards their stakeholders.
What does 'accountability' mean?

2  Explain how businesses are accountable to the following stakeholder groups:

   a   customers
   b   suppliers
   c   employees
   d   local community
   e   government.

3  When attempting to meet the needs of one stakeholder, the needs of another stakeholder could be negatively affected. This is a form of 'stakeholder conflict'. Copy Table 5.1 and complete it to show a conflict that may exist between the stakeholders identified, and then suggest a way this conflict can be reduced or resolved.

|  | Stakeholders | What is the potential conflict? | How might this be reduced or resolved? |
|---|---|---|---|
| A large public limited company has decided to award a pay increase to senior managers but not to any other employees in the company. | Employees and owners |  |  |
| A car manufacturer has decided to increase the capacity of its factory. | Local community and suppliers |  |  |
| A small fruit farm has decided to stop selling some of its least popular products. | Customers and owners |  |  |

**Table 5.1:** Stakeholder conflict and resolution

4
> **CEK Furniture (CEK)**
>
> CEK is a multinational organisation that sells self-assembly home furniture through its 326 stores in 36 countries. It has just completed a takeover of Pawfection, a large pet supply store that specialises in pet food and accessories.

Evaluate the impact on the stakeholders of CEK of the decision to take over Pawfection.                    [12]

## REFLECTION

A simple way to develop metacognitive skills that support you with self-assessment is to create a self-assessment grid that lists key things to look for in your work. Copy Table 5.2 and, using your answer for Question 4, check if you have done the following:

| Skill | What AO is this demonstrating? | Explain why this needs to be included |
|---|---|---|
| • Shown knowledge of stakeholders | | |
| • Applied your answer to furniture | | |
| • Applied your knowledge to a pet supply store | | |
| • Applied your answer specifically to CEK's decision to take over Pawfection | | |
| • Assessed the impact of this takeover on at least two stakeholders | | |
| • Identified stakeholders who are likely to view this takeover positively and those who are likely to view it negatively | | |
| • Made a decision on whether stakeholders are likely to take a positive or negative viewpoint overall | | |
| • Provided a justification for your overall decision | | |

**Table 5.2:** Self-assessment for Question 4

5   Do you think it is important for a business to consider its stakeholders when making decisions about its future business activities? Explain your answer.

## « RECALL AND CONNECT 2 «

Look back over the case study for CEK in Question 4.
What type of business growth is shown in this example?

## REFLECTION

Think about yourself. You are a stakeholder in your school/college.
What are your objectives as a stakeholder? How do these differ from those
of the other stakeholders in the school/college (for example, your teachers,
owners, government)? Do your objectives as a stakeholder conflict with those
of the other stakeholder groups? Considering your role and interactions with
different business organisations can be a really helpful way of learning how
to apply the theory you learn as part of your studies to real-world examples.

## SELF-ASSESSMENT CHECKLIST

Let's revisit the Knowledge focus and Exam skills focus for this chapter.
Decide how confident you are with each statement.

| Now I can | Show it | Needs more work | Almost there | Confident to move on |
|---|---|---|---|---|
| analyse the meaning of 'stakeholder', both internal and external | Take any case study in this chapter and identify the internal and external stakeholders. | | | |
| analyse the roles, rights and responsibilities of key business stakeholders | For a business of your choice, select three stakeholders and explain their roles, rights and responsibilities. | | | |
| assess the impact of business decisions on stakeholders and the need for business accountability | Conduct research and find an article related to a business in your country. Explain how the decisions made by this firm impact on its stakeholders. | | | |
| assess the impact of stakeholder aims on business decisions | Using the news article you have found, outline how the stakeholders for the firm can impact on the decisions of the business. | | | |
| identify conflicting stakeholder aims and objectives | Create a revision card outlining how the aims of four different stakeholders can conflict. | | | |
| evaluate how a business might respond to these conflicting aims | Using the examples on your revision card, explain how a firm might try to resolve these conflicts. | | | |

**CONTINUED**

| | | | | |
|---|---|---|---|---|
| start to develop an approach to metacognitive practice when answering exam questions with a focus on monitoring progress | Create a self-assessment grid for Question 3 in Section 5.1. | | | |

# Exam practice 1

This section contains both past paper questions from previous Cambridge exams and practice questions. These questions draw together your knowledge on a range of topics that you have covered up to this point and will help you prepare for your assessment.

The following questions have example student responses and commentaries provided. For each question, work through the question first, then compare your answer to the example student response and commentary.

**1 a** Define the term 'value added'. [2]

*Cambridge International AS & A Level Business (9609) Paper 12 Q4a, November 2018*

| Example student response | Examiner comments |
|---|---|
| When value is added to a product. | This answer does not show any real understanding of value added and is worth **zero** marks. The answer needs to show an understanding of the two elements of value added (cost of inputs and price of the finished product). |

**b** Explain **one** way a restaurant could increase its value added. [3]

| Example student response | Examiner comments |
|---|---|
| It could reduce the cost of its food by changing the supplier. | This answer provides one very clear method (reducing cost). This is done in the context of a restaurant (food) about how costs can be reduced. However, the reason why a reduction in cost leads to an increase in value added is not fully explained. Awarded **two** marks. |

**2 a** Evaluate the extent to which the stakeholders of a large clothing retailer might want the business to become more ethical and socially responsible. [12]

| Example student response | Examiner comments |
|---|---|
| One stakeholder is the customer. The customer might want the business to become more ethical and socially responsible because they will feel good about buying their clothes there. This means that the customers will gain satisfaction from their clothing purchases and are likely to return to make more purchases. However, if the clothing retailer becomes more ethical and socially responsible this might mean that the clothes become more expensive for the customer to buy. This is because ethically sourced items usually have a higher cost and so the clothing retailer might pass this on to customers in the form of high prices, which the customer will not be happy with, especially customers who might have a limited amount of income to spend on clothing. | There is clear knowledge of what that means to the stakeholders throughout, linked to the objectives of the stakeholders. |
| | Throughout the answer there is a reference to clothing and a clothing retailer, which provides some application. However, it would have been helpful for the student to include some other real-world examples here to develop their skills of application further. |
| Another stakeholder are the employees. They might be happy that the clothing retailer is becoming more ethical and socially responsible, because it could mean that it starts introducing better working practices for the employees such as a fair wage or safer working conditions. This means that the employees will take more satisfaction in their day at work. However, by working for a firm that is more ethical and socially responsible, because its costs are probably going up due to the increased costs of being ethical, it could mean it has to cut costs elsewhere, maybe through a reduction of employees. As long as it looks ethical to the customers, such as through the introduction of new ethically sourced clothing, customers may not even see potential unethical practises such as making staff redundant to pay for the new ethical products. Employees might then become concerned about the safety of their jobs, which is its objective. | Analysis can be seen throughout, where the student explores a clear implication/impact on the stakeholder group being discussed. |
| | The judgement at the end of the answer provides a clear suggestion on how the stakeholders will be impacted both in the short and long term. This is strengthened by the acknowledgement that the change may not be for positive reasons, which could affect the extent to which the stakeholder views the change in business direction. |
| Overall, I think that the stakeholders of the clothing retailer will generally be happy if the business decides to become more ethical and socially responsible. This is because it is likely to lead to better-quality clothing for the customers and better working conditions for the employees. However, in order to make sure the stakeholders are on board with this decision, the owners of the clothing retailer would need to communicate the changes involved in being more ethical carefully to their stakeholders so any concerns that they have are alleviated, meaning they are in positive position about the change in business direction. | To improve the answer, there could be some consideration of why the suggested changes in communication by the owners would alleviate the stakeholders' concerns. |
| | The evaluation is contextual, but not developed in the answer. |
| | *9/12 marks* |

3

## Fish and Chips (FC)

Min is a sole trader who is the owner and overall manager of FC. Min started the business as a restaurant, but FC has grown so that it now operates in the primary, secondary and tertiary sectors. Min sees this as FC's unique selling point (USP). Min allocates costs and revenues to each section of the business. She then calculates the profit margin for each section (see Table 1).

| Sector | Activity | Employees | Annual revenue | Profit margin |
|--------|----------|-----------|----------------|---------------|
| Primary | Catching fish using FC's own boat | One captain<br><br>Two fishermen | $50 000 | 2% |
| Secondary | Cooking fish in FC's own kitchen | One head chef<br><br>Two assistant chefs | $70 000 | 1% |
| Tertiary | Serving the cooked fish with chips and vegetables in FC's own restaurant | One restaurant supervisor<br><br>Three servers<br><br>One cleaner | $200 000 | 15% |

**Table 1:** Overview of FC

Min considers herself to be an excellent manager, having studied business at university. She manages her employees using Herzberg's 'Motivation' theory. Min has had an objective of growth, but she is now happy with the size of FC. She intends to change the objective to profit maximisation.

a  Analyse **two** appropriate ways that could be used to measure the
   size of FC.                                                    [8]

*Cambridge International AS & A Level Business (9609) Paper 23 Q2c,
     November 2018*

| Example student response | Examiner comments |
|---|---|
| One appropriate way that could be used to measure the size of FC is its revenue. It has made $200,000 in revenue from its tertiary-sector operations. This means that Min would be able to compare how her business is doing with other businesses by seeing if FC makes more or less revenue than them. However, this could be challenging to use as a measure as Min may not have access to the accounts of other businesses so she may not be able to measure FC's size using revenue. | Two appropriate ways to measure the size of FC are provided (revenue and market share). |
|  | The first paragraph contains some data from the case study, which is relevant to the point being discussed and is used well to explain how FC could use its revenue figure to measure its size. The second paragraph contains no reference to the case study, which would be required to improve this answer. |
| Another appropriate way that could be used to measure the size of FC is by looking at its market share. However, market share is not a good measure of size as it can look like a business has gained a greater market share in a market that is shrinking, so figures can be misleading. | There is a clear explanation of how revenue figures could be used to determine size, and the implications of this measure of size are detailed and thorough. The first paragraph provides all the rewardable analysis seen in this answer. |
|  | In the second paragraph, there is some good understanding of the use of market share as a way of measuring size discussed, and some appreciation of the implications of using this measure is shown. However, this is not developed so is not rewarded. |
|  | *6/8 marks* |

Here is another practice question which you should attempt.
Use the guidance in the commentaries in this section to help you
as you answer the question.

b  Evaluate which stakeholders might be most affected by the change
   in FC's business objective from growth to profit maximisation.    [12]

# 6 External influences on business activity

The command word 'analyse' requires a detailed answer with a clear line of argument. Useful ways to do this include looking at the reasons for, causes of, impact of, or consequences of factors or issues referred to in the question.

Another important exam skill is writing to time. The questions in this chapter cover elements of Paper 3 with a series of short-answer and essay questions based on different businesses, included in the text. Questions in Paper 3 have different mark allocations. It is crucial to check how many marks a question is worth before you answer so you know roughly how much time to spend and how much detail is required. There are 60 marks available on Paper 3, which is 1 hour and 45 minutes in length. You need to allocate time to complete the questions in this time – don't forget to allow 10 to 15 minutes to read the case study first.

# 6.1 Political and legal influences

1   Explain **three** reasons why a government might choose to privatise a state-owned business.

2   Provide **two** examples of situations in which a government may wish to bring a private sector business under public ownership.

3   a   Copy and complete Table 6.1. Add one of the areas of legislation from the word box to each row of the table so that it fits with the correct example of how the government may use the legislation to control areas of business practice.

conditions of work     wage levels     marketing behaviour
competition     location decisions

| Area of legislation | Purpose/example of use |
| --- | --- |
| | Covers occupational health and safety in the workplace |
| | Prevents heavy industry or firms that might cause pollution to operate close to high-density housing |
| | To provide a minimum living standard for all employees |
| | Prohibits anti-competitive agreements between businesses and the abuse of a dominant position in a market |
| | Makes it an offence for businesses or salespeople to sell a product or service based on misinformation |

**Table 6.1:** Legal constraints on business activity

   b   Having completed Table 6.1, research business legislation in your country in any of the areas mentioned in the table. Then explain how each might affect a business that you know well.

4   If the average wage level increased in a country, explain how it could provide both an opportunity and a threat to the following businesses.

   •   McDonald's

   •   HSBC (a bank)

   •   a Michelin-starred restaurant.

This next question contains the command word 'analyse'. Remember that this means to examine in detail, to show meaning or to identify elements and the relationship between them. This is a popular command word. You are provided with a small piece of text (as included in the following study) and then asked to use this information to analyse the impact of something on an organisation. When using this command word, one approach is to consider one of the three elements of analysis: cause (the government makes seat belts mandatory through a law designed to improve road safety that must be complied with); impact (all motor vehicles in India will now have to be fitted with seat belts); or consequence. For the 'consequence' element of the question you could divide the question in two and provide examples of businesses that have benefitted from the law change, followed by businesses that have been disadvantaged by the law change. For each section you must make a direct connection between the law change and the business. No conclusion is necessary for an 'analyse' question.

You should spend 14 minutes completing this Paper 3 response. Set your stopwatch for this time and stop writing when the 14 minutes have passed.

5

> **Government makes seat belts mandatory**
>
> In September 2022, a new law made the wearing of seat belts compulsory in India. Under the new law those not wearing belts are to be fined 1000r and all new cars will also need to be fitted with airbags for each seat. The law is not expected to apply to existing motor vehicles sold before this date, but passengers travelling in cars with seat belts will be required to wear them.

Analyse **one** opportunity and **one** threat that the new seat belt law may bring to a car manufacturer in India. [8]

## REFLECTION

In your answer to Question 5, have you included one of the elements of the command word: cause, impact or consequence? How did you decide on the cause, the impact or the consequences of the law? Can you think of how the new seat belt law would have provided another opportunity or threat for a different industry in India? Maybe consider delivery companies or a taxi firm.

Did the allocation of 14 minutes for this question allow you to complete your answer in the time given? How will this timing task this help you determine how much time to allocate to answering questions?

## « RECALL AND CONNECT 1 «

How might the primary objective of an organisation change when ownership is transferred from the public to the private sector or from the private to the public sector?

# 6.2 Social and demographic influences

| UNDERSTAND THESE TERMS |
| --- |
| • social audit |
| • demographic |
| • globalisation |

1   Copy and complete Table 6.2. Provide an example of **one** opportunity and **one** threat to businesses for each of the social and demographic changes identified in the table.

| | Opportunity | Threat |
| --- | --- | --- |
| Ageing population | | |
| Increase in workers wishing to work part-time | | |
| Growing awareness of corporate social responsibility (CSR) | | |
| Greater number of young people attending university | | |

**Table 6.2:** Social and demographic changes

2   Investigate the social audit of a business that you know well and identify some of the benefits and costs to the business of the audit.

3   A popular hotel decides to operate a system of flexible working. It hopes this will be popular with staff and boost productivity. One of the policies under consideration is for staff to choose their own hours. Explain **one** way in which this policy may motivate staff.                [3]

# 6.3 Technological influences on business activities

| UNDERSTAND THESE TERMS |
| --- |
| • information technology (IT) |
| • job enrichment |

1

> ### The iPhone decade: How Apple's phone created and destroyed industries and changed the world
>
> In the period 2010–2020, Apple's iPhone was transformed from a niche product for early adopters to a dominant economic force. Apple sold at least 1.4 billion iPhones during the decade, according to its official sales figures.
>
> The 2010s could be viewed as the iPhone decade: when smartphones went mainstream, created billion-dollar corporations, rearranged existing industries and changed the world. For example, Samsung, Google and Android partners took a fair amount of inspiration from Apple's iPhone to incorporate some of the Apple's best ideas for use in their own devices. The iPhone has also created arguably as many new industries as it has destroyed. For example, ride-hailing companies Lyft and Uber are collectively worth more than $60 billion, and they exist only thanks to the always-on GPS location and high-speed wireless connections that became common with the iPhone.

Copy and complete Table 6.3. Identify **three** examples of firms or organisations that have benefitted from Apple's technological developments and **three** that have been harmed.

| Business that have benefitted | Businesses that have been harmed |
|---|---|
|  |  |
|  |  |
|  |  |

**Table 6.3:** The 'Apple decade'

## 6.4 Influence of competitors and suppliers

Read the following case study and complete Question 1. Assume this is a question in Paper 3. Set a timer to see how long it takes you to write an answer to this question.

1

> ### Uber granted 30-month license to continue operating in London
>
> We're delighted to announce @Transport for London has granted Uber a new 30-month licence in London. TfL rightly holds our industry to the highest regulatory and safety standards and we are pleased to have met their high bar. 09:00, Mar 26, 2022.

Analyse **one** likely action that Uber's competitors may take following the decision to grant Uber a new 30-month licence. [5]

How long did it take you to write an answer to Question 1? Do you feel that you used your time well? How did timing how long it took you to write an answer compare to writing an answer earlier in the chapter where you were given a strict time limit?

Next try Question 2. Before you write the answer, give yourself a time limit to complete the question in. (*Hint – the suppliers are the people who drive their own cars for Uber.*)

2   Analyse **one** likely action that Uber's suppliers may take following the decision to grant Uber a new 30-month licence.   [5]

# 6.5 International influences

1   A business makes and sells musical instruments in country A.
Explain **three** ways the business may be affected by a rise in international trade.

2
> **Coca-Cola's global reach**
>
> Coca-Cola is a global business that operates in more than 200 countries. It claims to operate on 'a local scale in every community where we do business'. It is able to create global reach with local resources because of the strength of the Coca-Cola system, which comprises the main company and nearly 300 bottling partners around the world, which are not owned by Coca-Cola.

Identify the key features of a multinational company.   [2]

3   Explain **one** negative effect on workers in a country of its government attracting overseas investment.   [3]

4   Explain **one** benefit to Coca-Cola of publicising their approach to Corporate Social Responsibility (CSR).   [3]

5   Evaluate whether a developing nation would benefit from a multinational such as Coca-Cola investing in production facilities in their country.   [12]

**《 RECALL AND CONNECT 2 《**

The growth of a business can be organic or through mergers and acquisitions. Is a large firm becoming multinational an example of a business growing organically or non-organically?

## 6.6 Environmental influences on business activity

1 Identify how the following stakeholders might use an environmental audit.

    a    business

    b    managers

    c    pressure groups

    d    investors

    e    employees.

**UNDERSTAND THESE TERMS**

- environmental audit
- sustainability

2

> **An environmental audit**
>
> In 2021, a South American chamber of commerce ordered a full environmental audit of industrial activity completed by industries operating in the public sector with the aim of recommending policies and action plans for improving its management and performance.

Analyse **two** reasons for the chamber of commerce's conducting an environmental audit of public sector businesses. [8]

**UNDERSTAND THESE TERMS**

- social audit
- environmental audit
- demographic change
- technological change

### ≪ RECALL AND CONNECT 3 ≪

The 'triple bottom line' is used by businesses to ensure that the interests of all stakeholders and not just shareholders are considered in a firm's dealings. Describe the role of an environmental audit in the 'triple bottom line' approach.

### SELF-ASSESSMENT CHECKLIST

Let's revisit the Knowledge focus and Exam skills focus for this chapter.
Decide how confident you are with each statement.

| Now I can | Show it | Needs more work | Almost there | Confident to move on |
|---|---|---|---|---|
| understand how and why the state intervenes in business ownership through privatisation and nationalisation | Read the 'Business in context' feature in Chapter 6 of the coursebook and explain why the governments of Mauritius and Kenya might have different perspectives on the merits of nationalisation/privatisation. | | | |
| analyse why governments use legal controls over business activity and how these may impact on business decisions | Provide two examples of legal controls used by governments, e.g., minimum wage legislation, and describe two businesses impacted by them. | | | |

## CONTINUED

| | | | | |
|---|---|---|---|---|
| evaluate the impact of technology on business decisions | Investigate how technological changes have impacted learning at your school or a different business or product that you know well. | | | |
| evaluate the impact of competitors and suppliers on business decisions | Write out a different response to Question 1 in Section 6.4 using a business other than Uber. | | | |
| evaluate how changes in society can impact on business strategy | Investigate one business and then explain how it is likely to be impacted by political, economic or social changes within a society. | | | |
| examine the impact of the growing importance of sustainability on business decisions | Provide an example of a business that includes sustainability in its mission/vision statement. | | | |
| assess the nature, purpose and potential uses of environmental audits | Investigate a business that has completed an environmental audit and identify its purpose. | | | |
| further develop my understanding of the command word 'analyse' and practise using a cause, impact and consequence approach | Practise using the command word 'analyse' and identify how you can cover each element of it: cause, impact and consequence. | | | |
| understand how to manage my time across A Level Paper 3 – Business Decision-Making | Practise exam responses for different questions in Paper 3, using the allocated time available. | | | |

# 7 External economic influences on business activity

## KNOWLEDGE FOCUS

You will answer questions on:

**7.1** Government support for business activity

**7.2** How governments deal with market failure

**7.3** Macroeconomic objectives of governments

**7.4** How economic objectives and performance impact business activity

**7.5** Government policies to achieve macroeconomic objectives

## EXAM SKILLS FOCUS

In this chapter you will:

- understand connections between different concepts in this chapter

- manage test anxiety by using a study timetable.

One skill that you will need to master is the ability to link different parts of this course. When completing any question in the subject you will also benefit from bringing in other relevant parts of this course to support your understanding of the different syllabus areas.

Completing a study timetable is a useful way of managing test anxiety. Make sure your timetable includes manageable work periods, accompanied by self-evaluation and reflection. Your schedule must also allow sufficient time for each topic as well as significant rest periods. Allow sufficient time so that all units can be covered, avoiding the cramming process and allowing a long lead time for exam preparation. You should also include a set finish time that you do not work beyond.

# 7.1 Government support for business activity

**1**  Explain **four** ways that governments can provide special assistance for entrepreneurs and other owners of small businesses.

**2**  What are the advantages and disadvantages of government subsidies being given to existing businesses?

---

### ≪ RECALL AND CONNECT 1 ≪

How can governments influence business through legislation and regulation?

---

# 7.2 How governments deal with market failure

**1**  Suggest a suitable policy that a government might implement to address each of the following examples of market failure.

   **a**  High pollution levels in the country's main cities

   **b**  Traffic congestion in main cities and highways

   **c**  Businesses reporting difficulties in recruiting suitable workers for some positions, e.g., engineering positions

   **d**  Complaints of high prices and poor service from the nation's state-run water and energy companies.

> **UNDERSTAND THIS TERM**
>
> • market failure

# 7.3 Macroeconomic objectives of governments

> **UNDERSTAND THESE TERMS**
>
> • macroeconomic objectives
> • gross domestic product (GDP)
> • inflation
> • unemployment

**1**  What are the **three** main macroeconomic objectives of government?

**2**  Give an example of how some of these objectives may conflict with each other.

# 7.4 How economic objectives and performance impact business activity

**1**

> **DT Designs**
>
> Daniel is a graphic designer. He has always had a passion for art and design and has recently set up DT Designs in Country X, which offers creative services to businesses who are looking for new branding and packaging designs. Daniel has started to gain a positive reputation in the market for his innovative designs and his strong level of customer service.

Explain how DT Designs could be affected by each of the following:

**a** a sustained period of growth in the economy for Country X

**b** a recession in Country X

**c** low inflation in Country X

**d** an increase in the unemployment level in Country X.

**2** Does a recession always lead to negative impacts for a business? Explain your answer.

**3** Explain how a period of high inflation could affect a business.

# 7.5 Government policies to achieve macroeconomic objectives

**1**

> **Wooden Treasures (WT)**
>
> Wooden Treasures (WT) operate a workshop in City A, located in Country B. They manufacture and sell unique pieces of handmade, bespoke, household furniture using job production to match the individual needs of the customer. WT is owned by brothers Ahmad and Rayyan, who employ six skilled full-time workers, who are paid well above the national average wage. As a result, WT have to charge high prices for their furniture to cover the high production costs involved. WT are considering opening up another workshop in City D, which is 150 km north of City A in Country B. To do this, WT would need to find a source of finance for this, such as a bank loan.
>
> Currently, WT buys the wood they need to make their furniture from three different countries, all of which use different currencies to Country B.
>
> The government of Country B is considering the following changes to their supply-side policies:
>
> • increasing state provision at colleges for skills training
>
> • lowering rates of income tax to encourage workers to set up their own businesses and to encourage work incentives
>
> • increasing spending on infrastructure projects including a more reliable internet provision.

**UNDERSTAND THESE TERMS**

• monetary policy

• fiscal policy

• supply-side policies

• exchange rate policy

For each of the following, explain a likely impact of the change on WT:

a   An increase in income tax.

b   An increase in indirect taxes on spending, e.g., value added tax (VAT).

c   An increase in interest rates.

d   An exchange rate appreciation.

e   An exchange rate depreciation.

2   Evaluate the impact on WT of a change in government supply-side policies.   [12]

## REFLECTION

How long do you want to study for each day? When completing a study timetable, this question should be your starting point. Do not plan to spend more than eight to nine hours studying each day, even in the days leading up to your exam. This represents the upper limit of your productive study time, remembering that an effective schedule will include at least five to ten minutes' rest for each hour of study.

## ≪ RECALL AND CONNECT 2 ≪

What can governments do to protect entrepreneurs against falls in economic activity?

## SELF-ASSESSMENT CHECKLIST

Let's revisit the Knowledge focus and Exam skills focus for this chapter.
Decide how confident you are with each statement.

| Now I can | Show it | Needs more work | Almost there | Confident to move on |
|---|---|---|---|---|
| analyse how governments help business, encourage enterprise and deal with market failure | Provide examples from your own country of the impact of growth on the macroeconomic indicators. | | | |
| analyse the macroeconomic objectives of governments | Investigate the current rate of unemployment, inflation, GDP growth and trade balance in your home country. | | | |
| analyse the nature and causes of economic growth and its impact on business decisions | Provide examples of business (ones that sell luxury products) benefitting disproportionately from periods of growth, as well as examples of firms that prosper during recession. | | | |

## CONTINUED

| | | | | |
|---|---|---|---|---|
| analyse the business cycle and its impact on business decisions | Research an organisation you know well and provide examples of decisions made by the business at different stages of the business cycle. | | | |
| analyse the different causes of unemployment and inflation | Explain why recession causes cyclical unemployment but not structural/frictional unemployment. Identify causes of both cost-push and demand-pull inflation. | | | |
| evaluate how economic objectives and economic performance can impact business activity | Explain how a business that you are familiar with was impacted by the COVID-19 pandemic. | | | |
| evaluate the impact on business decisions of changes in monetary, fiscal, supply-side and exchange rate policies | Explain how a business that you are familiar with might be impacted by changes to central bank interest rates, changes in taxation and changes in exchange rates. | | | |
| understand connections between different concepts in this chapter | Use question cards to test your knowledge of the key terms in the chapter and then explore connections between them. Pair those that can be used in the same exam question, e.g., exchange rate depreciation and appreciation, fiscal and monetary policy, cyclical and structural unemployment, etc. | | | |
| manage test anxiety by using a study timetable | Having completed your schedule double-check that it is achievable in the time available. Are all of the subjects you need to study sufficiently covered? | | | |

# 8 Business strategy

## KNOWLEDGE FOCUS

You will answer questions on:

**8.1** Business strategy: Meaning and purpose

**8.2** Strategic management: Meaning and purpose

**8.3** Approaches to developing business strategy

## EXAM SKILLS FOCUS

In this chapter you will:

- understand how to complete a decision tree

- be introduced to the command word 'advise' and gain an awareness of how to answer an 'advise' question.

Some questions will require you to use some of the business tools that you have studied to help you answer the question. In this chapter you will practise using a decision tree to support your response to a question.

The command word 'advise' means to write down a suggested course of action in a given situation. You are required to provide an evaluation of the points for and against a particular decision, perhaps compared with an alternative course of action. The course of action to be taken must be clearly expressed and supported by evaluative comments which weigh up key arguments. It is sometimes used in conjunction with one of the business tools. For example, a question might ask you to use a tool like a decision tree or an Ansoff matrix to advise a business about a particular course of action. Your answer should focus on the findings of the business tool you use. This contrasts with questions using the command word 'evaluate', which require a detailed response addressing various possible options.

## 8.1 Business strategy: Meaning and purpose

**« RECALL AND CONNECT 1 «**

Why is it important to ensure that the objectives used in any business decision-making are SMART?

1   What is meant by the term 'business strategy'?

2   Business strategies are influenced by four different factors: resources available, strengths of the business, competitive environment and the business objectives. Explain how each of these factors can influence a business's strategy.

## 8.2 Strategic management: Meaning and purpose

1   Explain the meaning of:

   a   strategic analysis

   b   strategic choice

   c   strategic implementation.

2   When implementing a strategy, what factors may need to be in place for a business to be able to do this successfully?

3   How are the concepts of decision making and business strategy linked?

**« RECALL AND CONNECT 2 «**

Which managers/directors are responsible for the following business decisions?

•   Strategic decisions?

•   Tactical decisions?

## 8.3 Approaches to developing business strategy

**UNDERSTAND THESE TERMS**

•   blue ocean strategy
•   SWOT analysis
•   PEST analysis
•   Porter's five forces model
•   core competence framework
•   Ansoff matrix
•   force-field analysis
•   decision tree

**Stedding's Circus**

Traditional circuses are typically based on a range of acts using humans and animals performing together. Stedding's Circus created its own blue ocean strategy for a different experience, with traditional (human-based) show mixed with musical theatre. The company does not use animals in its acts, instead relying on professional gymnasts, which it believes is the circus's unique selling point. As an innovative business, the company is always looking for new markets and is exploring the creation of a circus skills training academy. More than 200 million people have watched the company's shows worldwide and sales have risen by 20% since 2015. The circus, however, is not without its critics, who claim that its building strategy is based on product development (what acts are included in the show) and not a marketing approach.

1   Copy Table 8.1 and add **one** of the SWOT labels to each of the descriptions of Stedding's Circus.

| strength | weakness | opportunity | threat |
|---|---|---|---|

| SWOT | Factors in the competitive environment |
|---|---|
| | Established reputation operating over 30 years, with an audience of over 200 million people worldwide |
| | Competition from other forms of entertainment such as theatre music productions |
| | A rise in concern for animal welfare causes among consumer groups |
| | A number of the world's leading sports nations invest in its gymnastic programmes |
| | Stedding's Circus's strategy is based on product development and not a marketing approach |
| | A rise in revenues of 20% since 2015 |

**Table 8.1:** SWOT analysis

2   Identify appropriate PEST factors that might relate to the circus.

3   Following a review of the plans for the circus skills training academy, the outcomes in Table 8.2 were calculated, with the state of the economy the determining factor in the academy's success. The training academy is expected to cost $35 000 to set up, and the expected outcomes are as follows.

| Economy | Outcome if academy started | Outcome without academy |
|---|---|---|
| Good (40% chance) | $200 000 | $140 000 |
| Poor (60% chance) | $60 000 | $50 000 |

**Table 8.2:** Predicted outcomes for circus skills training academy

Using the information in Table 8.2, construct a decision tree for Stedding's Circus.

## REFLECTION

Look back over Question 3. Have you drawn the decision tree correctly? Have you included learning to draw decision trees in your study schedule, and if so, how will you learn this? Can you draw a decision tree for a range of different projects?

4   a   Recommend whether Stedding's Circus should introduce a circus skills training academy.   [12]

    b   Advise Stedding's Circus on whether using decision trees is the most useful approach when developing their new business strategy.   [20]

## ≪ RECALL AND CONNECT 3 ≪

Can you explain the importance of business planning in making any investment decision?

a   Stedding's Circus operates in which economic sector?
b   What type of ownership structure does Stedding's Circus have?
c   Identify the objectives of the circus.

## SELF-ASSESSMENT CHECKLIST

Let's revisit the Knowledge focus and Exam skills focus for this chapter. Decide how confident you are with each statement.

| Now I can | Show it | Needs more work | Almost there | Confident to move on |
|---|---|---|---|---|
| analyse the meaning and purpose of business strategy | Investigate the mission and vision statement of a business that you know well and make connections between the published vision/mission and the overall strategy of the business. | | | |

**CONTINUED**

| | | | | |
|---|---|---|---|---|
| analyse the meaning and purpose of strategic management | Provide an example, from a business that you know well, of the business's overall strategy and identify how this might influence some of the strategic decisions made by senior management. | | | |
| evaluate approaches to developing business strategies including blue ocean strategy, scenario planning, SWOT analysis, PEST analysis, Porter's five forces model, the core competence framework, the Ansoff matrix, force-field analysis and decision trees | Complete a SWOT and PEST analysis, Porter's five forces model and an Ansoff matrix for Stedding's Circus or a different marketing campaign that you are familiar with. | | | |
| understand how to complete a decision tree | Practise completing a decision tree. A concert organiser is considering whether to purchase insurance in case it needs to cancel due to bad weather. It estimates there is a 10% chance of cancellation and the cost of the insurance is $1000. The predicted revenue from the event, if it goes ahead, is $12 000. | | | |
| be introduced to the command word 'advise' and gain an awareness of how to answer an 'advise' question | Show that you can use an Ansoff matrix to advise a business about a specific course of action. | | | |

# 9 Corporate planning and implementation

## KNOWLEDGE FOCUS

You will answer questions on:

**9.1** Corporate planning

**9.2** Corporate culture

**9.3** Transformational leadership

**9.4** Managing and controlling strategic change

**9.5** Contingency planning and crisis management

## EXAM SKILLS FOCUS

In this chapter you will:

- further develop your understanding of the 'evaluate' command word, with particular reference to 20-mark questions using this word

- understand how to manage your time across A Level Paper 4 – Business Strategy.

This chapter includes the command word 'evaluate'. This command word requires you to demonstrate AO1–AO4 skills and questions are generally awarded 12 or 20 marks. 'Evaluate' is a common command word for the essay-style questions in Paper 4, where each question is worth 20 marks. 'Evaluate' responses require a consideration of at least two different perspectives and typically a consideration of the perspectives of different stakeholders. You may also wish to consider the impacts of the question in both the short and long run, in order to add additional evaluation to your response.

A Level Business consists of Papers 3 and 4. In Paper 4 you will need to read a case study and then complete two compulsory questions. You will have 1 hour and 15 minutes to complete this paper. Remember to allow time to read the case material as well as time to plan your responses, before you decide how much time you will allocate to writing your answers.

# 9.1 Corporate planning

**UNDERSTAND THIS TERM**

- corporate planning

**1**  **a**  How do changes in the business environment make it necessary for businesses to continually revise their corporate plans?

  **b**  Describe the benefits and limitations of business plans and explain the similarities and differences between corporate and business plans.

# 9.2 Corporate culture

**UNDERSTAND THIS TERM**

- corporate culture

**1**  Explain how different corporate culture types can affect decision making.

# 9.3 Transformational leadership

**UNDERSTAND THIS TERM**

- transformational leadership

**1**  Explain **three** reasons why transformational leadership is important to a business during a period of change.

The next question contains the command word 'evaluate'. Remember that this means to judge, or calculate the quality, importance, amount or value of something.

The main difference between the 'evaluate' style questions you will find on Paper 1 worth 12 marks and those you will find on Paper 4 worth 20 mark is the focus on business strategy that is required on Paper 4. For a 20-mark evaluation question, there should be reference to the strategic nature of business, and analysis and evaluation must be linked to business strategy.

**2**  Evaluate how organisational culture could be used as a strategy to provide a source of competitive advantage for an organisation.  [20]

**REFLECTION**

What have you added to your response to differentiate it from a 12-mark response using the same command word?

## 9.4 Managing and controlling strategic change

### UNDERSTAND THIS TERM

- change management

1   What is the role of PEST and force-field analysis in managing and controlling change?

### ≪ RECALL AND CONNECT 1 ≪

Describe the importance of business strategy in managing and controlling change.

## 9.5 Contingency planning and crisis management

### UNDERSTAND THESE TERMS

- contingency planning
- crisis management

1   Explain the difference between contingency planning and crisis management.

2   Outline the benefits and costs to a business of using contingency planning.

### ≪ RECALL AND CONNECT 2 ≪

Provide reasons why a business might fail as a result of not putting in place contingency plans for any potential crisis management situation.

## SELF-ASSESSMENT CHECKLIST

Let's revisit the Knowledge focus and Exam skills focus for this chapter.
Decide how confident you are with each statement.

| Now I can | Show it | Needs more work | Almost there | Confident to move on |
|---|---|---|---|---|
| analyse the importance of corporate planning | Compile/design a corporate training programme for a business you are familiar with. This should include a list of the elements required. | | | |
| evaluate different types of corporate culture and its impact on decision-making | List the potential benefits and limitations of each of the following types of culture: role, task, power, entrepreneurial, person. Provide an example of an organisation where you might find each. | | | |
| evaluate the importance of transformational leadership | Investigate an organisation using transitional leadership and consider the impact on workforce engagement and innovation. | | | |
| analyse the management and control of strategic change | Identify an example of one significant change to an organisation that you know and apply the stages of the change process to the change. Assess the role of project champions in the process. | | | |
| evaluate the importance of contingency planning and crisis management | Explain the role of crisis management in a business you are familiar with in addressing the challenges presented by the COVID-19 pandemic. Describe the components of a contingency plan in that business. | | | |

## CONTINUED

| | | | | |
|---|---|---|---|---|
| further develop my understanding of the 'evaluate' command word, with particular reference to 20-mark questions using this word | Write down how the command word 'evaluate' differs from other command words used in essay-style questions. | | | |
| understand how to manage my time across A Level Paper 4 – Business Strategy | Practise exam responses for Paper 4 questions using the allocated time available. Use a stopwatch or clock to make sure that you spend no more than 30 minutes on responses in Paper 4. Allow yourself 15 minutes of reading time in addition to the writing time. | | | |

# Exam practice 2

This section contains both past paper questions from previous Cambridge exams and practice questions. These questions draw together your knowledge on a range of topics that you have covered up to this point and will help you prepare for your assessment.

For Question 1(a) read the case study, the question, the example student response and the commentary provided. Then, in Question 1(b), write your own answer to the question but using different legal changes from the ones in the example student response. Use the guidance in the commentary to help you as you answer the question.

1

### Garbanzo Restaurants (GR)

Leff Alfa left school with no formal qualifications. However, he had a passion for food and started working for a fast-food business in Country F. Leff worked hard and within five years was promoted to restaurant manager. By 2010, he had become dissatisfied with not being able to make strategic decisions. He decided to start up his own business. Leff is now the managing director of GR, a medium-sized private limited company in Country F. GR has a chain of 15 restaurants which sell high-quality, healthy food using locally sourced produce (ingredients). GR has expanded slowly. However, Leff is now considering ambitious growth strategies requiring significant capital investment.

### Restaurant 16

Leff has decided to open a new restaurant. He has identified two possible locations. Location X is an existing fast-food outlet in a shopping mall near a city. There are three other restaurants in the shopping mall. Location Y is in a tourist resort and would require more work to convert the building to a suitable restaurant layout. Leff has gathered information about the two locations. This is shown in Table 1.

## CONTINUED

|  | Location X | Location Y |
|---|---|---|
| Estimated time until opening of restaurant | 2 months | 6 months |
| Target market | Locals | Tourists |
| Capital cost of building work and equipment | $30 000 | $100 000 |
| Monthly fixed costs (including leasing cost) | $12 000 | $24 000 |
| Estimated average variable cost per customer | $2 | $2 |
| Estimated average revenue per customer | $8 | $10 |
| Expected average monthly number of customers | 3000 | 5000 |
| Number of customers per month needed to break even | 2000 | |
| Expected monthly profit | $6000 | |
| Length of contract for leasing the building | 1 year | 3 years |

**Table 1:** Information about the two locations

### Human resource problems

Suma, the human resource director, is worried about the high level of labour turnover and absenteeism at many restaurants, particularly among kitchen employees. These problems add to GR's recruitment and training costs. All new employees receive the minimum legally required training in food hygiene and health and safety. Most restaurant managers are recruited externally and Leff prefers individuals with strong personalities who 'get things done'. The restaurant market is highly competitive. Consequently, Leff aims to keep labour costs low and maintain as much labour flexibility as possible. Many kitchen employees and waiters are paid the legal minimum wage. However, waiters can supplement their income through the tips that customers give for good service and food.

### Budgeting for success

Leff sets quarterly budgets for all restaurants. He uses an incremental budgeting approach. Every quarter he meets with individual restaurant managers to monitor performance and give them new budgets. Leff is unhappy with the performance of Restaurant 13, which has failed to meet budget targets for the last 18 months. See Table 2. At the most recent meeting, the manager of Restaurant 13 blamed the adverse variances on:

- increased recruitment and training costs due to higher labour turnover
- a new competitor opening a nearby restaurant 12 months ago
- a reduction in tourist numbers caused by appreciation of Country F's currency exchange rate
- an increase in costs of locally sourced food due to poor weather.

## CONTINUED

The manager told Leff that: 'Unrealistic budgets demotivate me and other employees and do not help with the allocation of resources.' Table 2 shows recent budget data for Restaurant 13.

| | Budget | Actual |
|---|---|---|
| Revenue | $120 000 | $115 000 |
| Cost of sales | $27 000 | $28 000 |
| Restaurant overhead costs | $60 000 | $65 000 |
| Allocated head office overheads | $15 000 | $15 000 |
| Profit | $18 000 | $7 000 |

**Table 2:** Restaurant 13 – Budget data for the three months to 30 September 2020

### Strategic options for growth

Leff has decided to expand GR. He has conducted a thorough strategic analysis of his business and as a result is considering two strategic options.

### *Strategy 1: Manufacture chilled meals*

GR restaurants already sell a range of chilled meals, produced and packaged in each restaurant, for customers to purchase and reheat later. A national supermarket is interested in selling these GR meals throughout Country F. GR would need to establish a manufacturing site to meet the potential demand for these meals. Leff estimates a capital cost of $3 000 000.

### *Strategy 2: Takeover of Abila*

Abila is a group of ten restaurants in Country F. The owners want to sell the business for $1 560 000. If GR purchased Abila it would have to rebrand the group and update the restaurants. This would cost a further $500 000. Leff believes that he can improve profitability of these restaurants through rationalisation. There would be many redundancies.

**a** Analyse how any **two** changes in the legal environment might affect GR. [8]

| Example student response | Examiner comments |
|---|---|
| The legal environment is the rules set by government to regulate business activity and acts as both a constraint and an enabler for the restaurant's activities. | The student has identified and understood two relevant changes. |
| Two changes to law that are likely to have an impact on the business might be changes to the level of minimum wage and laws covering health and safety legislation. GR, like many restaurants, has a proportion of its workforce receiving the minimum wage or just above this level. As a restaurant serving customers they are also bound by health and safety laws with respect to food labelling, expiry dates and food hygiene. | Importantly, the student took care to identify both opportunities and threats to the changes identified. |
| At first glance the restaurant is likely to face a reduction in profits through increasing labour costs in the industry. | The response also makes some use of the extract. However, there is far too much use of the context. Given that this is an 8-mark question, there are only two marks available for application. The use of too much context leaves an opportunity cost of this wasted time and effort. |
| However, Garbanzo's may also see some benefit from the rise in minimum wage levels, despite the higher costs involved. Evidence from management theorists suggests that higher wages may well motivate workers as well as help GR retain workers. The rise in the level of minimum wage may also provide an opportunity for GR to change the way that they pay their staff, negotiating with staff representatives a compensation package based on tips (received from customers), rather than a salary. Such a scheme would negate the impact of higher minimum wage as employees would instead receive a proportion of total restaurant receipts. The advantage of such a compensation package is that it will motivate staff to improve customer service, benefitting the business. | There are some implications mentioned to the business, and analysis is developed. However, again, there is far too much detail included. This is a very common mistake, and it is important to know when to stop writing as this time needs to be spent on other questions. |
| Any change to health and safety standards might also have a direct impact on Garbanzo. Any changes will require additional health and safety training to employees. Training incurs costs on the business as well as taking employees away from working directly. | |
| That said, this may be one area that GR might turn to their advantage, with the highest health and safety of food standards contributing to the company's reputation for high quality, healthy food. By improving staff training, GR can improve the quality of employees and make the restaurant more efficient, improving service and reducing complaints from customers. | There is an attempt to make a judgement at the end of the answer by providing a conclusion. This is another example of time being used poorly as the skill of evaluation will not be awarded on an 8-mark question using the command word 'analyse'. |
| In conclusion, therefore, while GR (as with other establishments) will be fearful of changes to minimum wage and/or health and safety they may be able to turn any changes to their advantage or at least minimise any costs involved. Any such measure will of course require the business to be proactive in any decision making and grasp the opportunities provided. | *8/8 marks* |

**b** Think of **two** other legal changes (such as unfair dismissal, consumer protection law, taxation changes or competition policy) and write your own answer to Question 1(a).

For Question 2(a) read the question, the example student response and the commentary provided. Then, in Question 2(b), write an improved answer to the question, using the guidance in the commentary to help you.

**2  a**  Assume Leff chooses strategy 2. Evaluate how to implement this strategy effectively.  [20]

*Cambridge International AS & A Level Business (9609) Paper 32 Q7, November 2020*

| Example student response | Examiner comments |
|---|---|
| The owners of Abila want to sell the business. In addition to the purchasing cost the new owners will need to rebrand the group and update the restaurants, costing a further $500 000. Strategic implementation involves putting a strategy (the purchase and rebrand) into effect with the purpose of improving profitability of these restaurants through rationalisation. | The response demonstrates a good understanding of the key terms. For instance, strategic implementation is accurately defined and the response notes that detailed corporate planning will be needed. |
| This is a major strategic decision involving significant change and substantial resources. The first part of implementing this plan will involve a detailed corporate plan and given the costs involved of the acquisition, any plan will involve the financial department. One of the first decisions is how the initial cost of $2 000 000 will be paid for. Such a purchase could be financed out of borrowing and/or cumulative profit. | The response notes that sourcing finance will be needed but does not address the role of other operational sections, e.g. the role of HR and operational planning in allocating resources. The response does, however, note that this is a major strategic decision involving significant change and substantial resources. |
| The question suggests that following the purchase Leff wants to rebrand the restaurant chain and to be successful any brand image needs to promote meal quality and, equally, once the restaurant is under new management/ownership, maintaining the quality of meals and customer service. With the restaurant business being a very competitive one Leff can also expect to have to deal with new entrants to the market as well as needing to address changes to the legal environment. Examples of changes to external influences might be restrictions on conditions of employment, including maximum working hours and minimum wage. Lastly, competition policy and health and safety at work legislation are also particularly pertinent for the restaurant industry. Leff believes that he can improve profitability of these restaurants through rationalisation and any push for rationalisation includes the likelihood of redundancies. | The response is also applied to GR. The cost of the deal ($2,000,000) is highlighted and the passage is used where appropriate. Dealing with changes to the legal environment is also explained and the response also includes some examples of legal changes that might affect the business. |
| The addition of ten restaurants will also create significant communication changes for the business. This is particularly so because the Abila restaurant chain would be used to its own way of doing things and suddenly receiving instructions from GR may not go down well with the Abila management, an issue hardly improved by the looming threat of redundancies hanging over the acquisition. Communication problems are unlikely to be the only challenge facing the new business with any takeover potentially running into difficulties trying to merge the cultures of the new acquired restaurants under the GR umbrella. | |

| Example student response | Examiner comments |
|---|---|
| That said, there are also likely to be benefits of such a move. One of the benefits might include business planning, e.g., reducing risk from a larger pool of operating businesses as well as the financial support available from GR. This is sometimes called a financial economy of scale with larger businesses seen as a lower risk and finding it easier and cheaper to obtain finance when required.<br><br>There are clearly both risks and opportunities resulting from the takeover. GR will have to divert resources towards the project, especially finance and people, and any such diversion will potentially take away vital resources from GR's existing operations. This of course raises the question of whether there are sufficient finances available from retained earnings to maintain GR's current operations as well as finance the expansion. If not, at least part of the acquisition will have to be financed out of borrowing, adding debt interest to the firm's costs. Equally, if GR finances the purchase from retained profit, then existing shareholders may be unhappy about having to forego dividends this year in the hope of higher future dividends, which may or may not arrive. Clearly any attempt to finance the acquisition by taking on additional investors will be unpopular with existing owners who will not wish to see their current ownership of the business diluted. Does Leff have the expertise to make all the decisions regarding this expansion? | However, the response would have been further improved by a discussion of the use of brand image and the need to maintain quality meals, as well as deal with new entrants to the market. The difficulties of managing communication with the extra ten restaurants are mentioned but only briefly.<br><br>The advantages and disadvantages of the application are also briefly addressed. However, the answer only addresses individual elements of the implementation of the strategy. Stronger analysis would include a developed analysis of the strategy as a whole, rather than individual items.<br><br>The answer attempts to provide evaluation in places, but there is no clear judgement. It fails to note that successful implementation of the strategy will be vital to the success of GR as failure could put at risk the entire business but does identify some of the elements of the implementation, e.g. ensuring finance is in place, possible culture clash and possible employee resistance, and how best to deal with these issues. There is also a lack of context in evaluative points, which limits the marks that can be awarded.<br><br>*13/20 marks* |

**b** Now write an improved answer to Question 2(a).

# 10 Human resource management

You will answer questions on:

**10.1** Human resource management: purpose and role

**10.2** Workforce planning

**10.3** Recruiting and selecting employees

**10.4** Redundancy and dismissal of employees

**10.5** Employee morale and welfare

**10.6** Training and developing employees

**10.7** Management and workforce relations

EXAM SKILLS FOCUS

In this chapter you will:

- be introduced to the command word 'evaluate'

- further develop an approach to metacognitive practice when answering exam questions with a focus on monitoring progress against mark scheme requirements.

In this chapter you will be introduced to the command word 'evaluate'. 'Evaluate' means to 'judge or calculate the quality, importance, amount, or value of something'. This means that you need to give a detailed answer with a clear line of argument demonstrating the links/relationships between factors or the consequences of an event or decisions. You then need to provide a developed judgement or conclusion in the context of the business that draws together analytical and evaluative comments which weigh up key arguments.

Mark scheme awareness is an important skill to master. It is not just about knowing how the marks are allocated in a question but also what needs to be included in an answer to gain the allocated marks. A useful approach to understanding this is to create a small checklist of what you think you need to include in your practice answers so you can assess your progress. In this chapter you will be provided with a series of checklists to help you understand what is required to answer the questions in the chapter and to develop this skill to support you in monitoring your own progress.

# 10.1 Human resource management: purpose and role

| UNDERSTAND THIS TERM |
| --- |
| • human resource management (HRM) |

1   Why do you think effective HRM is important for a firm?

2   Using your answer to Question 1, which of the reasons you gave do you think is the most important for a firm? Explain your decision.

# 10.2 Workforce planning

| UNDERSTAND THESE TERMS |
| --- |
| • workforce audit |
| • labour turnover |

1   There are many factors that that will affect the number of employees required by a firm. Explain as many of these as you can.

2   State the formula for labour turnover.

3   What are **three** potential costs of a firm having a high labour turnover?

4   What are **three** potential benefits of a firm having a high labour turnover?

5   Suggest **four** ways a firm could reduce its labour turnover level.

6
> **Ultra Bank (UB)**
>
> UB offers online banking services for commercial use. At the start of the year, it employed 300 staff in one of its customer service centres. These employees are typically involved in answering customer phone calls and dealing with any technical difficulties when customers are trying to access their accounts online. Throughout the year, 165 workers have left the organisation.

a   Calculate the labour turnover rate for UB.                    [2]

Question 6(b) requires you to evaluate. The mark allocation for a 12-mark 'evaluate' question is as follows:

- AO1 Knowledge and understanding                    [2]
- AO2 Application                                     [2]
- AO3 Analysis                                        [2]
- AO4 Evaluation.                                     [6]

Plan an answer to Question 6(b) by writing down what needs to be included for each of the assessment objectives.

    **b**    Evaluate the impact on Ultra Bank of its high labour turnover.          [12]

## ≪ RECALL AND CONNECT 1 ≪

Becoming a company requires many legal formalities. Outline the **two** main documents that are required in most countries to establish a limited company.

# 10.3 Recruiting and selecting employees

**1**    Explain the purpose of a person specification.

**2**    Explain **three** methods a firm could use when selecting between applicants.

**3**    Explain **two** factors that could affect a firm's selection process.

Before you begin to write the answer to Question 4, write down how you think the eight available marks will be allocated in the mark scheme.

**4**

> ### AB Airlines (AB)
>
> AB is the national airline of Country Y. It currently employs over 30 000 workers and flies to 163 destinations, including international and domestic routes. It has been growing recently and needs to increase the number of pilots it employs to operate the new planes that it has purchased.

Analyse **one** benefit and **one** cost of external recruitment for AB when employing a new airline pilot.          [8]

---

**UNDERSTAND THESE TERMS**

- recruitment
- selection
- Recruitment agency
- job description
- person specification
- application form

Knowing what you need to do in an answer is an important skill when learning to understand the requirements of the mark scheme. The following is a checklist of items that may be covered in a mark scheme for Question 4. Check your answer. Have you done everything?

| Skill |
| --- |
| • Shown knowledge of a benefit of external recruitment? (AO1) |
| • Shown knowledge of a cost of external recruitment? (AO1) |
| • Applied your answer to AB? (AO2) |
| • Applied your answer specifically to the recruitment of an airline pilot? (AO2) |
| • Assessed the impact of the benefit and cost of using external recruitment to the business? (AO3) |

Are there any skills in the checklist that you did not include in your answer? How could you develop your answer to incorporate these?

**UNDERSTAND THESE TERMS**

- curriculum vitae (CV)
- resume
- reference
- assessment centre
- internal recruitment
- external recruitment
- employment contract

**REFLECTION**

Look at your answer for Question 4. Think about whether you would need to change the answer if you were asked to analyse a benefit and a cost of external recruitment to a grocery store when employing a new customer service assistant. Why would your answer need to be different?

# 10.4 Redundancy and dismissal of employees

1   State **three** reasons why an employee could be fairly dismissed.

2   Identify **three** reasons why an employee might have been unfairly dismissed.

3
| **TrainWay (TW)** |
| --- |
| TW is a large company which operates a number of train services in Country X. It employs a range of workers, including train drivers, ticket sellers and train inspectors. |

Analyse **two** possible consequences to TW if it were found to have unfairly dismissed a train driver.   [8]

**UNDERSTAND THESE TERMS**

- redundancy
- dismissal
- unfair dismissal

You need to be able to understand what skills are required in an answer to allow you to access the marks available. In Section 10.3, you were given a completed skills checklist for an answer. You should use the following template and create your own checklist of what you think you needed to include in your answer to Question 3. Use this to assess your own work.

| Skill |
| --- |
| •   Shown knowledge of ................................................... |
| •   Applied your answer to ................................................. |
| •   Analysed the impact of ................................................. |

## 10.5 Employee morale and welfare

UNDERSTAND THESE TERMS

- employee morale
- employee welfare
- work–life balance
- equality policy
- diversity policy

1   Explain **two** methods a firm can use to improve the work–life balance of its employees.

2   Explain **two** ways a firm can benefit from promoting diversity in its workplace.

## 10.6 Training and developing employees

1   State **three** features of an induction training programme.

2   State **two** benefits and costs to a firm of using on-the-job training.

3

> **FizzPop (FP)**
>
> FP produces a variety of beverages that are sold around the world. These are made in over 100 factories that are located in many different countries. The workers in the factories are involved in overseeing the machinery that combines the ingredients to make the beverages, as well as monitoring the quality of the output.

Evaluate whether FP should use on-the-job training for a new quality control supervisor in one of its factories.                    [12]

## 10.7 Management and workforce relations

1   Industrial disputes can cause problems to a workplace, including poor employee–employer relations and a reduction in productivity levels. Explain **two** methods of industrial action that trade union leaders can suggest are used by their members during a dispute with their employers.

**≪ RECALL AND CONNECT 2 ≪**

You need to think about the type of worker and the job they will be performing when considering what type of training might be most suitable. It might not be financially viable for a firm to spend a lot of its capital using off-the-job training for a worker who only requires a very basic skill or is unlikely to be in the job for a long time, such as a seasonal fruit picker. Explain the impact on **three** stakeholders if a firm decides to increase the amount of training it does for new workers.

## SELF-ASSESSMENT CHECKLIST

Let's revisit the Knowledge focus and Exam skills focus for this chapter.
Decide how confident you are with each statement.

| Now I can | Show it | Needs more work | Almost there | Confident to move on |
|---|---|---|---|---|
| analyse the role and purpose of the human resource managers in an organisation | Explain the impact of not having good human resource management in an organisation of your choice. | | | |
| analyse the importance of employee recruitment and selection to an organisation | Select three different firms and outline how they would recruit and select for two different job roles within the firm. | | | |
| evaluate the different methods of recruitment and selection | Create a revision card detailing the benefits and costs of different methods of recruitment and selection. | | | |
| assess the main features of employment contracts | State and explain the purpose of three features of an employment contract. | | | |
| discuss the importance of training and development in increasing efficiency and motivation | Outline three ways each method of training (induction, on-the-job and off-the-job) can be used to increase efficiency and motivation. | | | |
| evaluate the importance of employee morale and welfare | Describe three consequences for a firm of not looking after its employees' morale and welfare. | | | |
| be introduced to the command word 'evaluate' | Explain how the skills required to answer an 'evaluate' differ from those needed to answer an 'analyse' question. | | | |
| further develop an approach to metacognitive practice when answering exam questions with a focus on monitoring progress against mark scheme requirements | Create an answer checklist for Question 3 in Section 10.6. | | | |

# 11 Motivation

## EXAM SKILLS FOCUS

In this chapter you will:

- learn how to manage test anxiety by planning your answer using the PEEL method

- explore the use of the STEPS technique to improve application skills.

In an exam, it is tempting to go straight into writing your answer. The problem with this is that you do not give your brain enough time to consider the response. Spending some time planning your answers will give you time to relax and really consider what it is you are writing. It will help you think about the best points to include in your answer and how to structure these, meaning that the communication of your knowledge should be clearer.

Understanding the skill of application is essential. For the majority of exam questions, you will be required to refer to the case study (also called 'context'), and to do this your answers need to be *applied* to the case study you are given and *only* the case study you are given. This chapter introduces the STEPS tool, which you can use to help develop your understanding of the case study and explore ways you can apply your answer.

# 11.1 What is motivation, and why does it matter?

1  Why does motivating the workforce matter for a business? What would happen if workers were not motivated?

# 11.2 Human needs

1  Explain how human needs can be satisfied at work.

# 11.3 Motivation theories

1  Copy out Table 11.1 and make notes under each heading to help you understand the motivational theories from Taylor, Herzberg and Mayo.

| Theorist | What are the main features of the theory? | Are any key terms related to the theory? | What impact does this theory have on motivation? | Are there any other points to note? |
|---|---|---|---|---|
| Taylor | | | | |
| Herzberg | | | | |
| Mayo | | | | |

**Table 11.1:** Assessing the work of Taylor, Herzberg and Mayo

2  Figure 11.1 shows Maslow's hierarchy of needs.

a  Copy the diagram and complete the missing labels for each level of the hierarchy.

b  Explain how the needs of workers can be met at each level of the hierarchy by a business.

c  What are the limitations of Maslow's approach to motivation?

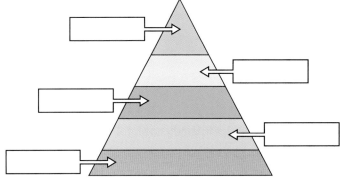

**Figure 11.1:** Maslow's hierarchy of needs

3

> **Nadia's Garden Club (NGC)**
>
> NGC is a small social enterprise. Nadia employs young people who are finding it challenging to enter the workforce and helps them gain new skills and qualifications to support them in securing jobs with other employers in the future. Typically, employees remain at NCG for two years. The social enterprise encourages its workers to grow and sell organic vegetables through a small vegetable plot and shop owned by Nadia.

Analyse **two** benefits to Nadia of using McClelland's content theory of motivation with her employees.                                   [12]

A simple way of planning analytical paragraphs is by using the PEEL method.

- Point: what is the point you wish to cover in this paragraph?
- Explain: explain this point a bit further (develop).
- Evidence: make sure you have included some case study evidence/application.
- Link: make sure you link it back to the question.

Table 11.2 provides an example.

| Point | Explain | Evidence | Link |
|---|---|---|---|
| Getting workers in the future | Need for achievement; want to reach goals, progress | Employees gain qualifications | Human need: praise and recognition |

**Table 11.2:** The PEEL method

You could then use this plan to write your paragraph.

A benefit to Nadia is that she may be able to attract workers to her business in the future. One area of McClelland's theory that Nadia could use is the <u>need for achievement</u>. This states that employees want to <u>reach goals as part</u> of their working day and <u>make progress</u> in what they do. Nadia offers her employees the opportunity to <u>gain skills and qualifications</u> when growing organic vegetables. This allows the workers to reach their achievement goals as they will have completed a qualification. This then allows the employees to meet their own <u>human needs for praise and recognition</u>, which is likely to mean they are motivated to work, benefitting NGC by developing a good reputation as a place to work for future employees. This is essential given that employees tend to only stay for two years, so Nadia needs to ensure she continues to attract the employees she needs in the future.

Try this for yourself: in answer to Question 3 you could copy the PEEL method, as shown in Table 11.2, for another point.

Now write the paragraph based on this plan.

How did you feel writing your answer after spending some time planning? Consider whether the planning time made you feel calmer and more organised or if you need to spend more time practising this technique to help you build your confidence in using it.

4   Copy Table 11.3 and match the features of Vroom's expectancy theory to the correct descriptions.

| Feature | Description |
| --- | --- |
| Valence | The confidence of employees that they will actually get what they desire, even if it has been promised by the manager. |
| Expectancy | The depth of the desire of an employee for an extrinsic reward, such as money, or an intrinsic reward, such as satisfaction. |
| Instrumentality | The degree to which people believe that putting effort into work will lead to a given level of performance. |

**Table 11.3:** Vroom's expectancy theory

## ≪ RECALL AND CONNECT 2 ≪

Company J has 400 000 shares issued into the market. The current share price is $0.30. What is the total market capitalisation value of Company J?

**UNDERSTAND THESE TERMS**

- piece rate
- self-actualisation
- motivators (motivating factors)
- hygiene factors
- job enrichment

# 11.4 Motivation methods in practice

1   In which situations might a business use each of the following financial motivation methods?

- a   time-based wage rate
- b   piece rate
- c   salary
- d   commission
- e   bonus
- f   performance-related pay
- g   profit sharing
- h   fringe benefits.

**2** Create a mind map to identify the advantages and disadvantages of each payment method discussed in Question 1.

The AO2 Application objective requires students to 'apply knowledge and understanding of business concepts, terms and theories to problems and issues in a variety of familiar and unfamiliar business situations and contexts'. You need to be able to apply your subject knowledge clearly to the case study and context presented to you. A useful method for improving your application is by following STEPS, as follows.

| **S**takeholders | • What do you know about the company's stakeholders? What are its customers called? Diners? Shoppers? Tourists? Be specific. |
|---|---|
| **T**ext | • Can you use any information or data from the case study text in your answer? |
| **E**xternal environment | • Are there elements of the external environment that will affect the business more than others? Changes in the economy? Demographics and social factors? Competitors? |
| **P**roduct/service | • Refer to the nature of the product/service in the case study. |
| **S**ize | • Consider the size of the business: this will impact on its ability to access resources such as capital, and may also affect its choice of objectives. |

Making some notes on STEPS for a few minutes when you get given a case study can help you gain a more developed appreciation of the context, allowing you to think of ways you can demonstrate the skill of application.

**3**

> **SuperSaver Supermarket (SS)**
>
> SS owns 75 supermarkets in Country D. It sells a range of high-quality but affordable groceries. It does this by purchasing its stock in bulk, as well as holding a limited number of well-known brand-name products, preferring to sell its own brand-name products. It employs over 2000 workers in its stores, ranging from shop-floor workers through to team leaders and store managers.

Evaluate whether financial motivators are the most effective way of improving employee motivation in a supermarket. [12]

**a** Make some notes on some elements of STEPS for the SS Supermarket case study; you may not be able to do all element of STEPS as there is limited information.

**b** The following paragraph is theoretically correct, but only scores one mark as it has no application within it. Using your understanding of the SS Supermarket case study and your STEPS notes, write out an improved version of this paragraph so it includes application in appropriate places.

> Financial motivators are a useful method of improving the motivation of workers as they help workers meet their basic needs. By providing financial motivators such as increased pay or bonuses, workers will be more motivated. This will make them more productive, meaning they will perform better. This is a benefit for a business because it should mean that there are more goods for sale.

It is vital when bringing impacts of motivation back to the business, especially when discussing productivity, that you are very clear about how the business would measure productivity and the overall impact of this on the business and its potential objectives.

4 Explain the difference between job rotation, job enrichment and job enlargement.

5 How can training be used as a method of non-financial motivation?

6 Explain how methods of employee participation can be used to motivate workers.

## UNDERSTAND THESE TERMS

- job redesign
- development
- employee participation
- teamworking
- empowerment
- development
- quality circle

## ≪ RECALL AND CONNECT 3 ≪

Explain how a business can grow through external methods.

## REFLECTION

In this chapter you have been introduced to two different techniques to support you in your exams – PEEL and STEPS. Do you think these techniques are useful for you? How can you practise using these to develop your confidence further?

## SELF-ASSESSMENT CHECKLIST

Let's revisit the Knowledge focus and Exam skills focus for this chapter.
Decide how confident you are with each statement.

| Now I can | Show it | Needs more work | Almost there | Confident to move on |
|---|---|---|---|---|
| understand what motivation is and why motivated workers are important to business | Explain four reasons why having motivated workers is important for a business. | | | |
| discuss contributions of motivational theorists and their relevance to business | Create a two-page factsheet detailing the contributions of the motivational theorists in this chapter and their relevance to business today. | | | |

**CONTINUED**

| | | | | |
|---|---|---|---|---|
| understand the different methods used to motivate workers | Go back to the mind map you created in Section 11.4 (Question 2) and add in the non-financial methods of motivation that can be used by a business. | | | |
| evaluate the appropriateness of different payment systems and evaluate their impact on motivation | Find real-world examples of job roles that would be appropriate for each payment system and explain your reasons for this. | | | |
| analyse the role of non-financial methods of motivation and evaluate their impact | Find real-world examples of job roles that would be appropriate for each method of non-financial motivation and explain how these methods would motivate the worker. | | | |
| learn how to manage test anxiety by planning my answer using the PEEL method | Look through a selection of past papers and mark schemes on the Cambridge Assessment International Education website and practise using the PEEL method on some of the extended response questions. | | | |
| explore the use of the STEPS technique to improve application skills | Look through a selection of past papers and mark schemes on the Cambridge Assessment International Education website and use the STEPS technique to develop your confidence in using it for exam case studies. | | | |

# 12 Management

In this chapter, you will practise planning your answer before you write, as this can be a useful method for reducing anxiety. This will be done alongside the use of assessment objectives so you can start to combine the skills you have developed in previous chapters. It may feel like planning is not a good use of time in an exam, as it means you have less time to write your actual answer. However, time spent planning usually means you can write your answer more efficiently as you have a clearer idea of what you are hoping to write.

# 12.1 Management and managers

**1** **a** What are the traditional functions of managers?

    **b** What did Fayol state the **five** functions of managers are? Explain what each function means.

    **c** What **three** categories did Mintzberg classify manager roles as?

**2** Create a knowledge organiser for each of the **four** main management styles. Use the format in Figure 12.1 to help you: just be sure to change the management style in the centre of each one you create. You need to fill in each of the boxes with as much information as you can to help you revise the topic.

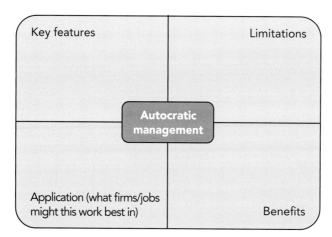

**Figure 12.1:** Knowledge organiser example

Planning an answer should be a relatively quick process as it is just a way to organise your thoughts before you start writing your response to an exam question. Follow these steps for Question 3:

- Step 1. Identify the skills/assessment objectives you will be assessed on in the question (this can be identified by the command word in the question).

- Step 2. Read and understand the question you are being asked.

- Step 3. Underline what topic you are being assessed on.

- Step 4. Write down anything that comes to mind when you think about the topic.

- Step 5. From all the things you have written down, pick the one or ones that you think are the most relevant in supporting you to answer the question.

- Step 6. Structure your paragraphs, ready to write them in full (use the following example to support you with this).

| Knowledge and understanding (AO1) | Application (AO2) | Analysis (AO3) | Developed analysis (Developed AO3) |
|---|---|---|---|
| Discuss ideas with workers | Managers of SV hotel | Get better ideas on running hotel | Staff feel happier that ideas are being used–better motivation–therefore customer service |

3

**Sandy View Hotel (SV)**

SV is located in a beach resort in Country A. The hotel is open all year round, although it finds it has very few customers during the winter months. SV employs a range of workers, including a manager, cleaners, catering staff and receptionists. Adam, the manager, has the responsibility for running the hotel on a daily basis. He has always adopted a democratic leadership approach with the workers.

Analyse **one** advantage and **one** disadvantage of Adam's management style on the operations of SV. [8]

## ≪ RECALL AND CONNECT 1 ≪

What are the **four** different methods of business integration that can be used to grow a business?

## 12.2 McGregor's Theory X and Theory Y

### UNDERSTAND THESE TERMS

- Theory X
- Theory Y

1  Copy the following table into your notebook. For each of the statements, decide whether it is a view held by a Theory X manager or a Theory Y manager and then tick the correct column.

| Statement | Theory X | Theory Y |
|---|---|---|
| **a** Workers dislike work and are lazy. | | |
| **b** Workers can derive as much enjoyment from work as from rest and play. | | |
| **c** Workers will avoid responsibility. | | |
| **d** Workers are not creative. | | |
| **e** Workers will accept responsibility. | | |
| **f** Workers are creative. | | |

**Table 12.1:** Theory X and Theory Y statements

### ≪ RECALL AND CONNECT 2 ≪

Explain **two** differences between public and private sector organisations.

### REFLECTION

Think about the exam skills question in this chapter. How did planning the answer before you wrote your response help manage any anxiety you might have had in this task? Are there ways you could develop your approach to planning that can help you with reducing test anxiety with any future questions?

## SELF-ASSESSMENT CHECKLIST

Let's revisit the Knowledge focus and Exam skills focus for this chapter.
Decide how confident you are with each statement.

| Now I can | Show it | Needs more work | Almost there | Confident to move on |
|---|---|---|---|---|
| analyse the main functions of managers | State three functions of managers. | | | |
| assess the importance of good management to the success of a business | Explain what would happen to a business if there was bad management. | | | |
| evaluate the differences between the views of Fayol and Mintzberg on the role of management | Create a table that shows the difference between the views of the two theorists. | | | |
| analyse the key differences in management styles | Develop a revision mind map detailing the key features of the different management styles. | | | |
| evaluate the appropriateness of these styles to different business situations | Look at a selection of case studies from this chapter of the coursebook and consider which management style might be most appropriate in each case and try to explain why. | | | |
| analyse the differences between McGregor's Theory X and Theory Y | List three examples of job roles that would be suited to each of McGregor's theories. | | | |
| learn how to manage test anxiety by using a structured answer plan linked to assessment objectives | Look through a selection of past papers on the Cambridge Assessment International Education website and practise planning some answers before you write them as part of your revision. | | | |

# Exam practice 3

This section contains both past paper questions from previous Cambridge exams and practice questions. These questions draw together your knowledge on a range of topics that you have covered up to this point and will help you prepare for your assessment.

Question 1 has example student responses and commentaries provided. For each part of the question, work through the question first, then compare your answer to the example student response and commentary.

**1  a**  Define the term 'contract of employment'.                    [2]

*Cambridge International AS & A Level Business (9609) Paper 13 Q2a, November 2019*

| Example student response | Examiner comments |
|---|---|
| It sets out the terms and conditions for employment. | This answer shows a simple understanding of what a contract of employment is and is worth **one** mark. The term includes two words that need to be explained: 'contract' and 'employment'. This answer only gives a definition of contract and not employment. |

**b**  Explain **one** advantage to employees of having a contract of employment.                    [3]

| Example student response | Examiner comments |
|---|---|
| An advantage is that the employee knows what is expected of them, for example what their duties are and how many days a week to work. | This is a sound explanation of an advantage of having a contract of employment and this is fully explained. The student clearly understands that having written employment details is useful and the advantage is that they know what is expected of them. The answer is awarded **three** marks. |

For Question 2(a) read the question, the example student response and the commentary provided. Then, in Question 2(b), write an improved answer to the question but using a different benefit from the one in the example student response. Use the guidance in the commentary to help you as you answer the question.

2  a  Explain **one** benefit of a cooperative to its members.          [3]

| Example student response | Examiner comments |
|---|---|
| One benefit is that members get to have a vote. | Stating that members have a vote shows some knowledge of a cooperative. This answer is worth **one** mark. An improved answer would need to provide a descriptive benefit, such as 'members are involved in the running of the cooperative'. This would then need to be developed in further detail to be worth three marks. An example of this would be 'so they can feel motivated by the responsibility of this'. |

   b  Think of another benefit of a cooperative to its members and write your own answer to Question 2.

Question 3 has example student responses and commentaries provided. For each part of the question, work through the question first, then compare your answer to the example student response and commentary.

3  a  Analyse **two** advantages to a financial services business of improving employees' work–life balance.          [8]

   *Adapted from Cambridge International AS & A Level Business (9609) Paper 13 Q5a, November 2019*

| Example student response | Examiner comments |
|---|---|
| One advantage of improving employees' work-life balance is that it will create a healthy working environment. The employees will be able to balance the time they spend at work with the time they spend at home, so they will be more motivated to work and will be more productive. | This answer shows a good knowledge of work–life balance. |
| | Application to a financial services business is weak. There needs to be more reference to the business (e.g., instead of saying 'more productive', say 'able to provide better customer service to the clients'). |
| Another advantage is that by improving the work-life balance of the employees, there will be better relationships between employees and their managers. By maintaining a supportive working environment through things such as providing additional training opportunities for employees to gain qualifications in financial services, the employees will feel they are getting personal growth. If they feel their needs to develop are being met, they are likely to be happier and feel appreciated by their managers for investing in them. This will mean that relationships will be stronger in the workplace, which is likely to lead to much higher levels of employee retention, reducing potential recruitment costs in the future. | In the first paragraph, the advantage given is implied and not well-developed. The impact on the business of the employees being more productive needs to be more developed. The second paragraph is much more developed, and the advantage is well explained. |
| | *6/8 marks* |

**b** Evaluate why it is considered important for businesses to have effective policies on diversity and equality. [12]

*Adapted from Cambridge International AS & A Level Business (9609) Paper 13 Q5b, November 2019*

| Example student response | Examiner comments |
|---|---|
| Having policies related to diversity and equality means that the business is seen as a fairer workplace. This is important because if it has a focus on equality, then the workers will feel assured that any promotions that are given out are awarded based on merit and qualifications and not on race or gender. This could be essential for employee morale and motivation and ensures that the best candidate for the job is selected. This will lead to a more successful organisation. However, a business should not need to have a policy on diversity and equality to know that it should not discriminate on race or gender as this is not an acceptable way of giving out promotions and is bad business practice.<br><br>Having effective policies on diversity and equality can make a business look good to customers. A customer may look at a business website and see that it has policies on diversity and equality and then may decide this is the type of business that they want to buy from as it is showing good corporate social responsibility. As a result, the business will receive more sales revenue and, given that having policies on being diverse won't cost that much, it should mean the business gains higher levels of profit.<br><br>Overall is it essential for a business to have effective policies on diversity and equality. If it has policies then all stakeholders are able to read and see these so that everyone knows what is expected from them and their role within the business. This should mean that discrimination is reduced and all processes are fairer and do not break the law, which can be very costly for a business if it was taken to court by someone who did not get a promotion because of race discrimination. | Some knowledge of diversity and equality has been shown in the answer.<br><br>The answer is applied to different areas of the business (marketing and human resources). It is explained with good business examples and the knowledge is clearly applied to the answer in a realistic way.<br><br>There are some impacts on a business discussed, but these are not very detailed in the first paragraph. To develop this skill further, some reference to benefits that are specific to diversity and equality policies would be required (e.g., they are a legal requirement, increased understanding of diversities within the workforce, reduction in discrimination on workplace culture). The second paragraph provides better evidence of business impacts.<br><br>A judgement is made, and an attempt to justify this has been made. There is evidence of developed evaluation, but this requires explicit application to be at the highest level, which this answer is not. To strengthen the answer, it would be helpful to have more reference to the importance of these policies to a business and more justification of the factors (e.g. what the level of importance might depend upon, such as the nature of the business, e.g. a service sector business might need better public perception than a manufacturing business).<br><br>*9/12 marks* |

Now that you have read the example student responses to Question 3, here is a similar past paper question which you should attempt. Use the guidance in the commentary to help you as you answer the question.

4    a    Analyse **two** ways a business might satisfy the self-actualisation needs of its employees.                                                              [8]

     b    Evaluate the significance of McGregor's Theory X and Theory Y for managers in a hospital.                                                                       [12]

For Questions 5(a) and (b) read the case study, the questions, the example student responses and the commentaries provided. Then, in Question 5(c), write an improved answer to Question 5(b) but using a different entrepreneurial quality from the one in the example student response. Use the guidance in the commentary to help you as you answer the question.

5

> ### Priya's Bookshop (PB)
>
> Priya lives in Town R, which is situated in beautiful countryside with nice walks nearby. Many tourists visit Town R. The town's council would like Town R to become branded as a 'booktown', a town with many bookshops selling new and used books. The council announced a new financial scheme offering grants to attract entrepreneurs willing to open a bookshop. Priya applied for a grant to start up PB. Part of her grant application included a cash flow forecast, shown in Table 1.
>
> | | Month 1 | Month 2 | Month 3 |
> |---|---|---|---|
> | Cash in | | | |
> | Owner's capital | $15 000 | 0 | 0 |
> | Grant | $20 000 | 0 | 0 |
> | Revenue | $4000 | 6 | $11 000 |
> | Cash out | | | |
> | Initial set up costs | $20 000 | 0 | 0 |
> | Utilities (power, water etc.) | 0 | 0 | $2000 |
> | Employee costs | $1000 | $1000 | $3000 |
> | Purchases | $6000 | $3000 | $4000 |
> | Marketing | $10 000 | $5000 | $4000 |
> | Opening balance | 0 | $2000 | –$1000 |
> | Closing balance | $2000 | –$1000 | X |
>
> **Table 1:** Cash flow forecast, first three months of trading

> ## CONTINUED
>
> Priya's grant application was successful and she opened PB well aware of the need for both cash and profit. Priya now wants to raise awareness of PB in Town R. Priya did some market research and decided to use market segmentation. This will help her to decide on the promotional methods she could use for her bookshop. See Table 2.
>
> | Age group (years) | Percentage of residents in age group | Percentage of age group who are female |
> |---|---|---|
> | 0–15 | 19 | 50 |
> | 16–64 | 63 | 55 |
> | 65+ | 18 | 60 |
>
> **Table 2:** Age and gender of residents in Town R

a   Explain the term 'market segmentation'.                                          [3]

| Example student response | Examiner comments |
|---|---|
| When a market is split into groups based on features such as age, gender and interests. This makes it easier for a business to target its marketing efforts based on these similar characteristics. | This answer shows a more developed understanding of market segmentation. The answer shows a good understanding of the concept of segmentation, but has not fully explained the term 'market'. As they have not explained both words in the question, it cannot gain full marks. This is given **two** marks. |

b   Explain **one** entrepreneurial quality that Priya has shown.                    [3]

| Example student response | Examiner comments |
|---|---|
| Priya is motivated and likes to take risks. | The student has given a list of two entrepreneurial qualities. This is awarded **one** mark as only one entrepreneurial quality can be awarded marks. This answer needs to be developed further through a clear explanation with reference to how Priya has displayed this quality using evidence from the case study. |

c   Think of another quality not mentioned in the example and write your own answer to Question 5(b).

For Question 5(d) work through the question first, then compare your answer
to the example student response and commentary.

**d** Evaluate the most suitable promotional method that Priya could use
to raise awareness of PB in Town R.                          [12]

| Example student response | Examiner comments |
|---|---|
| One suitable promotion method that Priya can use is local radio. PB is a local bookshop in a small town with lots of competition, so Priya would need to use a promotional method that has a wide reach and sets her apart from her competitors. Local radio will allow her to do this as she could have a memorable song made that people who listen to the radio will remember. As a result, people in the local areas will hear about Priya's bookshop and come and buy books from her. However, advertising on the radio is an expense that a new, small business may not be able to afford and there is no guarantee that people who listen to the local radio even like to read books or buy books, so Priya may find that there is very minimal impact of advertising on the radio without doing much more market research. | The student shows excellent knowledge of promotional methods and how these can be used. |
|  | Throughout the answer, there is evidence of the aspects of the case study being used to explain the suitability of the methods. There is no doubt that the student is talking about Priya's bookshop, and no other business. |
| Another suitable promotional method that Priya could use is by putting leaflets in local hotels and asking them to share them with their customers. Town R is popular with tourists, and Priya could try and capture this market, which her competitors may not be doing. This would give her a market of her own so tourists who come to Town R to visit bookshops would see her leaflet in the hotel and then go and visit PB as it is the bookshop they become aware of. This should lead to good revenues for Priya. However, the issue with using leaflets in the hotel is that it will only attract tourists as locals do not stay in hotels. This means that Priya's market may be very limited and the tourists may only be in the area for a small period of the year as the weather might not be good enough for them to come and take advantage of the lovely countryside. This means that Priya's revenues will be very low in the out-of-season months. | In the first paragraph, the student takes a two-sided approach to the answer. This is a helpful approach to take when looking at the suitability of suggestions being made. There are good examples throughout of the impacts that will occur for the business when using each method of promotion, which are clearly measurable. However, the inclusion of more than one promotional method in the answer is unnecessary as analysis of only one can be awarded. |
|  | There is evidence of clear evaluation throughout the answer. At the end of the first two paragraphs, there is strong evaluation shown because the evaluative comments are in context ('a new small business may not be able to afford' and 'tourists may only be in the area for a small period of the year'). There is an attempt at a judgement at the end of the answer, but this is not explained and there is no link back to the case study. All evaluation requires justification. |
| Overall, I think Priya should use leaflets as these are cheaper than radio advertising. | *11/12 marks* |

# 13 Organisational structure

Answering one- or two-mark questions normally requires one or two (depending on the number of marks available) knowledge points. For two-mark questions the key is to include two clearly different points to avoid repetition. The command word is often 'identify', as you will see in an Exam skills question in this chapter. When answering three-mark questions with the command word 'explain', you will need to provide a sound explanation and also include an example or use of the case study material to show clear knowledge and application.

Another useful skill that you can develop is learning to mark other students' responses, in particular understanding how marks are awarded for each of the assessment objectives. This is a great way to develop your own responses. This chapter includes an activity for you to practise this.

## 13.1 Organisations need structure

1   Explain what is meant by the term 'organisational structure'.

2   What would happen if a business did not have a clear organisational structure?

3   What are the main features of an organisational structure?

## 13.2 Types of organisational structure

1   Copy out and then match the two sides of Table 13.1 so that each sentence relating to organisational structures is correct.

| Type of structure | Definition |
|---|---|
| Functional structure | Suitable for small businesses and illustrates a narrow chain of command. |
| Entrepreneurial structure | An organisational structure illustrating levels of hierarchy, spans of control and a chain of command. |
| Geographical/product structures | An organisation characterised by a divisional structure, rather than a structure based on function. |
| Hierarchical structure | An organisational structure showing relationships as a grid, rather than the traditional structure. |
| Matrix structure | A hierarchical structure showing job titles and lines of authority. |

**Table 13.1:** Organisational structures

---

REFLECTION

How confident are you about different organisational structures? You could reinforce your understanding of each structure by completing the question again but adding different definitions for each organisational structure.

---

2   Explain **two** differences between organisational structures based on hierarchy and those based on a matrix.

3   What are the advantages of a flat organisational structure with wide spans of control?

4 What are the advantages and disadvantages of delayering to a business?

5 Explain **two** ways that a centralised organisational structure might affect the motivation of employees.

6 Table 13.2 identifies features of different organisational structures. Copy out the table and identify which organisational structure(s) each feature relates to.

| Organisational structure feature | Type of organisational structure |
|---|---|
| Employees are usually grouped together by their particular specialisation. | |
| Focus on particular market segments. | |
| The structure is a vertical one and this often does not allow for good connections between departments. | |
| Crossover of ideas between people with specialist knowledge in different areas tends to create more successful and innovative solutions. | |
| This type of structure is likely to have very long chains of command. | |
| Team members may have two managers to report to. | |
| Communication is often one-way (top-downward). | |
| Spans of control are likely to be very wide. | |

**Table 13.2:** Features of functional organisational structures

REFLECTION

How have you learnt the different types of organisational structure in any business? Can you draw an organisational structure organised by function and one organised by product? After drawing these, make a list of businesses that might use each type of organisational structure and write one strength and one weakness of each.

**7** Analyse **two** advantages to a firm of the organisational chart shown in Figure 13.1. [8]

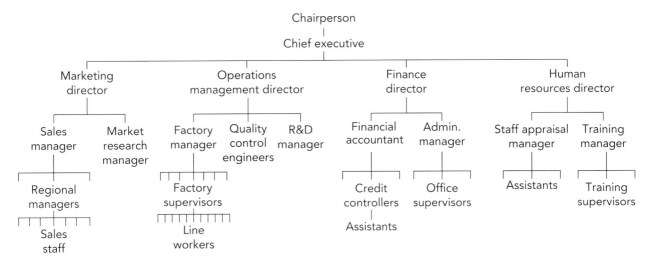

**Figure 13.1:** An example of an organisational structure

REFLECTION

How would your response have been different using either of the command words 'analyse' or 'evaluate?' What makes 'analyse' appropriate for this question?

**≪ RECALL AND CONNECT 1 ≪**

**a** Can you explain the relationship between business objectives and organisational structure, specifically relating to flexibility and business growth?

**b** Does the type of business structure influence the suitability of different organisational structures?

## 13.3 Delegation and accountability

**1** Explain **one** reason why the level of delegation in an organisation may increase when the span of control increases.

**2** Explain how delegation can improve the motivation of employees.

**3** Explain which **one** of the following is **not** a feature of delegation.

    **a** It gives senior managers time to focus on more important tasks.

    **b** It shows trust in and improves motivation of subordinates.

    **c** It helps develop and train employees for more senior roles.

    **d** It ensures that senior managers maintain direct control of all tasks.

UNDERSTAND THESE TERMS

- delegation
- accountability

4 Explain which **one** of the following steps should be taken in the accountability process.

   a Provide clear expectations and establish a one-way communication process.

   b Provide clear expectations and establish a two-way communication process.

   c Agree the process, including limits to the process.

   d Ensure that senior managers maintain direct control of the process.

### REFLECTION

How will you remember the relationship between spans of control, levels of hierarchy and the conflicts between trust and control when delegating? You could create revision cards for each term and then test yourself on the contents. Remember that by writing down meanings and definitions, they are more likely to remain embedded in your memory.

### ≪ RECALL AND CONNECT 2 ≪

a Explain how managers may need to delegate more tasks to their staff as the business grows.

b Which management styles are most likely to use delegation and accountability? Which styles are least likely to practise delegation and accountability?

## 13.4 Control, authority and trust

### UNDERSTAND THESE TERMS

- control
- authority

1 Explain the relationship between authority and responsibility.

2 Why might some managers be reluctant to give up control of a task to a subordinate?

### ≪ RECALL AND CONNECT 3 ≪

Explain the role of control, authority and trust in motivational theories.

# 13.5 Centralisation and decentralisation

| UNDERSTAND THESE TERMS |
| --- |
| • centralisation |
| • decentralisation |

1   Explain why decision-making in geographically decentralised structures might lead to more effective local decision-making.

The following Exam skills question provides an opportunity to mark a student response.

2

> **Milk Lion (ML)**
>
> ML is a well-established business selling luxury milkshakes, founded by Gabriel, with a highly centralised organisational structure. This structure means that most decisions are made by a team of senior managers with over 20 years of experience in the field. They are the current market leader in their nation but Gabriel's plan is for the business to grow through opening new shops overseas in Country Y. The company has never operated overseas before and Gabriel believes that the current centralised structure has worked until now, so why change the model when operating overseas? Others in the business, particularly the overseas franchise managers, believe that this model will need to evolve as the business gets larger and spans of control grow. There remains, however, general support for the centralised buying of milk and other ingredients to continue given the current economies of scale that the process provides. Last, ML is also unsure over the direction of the branding of the business moving forward, with Gabriel believing that the current centralised model helps maintain the current brand reputation, while some members of the business believe that any new marketing campaigns should reflect the local character of the country.

Analyse **two** possible advantages to ML of centralisation as the business continues to expand.                                                   [8]

'Analyse' questions include marks for AO1 Knowledge and understanding, AO2 Application and AO3 Analysis. Read the following sample answer and indicate whether each sentence shows AO1, AO2 or AO3. One way of assigning an AO is to think about *what*, *where* and *how*. For AO1, 'what' means the key business concepts or theory. For AO2, 'where' refers to specific use of the text (or examples). For AO3, 'how' refers to how this affects the business or one of its stakeholders. What skills can be seen in the following answer?

> One advantage of a centralised management structure is that quicker decisions can be made. In the case of ML this means that a majority of crucial decisions are made by a team of senior managers with over 20 years of experience in the drinks market, which should make it easier to achieve consistency in providing a premium brand to the market, which is important in making their decision to franchise their operations successful.
>
> Another advantage of centralisation might be cost savings of being able to buy milk in larger quantities. If the milk and other ingredients are purchased centrally from suppliers and farmers by ML for all their shops and on behalf of their franchisees, they will be purchasing these items in bulk which usually leads to lower unit costs, which can enable ML to compete against global brands, possibly through the ability to now offer lower prices.

## « RECALL AND CONNECT 4 «

Can centralised organisational structures still be effective when businesses grow through integration?

# 13.6 Line and staff management functions

1  Explain the difference between line and staff managers.

## REFLECTION

Are you able to analyse the distinctions between line and staff management functions and the potential conflicts between them? What study methods will you use to understand the difference?

## UNDERSTAND THESE TERMS

- line managers
- staff managers

## SELF-ASSESSMENT CHECKLIST

Let's revisit the Knowledge focus and Exam skills focus for this chapter.
Decide how confident you are with each statement.

| Now I can | Show it | Needs more work | Almost there | Confident to move on |
|---|---|---|---|---|
| explain why organisations need a structure | Explain what would happen to a business if it failed to review its objectives and organisational structure as the firm grows in size. | | | |
| analyse the relationship between business objectives and organisational structure | Investigate the mission and vision statements of businesses with different organisational structures to understand differences in their business objectives, e.g., Phillips (matrix), Nike (hierarchical), azcentral (entrepreneurial), GE (geographical) | | | |
| analyse the different types of organisational structure and their advantages and disadvantages | Investigate the organisational structure of a business you know well and list some strengths and weaknesses of the structure. Use specific business terminology in your responses. | | | |
| assess the main features of a formal organisational chat | List the main features of a formal organisational chart; then test your understanding of these terms: delegation, span of control, levels of hierarchy, chain of command, bureaucracy, centralisation, decentralisation. | | | |

**CONTINUED**

| | | | | |
|---|---|---|---|---|
| evaluate the conflict between trust and control in delegation | Write a short paragraph providing an example of delegation and an example of a manager keeping all tasks to themselves. Explain why some managers are better able than others to manage the conflict between trusting their employees and maintaining control. | | | |
| understand the difference between authority, accountability and responsibility | Write out revision or question cards for each term and then test yourself on the meaning of each term. | | | |
| examine the appropriateness of centralised and decentralised structures | List some businesses you know well and label each as either a centralised or decentralised structure (research online if needed). What makes a centralised system more appropriate for some businesses and a decentralised system more suitable for others? | | | |
| outline the differences between line and staff authority | Write an organisational structure (by function) for a business you know well and then highlight the span of control for each line manager as well as the role of each staff manager. | | | |
| learn to distinguish between different question types with a focus on answering short-answer and eight-mark 'analysis' questions | Practise writing answers to some of the questions in the Exam practice sections. Compare your own response with the example student responses in these practice sections. | | | |
| learn how to mark a student response, focusing on how marks are awarded for different assessment objectives | Practise grading some of the example student responses included in this book, allocating either AO1, AO2 or AO3 where you see evidence of each. | | | |

# 14 Business communication

The command word 'explain' is used in low-mark question and the command words 'advise' and 'evaluate' are used in medium- to high-mark questions. They each require different things and there will be an opportunity to practice answering questions using these command words in this chapter.

Break down what you need to revise into solid chunks of smaller concepts. This involves scanning the syllabus or the *Cambridge International AS & A Level Business Coursebook* to understand the different parts of this course. Finally, for each section of this course answer a practice question.

## 14.1 Purposes of communication

1   Copy and complete Table 14.1, describing the **five** features of effective communication.

| | Feature of effective communication |
|---|---|
| 1 | |
| 2 | |
| 3 | |
| 4 | |
| 5 | |

**Table 14.1:** Features of effective communication

2   Explain **three** situations when effective communication is essential.

### REFLECTION

Review your response. Were you able to make the distinction between the features of effective communication (Question 1) and the purposes of effective communication (Question 2)? It is very easy to get confused when answering short-answer questions of this nature, so you should always spend a few moments to reflect on your answers before moving on.

### ≪ RECALL AND CONNECT 1 ≪

Can you identify **three** situations in which effective communication between the organisation and outside stakeholders is essential?

## 14.2 Methods of communication

### UNDERSTAND THESE TERMS

- visual communication
- spoken communication
- written communication
- electronic communication

1   Provide as many examples as you can of electronic communication used in business.

2   Choose the word 'weakness' or 'strength' for each of the following statements regarding electronic communication.

    a   Global communication is possible through the internet.

    b   Employees are sometimes tempted to use the technology for personal use.

    c   Electronic communication has the potential for security and technical issues.

    d   Electronic messages are transmitted in just a few seconds.

3   Explain which of the following is a weakness of spoken communication.

    a   It allows for two-way communication and feedback.

    b   Spoken communication is the most specific of all communication techniques.

    c   Spoken communication is the quickest to transmit.

    d   There is no written record of the communication.

4   Explain which of the following is a strength of spoken communication.

    a   It allows the sender to reinforce the message with a written record of the communication.

    b   Spoken communication can be ambiguous.

    c   It can be instantaneous as there is no delay between sending and receiving the message.

    d   Spoken communication can be time-consuming, especially when the message needs to be communicated to multiple recipients.

5   Explain which of the following is a strength of written communication.

    a   It allows for greater detail to be transmitted, including facts, charts, diagrams, etc.

    b   It allows for non-verbal communication to be used which supports the message being transmitted.

    c   It allows for instant feedback to be communicated.

    d   It is not effective in providing a permanent record which might be used legally, e.g., with employer contracts.

6   Explain which of the following is a weakness of written communication.

    a   Written messages can be used over again to make understanding easier.

    b   It does not allow for non-verbal communication to be used which supports the message being transmitted.

    c   It allows more detailed information to be transmitted, including facts, charts, diagrams, etc.

    d   It provides a permanent record which might be used legally, for example with employer contracts.

7   A firm uses a range of different types of communication, including
    written, spoken, visual and electronic. Explain the effectiveness of each
    for the following purposes.

    a   the annual report to shareholders

    b   a disciplinary meeting with an employee

    c   interviewing for an internal promotion

    d   an announcement that applies to all staff

    e   key instructions to a specific member of staff

    f   a social gathering of close friends within the same department.

## REFLECTION

How have you revised this section of the syllabus, particularly the difference
between written and electronic communication, between formal and informal
communication and between spoken and non-verbal communication?

## ≪ RECALL AND CONNECT 2 ≪

To what extent does effective communication within any business come from
setting the correct corporate culture?

# 14.3 Formal communication channels

## UNDERSTAND THESE TERMS

- one-way communication

- two-way communication

- horizontal communication

- vertical communication

1   Explain the difference between one-way communication and two-way
    communication.

2   Outline the disadvantages of using each of the following methods
    of communication:

    a   one-way communication

    b   two-way communication

    c   vertical communication

    d   horizontal communication.

# 14.4 Barriers to effective communication

The following Exam skills questions provide an opportunity to practise using the command words 'explain', 'advise' and 'evaluate' . Question 1 uses the command word 'explain'. Explain means 'to set out purposes or reasons / make the relationships between things evident / provide why and/or how and support with relevant evidence'. You should aim to give more detail than 'define' by, for example, applying your answer to the case study context.

Question 2 uses the command word 'advise'. Advise means to 'write down a suggested course of action in a given decision'. You need to provide an evaluation of the points for and against a particular decision, perhaps compared with an alternative course of action. The course of action to be taken must be clearly expressed and supported by evaluative comments which weigh up key arguments.

Finally, the command word in Question 3 is 'evaluate'. Evaluate means to judge or calculate the quality, importance, amount or value of something. You should aim to make a reasoned judgement and include a supported conclusion. To do this, you need to provide a developed judgement or conclusion in the context of the business that draws together analytical and evaluative comments which weigh up key arguments.

1

> **When communication goes wrong**
>
> In February 2021, the human resources department of KLY, a large information technology company, sent out a memo to all employees announcing that henceforth the company was being restructured and all employees would now be required to reapply for their current positions – at a level of pay and conditions to be negotiated. However, on closer examination, it was noted that the message was sent out in error. The policy covered only new temporary and contract staff, and the move was designed to bring those workers 'in house'. The human resources management department quickly sent out a second message clarifying its error, but by then the informal rumour mill had already started. Despite the clarification that all permanent positions were safe, morale and trust in the business was diminished.

**UNDERSTAND THIS TERM**

- communication barriers

Explain **one** type of communication that could be used by KLY. [3]

2 Advise the director of communications at KLY how to improve future communication. [20]

3

> **HSBC: 'Together We Thrive'**
>
> Even after a decade of trimming, HSBC is still vast, with $2.7 trillion of assets. Think of globalisation and you think of HSBC. The organisational structure of the UK-based bank can be described as a decentralised model, with divisions separated by geography rather than by function. HSBC operates in 65 countries, and its aim is to deliver a safe and secure banking experience at all times, including when communicating confidential information to customers.

Evaluate how cultural differences impact on communication within HSBC. [12]

## REFLECTION

How will you remember the functions of the command words explain, advise and evaluate? Write out revision cards with the function on one side and the command word on the other; then test yourself to help remember each.

## ≪ RECALL AND CONNECT 4 ≪

Does communication within business become more difficult as a business grows? Why is the level of difficulty likely to increase when the growth in the size of the business is derived from the result of a merger or acquisition?

# 14.5 Role of management in facilitating communication

1   Explain why many managers might prefer to use written communication over spoken methods when communicating important messages to other employees.

## ≪ RECALL AND CONNECT 5 ≪

a   Explain why communication is an important quality for an effective entrepreneur/business owner.

b   Explain the role of different management styles in ensuring that communication within any business is effective.

**UNDERSTAND THIS TERM**

- informal communication

## SELF-ASSESSMENT CHECKLIST

Let's revisit the Knowledge focus and Exam skills focus for this chapter.
Decide how confident you are with each statement.

| Now I can | Show it | Needs more work | Almost there | Confident to move on |
|---|---|---|---|---|
| analyse the importance to business of effective communication | Write out a short report, detailing some of the problems caused by poor communication within an organisation. | | | |
| evaluate the advantages and disadvantages of different communication methods | Provide strengths and weaknesses for spoken, written, electronic and visual communication. Describe a number of scenarios and then suggest the most appropriate communication method for each scenario. | | | |
| analyse the causes of barriers to communication and how to overcome them | Produce a chart or mind map describing **three** main barriers to communication, within organisations and provide one method that could be employed to resolve each specific issue. | | | |
| evaluate the differences between one- and two-way, vertical and horizontal, formal and informal communication | Investigate an organisational chart of an organisation you know and assess how messages are communicated using some or all of the following terms: one- and two-way, vertical and horizontal, formal and informal communication. | | | |
| evaluate the role of management in facilitating communication | Consider managers that you have worked with, either in a part-time job or at the school where you study. What made them either effective or poor in facilitating communication? | | | |

**CONTINUED**

| | | | | |
|---|---|---|---|---|
| show that you understand the 'explain', 'advise' and 'evaluate' command words and the difference between them | Practise using the three command words in responses to different Exam skills questions. | | | |
| plan your revision by using chunking strategies | Go through the revision timetable that you completed in Chapter 7 and for each unit of study sub-divide each unit into manageable 'chunks' of information to be learnt during each revision session. | | | |

# 15 Leadership

Understanding what is needed to receive marks in an exam is important but can be a challenge. Knowing the mark scheme and the language used, as well as understanding how the marks break down across a paper, will help you in your exams.

Much of what students refer to as test anxiety arises from a lack of confidence regarding study habits. The solution to exam preparation is not simply to study for longer but also to use strategies for improving your study habits. These could include starting your revision in plenty of time, writing a revision schedule with rest and reward periods, learning relaxation techniques, remembering to eat and drink, doing some exercise and getting plenty of sleep.

# 15.1 The purpose of leadership and qualities needed

**1** Copy and complete Table 15.1, matching the relevant leadership positions from the following word box to the correct definition.

| directors | managers | supervisors |
| workers' representatives |

**UNDERSTAND THIS TERM**

- leadership

| Leadership position | Definition |
| --- | --- |
| | Appointed by managers to watch over the work of others: responsible for leading teams and working towards a preset list of goals. |
| | Elected by shareholders, they are responsible for delegating tasks, recruitment and meeting the overall objectives of the organisation. |
| | Elected by the workers as trade union officials or work council representatives. |
| | Individuals responsible for people, resources or decision-making. They have authority over workers below them. |

**Table 15.1:** Leadership positions

**REFLECTION**

Can you think of a way of remembering each of the four leadership positions: perhaps thinking of a mnemonic using the first letters: d, m, s and w?

**2** What are the qualities of a good leader?

<< RECALL AND CONNECT 1 <<

Copy Figure 15.1. Use it to explain the role of leaders in managing the factors
of production to turn inputs into outputs.

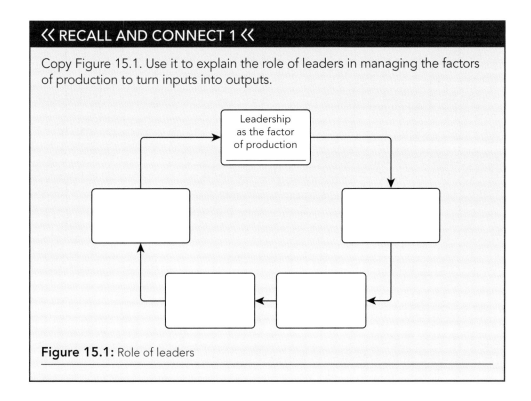

**Figure 15.1:** Role of leaders

## 15.2 Theories of leadership

1   Describe the **two** sources of power according to social psychologists in the Power
    and influence theory.

2   Explain which of the following are **not** normally considered leadership traits
    in 'Trait' theory.

    a   academic intelligence

    b   creativity

    c   charisma

    d   emotional intelligence.

3   Explain which of the following statements is **not necessarily** one of the skills
    of leaders according to 'Behavioural' theory.

    a   knowledge of the business practise or technique

    b   ability to interact with people

    c   conceptual skills

    d   experience in the field or organisation.

**« RECALL AND CONNECT 2 «**

**a** Compare the qualities required of successful entrepreneurs/intrapreneurs with those of successful leaders.

**b** Explain the difference between management and leadership.

# 15.3 Emotional intelligence

**UNDERSTAND THESE TERMS**

- emotional intelligence (EI)
- emotional quotient (EQ)

**1** Copy and complete the following sentence.
The greater a person's emotional intelligence, the higher their _____
_____ .

**2** Copy and complete Table 15.2, illustrating the four competencies of emotional intelligence according to Goleman's theory, with an explanation for each.

| Competence | Explanation |
|---|---|
|  |  |
|  |  |
|  |  |
|  |  |

**Table 15.2:** Emotional intelligence competencies

**3** By contrast, how does Goleman's theory suggest that a manager with low levels of emotional intelligence would act?

The following exam skills question provides an opportunity to practise marking a sample student response. An excellent way of learning the mark scheme is to grade a sample response using the marking criteria of knowledge (K), application (AP) and analysis (AN).

**4**

> ### U-study (US)
>
> One year after graduating from university, Lydia set up her own business providing tutoring online. She employs four administrative staff (paid by salary) and a number of part-time tutors, who receive $15 an hour. Tutors work from their own homes but Lydia monitors their progress regularly, holding fortnightly meetings with the whole 'tutoring team'. She believes that one of her most admirable qualities (as a leader) is her ability to listen to employees and she also has an understanding of their concerns. She wants to inspire her young employees to feel a part of the business and this means that she tends to take a 'hands off' approach to her staff, largely leaving each to complete their tasks without micromanagement. She believes that this is the correct approach and ensures morale among the staff remains strong, but she also recognises that her laissez-faire leadership style may sometimes be unsuitable for the occasion and is working to change this as necessary.

Analyse **two** ways in which emotional intelligence may help Lydia be an effective leader.                                                                 [8]

Copy the sample response to Question 4 and then by each sentence write either knowledge (K), application (AP) or analysis (AN).

Emotional intelligence can be described as the ability to understand, interpret and respond to the emotions of others. Effective managers will use emotions to communicate with and relate to their employees effectively and constructively. According to Goleman, the four competencies of emotional intelligence are self-awareness, self-management, social awareness and social skills. Lydia's start-up internet business employs a number of young staff who lack experience. All staff are part-time and so not necessarily always connected to the organisation, making it more important than ever to keep them motivated to ensure good customer relations.

Self-awareness would help Lydia to recognise emotions as they arise in response to an action or situation. As a result, she would be in a better position to address problems/future complications. For example, greater self-awareness may help her recognise that her current laissez-faire management style is not appropriate given that staff are unlikely to have many opportunities to meet as they are working from home, which can be alienating, and a leader should recognise this and take action to help develop a team spirit/engage employees.

Improved social skills would also help Lydia convey directions and know what to say in order to inspire and motivate others. An important skill for leaders, communication can be a deciding factor in whether the team listens or not. She should be able to handle any disagreements that arise between employees, customers and other parties. In conjunction with the above skills, leaders can use their emotional intelligence to develop a more effective workplace.

## ≪ RECALL AND CONNECT 3 ≪

Identify the role of emotionally intelligent management teams on employee motivation levels.

## REFLECTION

How did you find completing Question 4? Did you understand how the marks were allocated and how to use the command word?

## SELF-ASSESSMENT CHECKLIST

Let's revisit the Knowledge focus and Exam skills focus for this chapter.
Decide how confident you are with each statement.

| Now I can | Show it | Needs more work | Almost there | Confident to move on |
|---|---|---|---|---|
| analyse the purpose of leadership | Imagine you are devising a training programme for young trainee leaders. Make a list of the units you would include for them to study so that by the end of the course they have learnt all of the tasks they will have to fulfil as future leaders. | | | |
| analyse the qualities of a good leader | Think about the most effective leaders that you have worked with or read about. Make a list (using full sentences and paragraphs) describing the qualities that makes these people effective leaders. | | | |
| evaluate key leadership theories | Produce revision cards for each of the key leadership theories and then test yourself to improve your learning. | | | |

**CONTINUED**

| | | | | |
|---|---|---|---|---|
| analyse the four competencies of emotional intelligence | Practise writing out the four competencies of emotional intelligence according to Goleman's theory on revision cards. Test yourself, or have a friend or family member test you, on their meaning. Can you think of a handy phrase or mnemonic to remember the four? | | | |
| learn how to mark a student response | Mark some of the sample answers to the exam questions in this resource by writing either K, AP, AN or E (if required) by each sentence to identify the AO skill awarded. | | | |
| manage test anxiety by improving my study habits | Make a list of study habits that you could improve to help manage test anxiety. | | | |

# 16 Human resource management strategy

Consider what knowledge you already have and what questions you have. Reach out to your teacher or use different sources to fill in the gaps in your knowledge. Test yourself regularly, using revision and question cards to cement your knowledge.

# 16.1 Approaches to HRM strategy

UNDERSTAND
THESE TERMS

1

### Holidayvillas.web

Holidayvillas.web was set up by two brothers, John and Paul. The business started ten years ago and initially consisted of just the two brothers, with John maintaining the website and Paul marketing the business. In the last three years the business has grown and has recruited a number of staff in part-time positions. It also relies on agency and temporary positions during busy periods. John is happy with the new recruits, believing that they provide flexibility for the company's needs (demand is largely seasonal). Paul, however, believes that the company's needs would be better served by recruiting full-time employees, paid on a salary basis.

Explain **one** advantage to Holidayvillas.web of training and developing its employees. [3]

- HRM strategy
- permanent employment contract
- temporary contract
- zero-hours contract
- gig economy
- flexible employment contracts
- flexi-time arrangement
- home working
- annualised hours contract
- shift work
- absenteeism
- MBO

### REFLECTION

How did you learn the different types of training (on-the-job, off-the-job and induction training) as well as the circumstances where each might be appropriate? Have you learnt the possible benefits of investment in training and development?

2 Advise Holidayvillas.web on whether it should continue to rely on flexible working contracts for its employees. [12]

### ≪ RECALL AND CONNECT 1 ≪

a Describe the impact of full-time employment contracts on employee morale.

b Describe the impact of the recruitment of temporary/contract workers on the running costs of a business.

# 16.2 The changing role of IT and AI in HRM

1 Describe some of the benefits of IT and AI in HRM departments, as well as some of the risks/costs of their use.

### ≪ RECALL AND CONNECT 2 ≪

a Will the role of IT and AI within HRM departments change as businesses grow?

b To what extent can a specialist human resources department be considered an economy of scale?

## SELF-ASSESSMENT CHECKLIST

Let's revisit the Knowledge focus and Exam skills focus for this chapter.
Decide how confident you are with each statement.

| Now I can | Show it | Needs more work | Almost there | Confident to move on |
|---|---|---|---|---|
| evaluate the difference between hard HRM and soft HRM | Provide examples of both hard HRM and soft HRM within a business that you are familiar with. | | | |
| evaluate the impact on business of flexible employment contracts and flexible working | Compile a list of the benefits and costs of flexible employment contracts and flexible working on a business. Consider whether some businesses/industries are more suitable to the recruitment of flexible working contracts than others. | | | |
| analyse employee performance by using a range of measures | Investigate different methods of employee performance management systems. Find examples used by a company you have worked for or by your school. | | | |
| assess ways in which employee performance might be improved | Assess ways that the performance management system you identified in the previous task could be improved. What are the strengths of the performance system used? | | | |
| analyse management by objectives, its implementation and usefulness | Make revision notes/cards identifying the benefits and costs of management by objectives. Include how a business might be able to implement this system into the organisation. | | | |

## CONTINUED

| | | | | |
|---|---|---|---|---|
| access the changing role of IT and AI in HRM | Make a list of how IT and AI might be used in the HRM department of your school for: receiving job applications and using chatbots, virtual reality simulators, fingerprinting and biometric recognition. | | ' | |
| monitor my progress by testing myself on what I have learnt so far | Create a mini-test to check your understanding of one of the concepts in this chapter. | | | |

# Exam practice 4

This section contains both past paper questions from previous Cambridge exams and practice questions. These questions draw together your knowledge on a range of topics that you have covered up to this point and will help you prepare for your assessment.

Question 1(a) has an example student response and commentary provided. Work through the question first, then compare your answer to the example student response and commentary.

1   a   Analyse why many human resource departments have developed
        policies for diversity and equality.                                    [8]

*Cambridge International AS & A Level Business (9609) Paper 12 Q7a,*
        *June 2018*

| Example student response | Examiner comments |
|---|---|
| Diversity policies can be described as the practice or processes aimed at creating a mixed workforce and placing a positive value on diversity in the workplace. Equality policies can be described as practices and processes aimed at achieving a fair organisation where everyone is treated in the same way without prejudice and has the opportunity to fulfil their potential. | The response contains accurate definitions of both diversity and equality. This knowledge is developed with a clear understanding of items that might be included in the policies. |
| Examples of policies for diversity and equality might include the adoption of a 'blind applications process', where age, ethnicity and gender data is excluded from the applications process. In some countries businesses are required to comply with laws requiring explicit policies relating to diversity and equality. | The response includes limited application of the concept of a diversity and equality policy to a business. This is seen briefly in the second paragraph 'blind applications process'. More application to business use needs to be included in the answer. |
| Many businesses have grown to recognise the positives of such policies, which might include the positive public relations associated with being perceived as an ethical or fair employer. HRM departments within many businesses, therefore, have simply responded to changing societal demands for more equality and diversity. This is because business is seen as a microcosm of society and HRM departments are at the forefront of attempts to produce inclusive environments and cultures in the work organisation. | There is an attempt to explore some of the benefits of the prescribed policies in terms of the impact on positive public relations and that they comply with the law. However, the response needs to provide greater development of the impact on a business in terms of those policies, e.g., in the first paragraph, what is the impact on the business if everyone has the opportunity to fulfil their potential? In the second paragraph, the impact of complying with the law could be developed. |
|  | *5/8 marks* |

For Question 1(b) read the question, the example student response and the commentary provided. Then, in Question 1(c), write an improved answer to the question, using the guidance in the commentary to help you.

**b** 'A significant investment in training and development is the best way to improve employee effectiveness in a retail business.' Evaluate this view.　[12]

*Adapted from Cambridge International AS & A Level Business (9609) Paper 12 Q7b, June 2018*

| Example student response | Examiner comments |
|---|---|
| Training and development is one of the responsibilities of a HRM department and aims to strengthen and update employee job-related knowledge and skills. Retail businesses are 'labour-intensive' businesses, where customer service skills are critical.<br><br>One example of this might be the way that training and development is a motivating factor with many employees and by investing in training companies may see improved employee performance.<br><br>With training being a motivational factor, companies that train and develop their staff might find it easier to recruit and retain staff. On the other hand, however, despite its effectiveness, investment in training and development does involve time and money and retail firms will need to consider whether this is time and money well spent. | The response shows some basic knowledge and understanding of training and development. However, the question also includes the key term 'employee effectiveness' so there also needs to be knowledge and understanding of this term in the answer, which there is not.<br><br>The response includes some application, for example, noting that retail businesses are labour-intensive and that a significant investment in training and development might improve employee effectiveness in a business. However, there needs to be more application throughout the answer as there is no real reference to business use of training and development (or relevant measures of employee effectiveness).<br><br>There is little attempt to analyse how the 'best way' to develop a training programme depends on a number of factors, e.g., the current state of employee performance and a comparison with competitors.<br><br>Some limited evaluation is shown, e.g. the recognition that training can be expensive, but there is no evaluation of alternative methods that might be used (instead) to improve employee effectiveness in a retail business (such as more money). Additionally, there is no judgement made as to whether the statement in the question is correct or not.<br><br>*5/12 marks* |

**c** Now write an improved answer to Question 1(b).

Question 2 has example student responses and commentaries provided. For each part of the question, work through the question first, then compare your answer to the example student response and commentary.

2 a Analyse the benefits of a job description **and** a person specification when recruiting a new employee. [8]

*Cambridge International AS & A Level Business (9609) Paper 12 Q5a, March 2018*

| Example student response | Examiner comments |
|---|---|
| A job description can be described as a detailed explanation of the roles and responsibilities of the post advertised. By contrast, a job specification lists qualities required of the successful candidate, e.g., qualifications, experience and personal qualities required to perform the roles and functions included in the job description.<br><br>For any business a job description is important when recruiting staff, because it sets out what the successful applicant would be expected to do so that applicants can assess whether they are capable of completing all of these roles before they apply.<br><br>Businesses will presume that applicants will ask for a job description before applying for the job and so an accurate job description might prevent the majority of unsuitable applicants from applying, thus saving the business time when shortlisting applicants.<br><br>The job specification, sometimes called the personal specification, also saves the recruiting business time and money, making it easier to shortlist applicants by comparing the attributes of each applicant against the qualifications, skills, experience and personal attributes of those identified in the job specification. | This response illustrates very good knowledge and understanding of both key terms in the question (job description and person specification).<br><br>There is no application in the answer. It is purely theoretical with no reference to a business context.<br><br>Some analysis is clearly shown in the response with the benefit to both candidates and recruiting business identified. However, the response should have shown more depth of analysis. For example, the response only focuses on the time-saving benefits, which could have been developed further in terms of how time-saving benefits can reduce business costs or the time can be used for something else.<br><br>*4/8 marks* |

b    Evaluate which leadership style is likely to be the most
     effective for a large clothing manufacturer.                    [12]

**Adapted from Cambridge International AS & A Level Business (9609)
Paper 12 Q5b, March 2018**

| Example student response | Examiner comments |
|---|---|
| There are a number of distinct leadership styles: autocratic, where all decisions are kept at top of the organisation or with the leader; democratic, where workers are encouraged to take part in decisions; and paternalistic leadership, where leaders take on a 'fatherly' role within the organisation. This style involves leaders simply setting the parameters for work and then leaving workers to complete the task as they see fit. Each leadership style can be effective in different situations. A large clothing manufacturer is likely to have a large workforce, making it difficult for democratic styles of leadership. The workforce at the factory is also likely to have relatively low skills and experience. This suggests that autocratic and/or bureaucratic leadership styles might be the most suitable. The type of decisions being made, i.e., instant decisions and responding to emergencies, would also tend to lean the factory towards a more autocratic style. Decisions relating to the long-term wellbeing of workers are less likely, with high turnover of staff again probably meaning a democratic style is unsuitable. | The response demonstrates good knowledge of three of the main leadership styles. Throughout the answer, there is also a suitable discussion of the different circumstances that might be appropriate for selecting a leadership style in a business context. |
| The organisational structure might also play a role here and it is not clear what structure the factory has. For a democratic style to be effective a flat structure will be needed. A tall structure is again more likely to be autocratic but may be democratic. | There is very limited analysis in this answer. There is little discussion around the impacts/effects of the leadership style selected on the business itself. For example, if the business has a large workforce, what is the implication for them of using a particular leadership approach? |
| Presumably, unless the workers are highly skilled, the factory is unlikely to delegate many tasks, which again fits better with the autocratic model. It is very likely, also, that attitudes to decision-making and the culture of the business may have shaped the leadership style over time, with workers expected to be told what to do, almost certainly meaning that democratic management styles are unlikely to take route in the factory. It is also difficult to see anything other than low levels of motivation on the production floor, which again suggests that an autocratic approach may be necessary. | The response notes that the size of the factory would make it difficult for democratic leadership. There is good recognition that autocratic and bureaucratic leadership styles are most suitable given that workers expect to be told what to do. |
| In conclusion, therefore, a large clothing factory is most likely to have autocratic leadership styles dominant. However, given that all managers are individuals, the firm will see some variation in its leaders, with the personality of each leader being different and some being more decisive, forceful, easy-going or open than others. | The response also contains a judgement at the end of the answer, and there is an attempt to justify this in context. However, a more effective evaluation of the leadership style most likely to be most effective for a large clothing manufacturer is seen in the first paragraph 'This suggests that autocratic and/or bureaucratic leadership styles might be the most suitable'. This is well-developed and contextual. |
| | *10/12 marks* |

Here is another practice question which you should attempt. Use the guidance in the commentaries in this section to help you as you answer the question.

3    Evaluate whether flexibility of operations might improve the sales of a toy manufacturing business.    [12]

*Adapted from Cambridge International AS & A Level Business (9609) Paper 12 Q7b, March 2022*

For Question 4(a) read the question, the example student response and the commentary provided. Then, in Question 4(b), write your own answer to the question but use the context of a small technology organisation, with a high proportion of highly skilled employees. Use the guidance in the commentary to help you as you answer the question.

4    a    'Non-financial motivators are the most effective way of improving employee motivation in a house building business.' Evaluate this view.    [12]

| Example student response | Examiner comments |
|---|---|
| Non-financial methods of motivation that a house building business might employ include job enlargement, job rotation, job enrichment, empowerment and training. Job enlargement involves employees being provided with additional tasks as part of their daily role, for example, a worker might perform different tasks on the building site. | The response includes an understanding of non-financial motivators, financial motivators and employee motivation as they relate to a building business. Too much time is spent at the start of the answer explaining all the key terms without applying them to the business context or using them to answer the question. |
| Financial motivation factors involve motivating employees with money and things associated with money. The main methods of financial motivation that could be used by a house building business are remuneration, bonuses, piece rate and fringe benefits. | |
| Employee motivation is defined as the level of energy, commitment, persistence and creativity that workers bring to their jobs. | There is limited application to the business context (house building business) in the answer. While there is some mention of a 'site' and relevant job roles such as 'electrical work, plumbing and bricklaying', the opportunity to include more application to the context has been missed in many cases. For example, is the use of piece rate really that suitable for those building houses as a house is not built from start to finish by the same person? The inclusion of the output type (houses) might have helped assess the suitability of the motivational methods better. |
| It would be tempting for a building company wishing to improve employee motivation to begin by reviewing its financial packages as this might be the easiest way to improve motivation levels and can be completed relatively quickly. The building firm may switch to productivity-based payment systems such as piece rate. This would mean that workers employed on site will be paid relative to what they produce rather than for the time spent working. While this method of payment would be suitable for a house building company, given that performance and productivity can be easily measured, the impact of this on motivation is less clear. | |
| The business may also consider non-financial methods of motivation. Methods such as putting workers into teams, encouraging greater participation among the workforce and offering end-of-project bonuses would all be appropriate for a property building company. | |

| Example student response | Examiner comments |
|---|---|
| A job rotation scheme might also help to reduce boredom if the tasks are not complicated and are very repetitive. Whether this could be applied to skilled roles such as electrical work, plumbing and bricklaying is more open to question.<br><br>The building company may find, of course, that not all employees will be motivated by the same approach. Herzberg, for example, states that non-financial motivators are more likely to be successful when the employees are earning at least enough money to satisfy their basic needs (what he describes as hygiene factors), while workers receiving this basic level will be more motivated by non-financial factors, what he describes as motivators. Applied to the building company, lower-paid construction workers are more likely to look for financial incentives to motivate them (hygiene factors), while higher-paid construction managers may want to fulfil their esteem needs/seek recognition/empowerment from their employer. Whether or not non-financial motivators are the most effective can depend on the level of security felt by employees. Employees on short-term contracts might be more focused on financial reward. | The answer contains no reference to how the methods suggested are effective in improving the motivation of the workers. The answer is descriptive and does not address this aspect of the question.<br><br>The response includes some judgements and conclusions including that not all employees will be motivated by the same approach/method with the level of pay a factor in determining whether workers are more likely to be financially motivated or non-financially motivated. The conclusion also recognises that a further factor is likely to be the level of security felt by employees.<br><br>*8/12 marks* |

b   Now write your own answer to Question 4(a) but for a small technology organisation, with a high proportion of highly skilled employees.

# 17 The nature of marketing

## EXAM SKILLS FOCUS

In this chapter you will:

- learn how to use a balance grid to help plan AO4 evaluation exam answers to develop metacognition

- develop your understanding of how the marks are allocated for a selection of questions to gain a greater understanding of how the mark scheme is applied to answers.

Developing your understanding of how to evaluate will take practice and it is important to try different techniques to help you master this skill. In this chapter you will be introduced to a balance grid, which is a planning tool that can help you develop your ability to look at a concept from two different viewpoints before developing a judgement. Time spent planning your written answer will support your thinking skills and allow you to consider what you are writing in more detail.

It is important to understand both which assessment objectives are being assessed in an exam question *and* how many marks are being awarded for each assessment objective. For example, if there are two marks available for knowledge, then you need to show at least two pieces of knowledge in your answer. Gaining an understanding of the marks being awarded will allow you to develop an awareness of how much depth or development you need to provide in your answers.

# 17.1 The role of marketing

**≪ RECALL AND CONNECT 1 ≪**

What do the letters in SMART stand for when setting objectives?

1   In your own words, explain the relationship between marketing objectives and corporate objectives.

2   How do marketing objectives link to the other departments in a business (operations, human resources and finance)?

# 17.2 Demand and supply

1   a   When looking at the concept of demand and supply, what does 'demand' mean? Write a definition of this term.

   b   There are many factors that can affect the demand for a product. Explain **four** factors that can affect the level of demand and give an example for each one.

2   What is the relationship between the change in price of a product and the demand for the product?

3   a   When looking at the concept of demand and supply, what does 'supply' mean? Write a definition of this term.

   b   There are many factors that can affect the supply for a product. Explain **four** factors that can affect the level of supply and give an example for each one.

4   Copy and complete Table 17.1 to indicate whether the change affects supply or demand, how it affects supply or demand and one example of how this might affect a business.

| Change | Does this affect supply or demand? | Does this cause supply or demand to increase or fall? | Explain how this change might affect a business |
|---|---|---|---|
| A decrease in rice grown following a bad harvest | | | |
| An increase in the cost of steel for a car manufacturer | | | |
| A decrease in customer incomes for a fast-food restaurant | | | |
| A government subsidy being awarded to electric scooter manufacturers | | | |
| An increase in wage costs for a fruit farm | | | |
| An increase in advertising for a sportswear retailer | | | |
| An increase in interest rates for a luxury shoe producer | | | |

**Table 17.1:** Supply or demand?

5

> **AF Pharma (AFP)**
>
> AFP is a large multinational organisation which manufactures pharmaceutical products, as well as undertaking research into medicines and consumer health-related products. The vast majority of its products are plant-based and are sourced from many different suppliers from around the world. AFP has an annual revenue of approximately €5 billion.

**UNDERSTAND THIS TERM**

• equilibrium price

Evaluate the most important factor affecting the supply of AFP's pharmaceuticals to customers.                    [12]

A balance grid is a way of considering how to balance your arguments or viewpoints when approaching questions that require you to weigh up a series of points. You can see an example of this grid in Table 17.2.

If we look at Question 5, one factor that could affect the supply of AFP's pharmaceuticals to customers could be the weather. You can see this has been placed in the Factor column in Table 17.2. From this, you can add notes outlining one way this factor could affect the customers (which is what is required in this question) and one way this factor may not affect the customers.

| Affect | Factor | Not affect |
|---|---|---|
| Raw materials: AFP may not be able to produce if bad weather causes poor crops of the source ingredients; there would be no product for the customers of AFP to buy. | Weather | If other supplies are available in other countries that are not affected by the weather, then there would be no impact on customers. |
| Judgement of factor: could affect supply but depends on how many of the materials are grown in that one crop. Probably not a significant factor in this case. | | |

**Table 17.2:** Balance grid for weather

Copy the following table and try this yourself using another factor that might affect the supply of AFPs pharmaceuticals – labour.

| Affect | Factor | Not affect |
|---|---|---|
| | Labour (workforce) | |
| Judgement of factor: | | |

**Table 17.3:** Balance grid for labour

The balance grid technique can be used to help you plan your answer before writing it. This should support you in writing better paragraphs that look at two sides of a developed argument before you arrive at an overall judgement, which in this case would be determining the factor that has the greatest impact on the supply of pharmaceuticals to the customers and why.

## ≪ RECALL AND CONNECT 2 ≪

What is the difference between internal and external stakeholders?
Give at least one example of each in your answer.

## 17.3 Markets

1   What is a market?

2   The purposes of industrial markets and consumer markets are very different. Explain the role of each market.

3   a   What is meant by the term 'customer (or market) orientation'?

    b   Explain **two** benefits to a firm of focusing on customer (or market) orientation.

4   a   What is mean by the term 'product orientation'?

    b   Explain **two** benefits to a firm of focusing on product orientation.

5   Do you think it is better for a firm to take a product orientation approach or customer orientation approach? Explain your answer.

| UNDERSTAND THESE TERMS |
| --- |
| • market growth |
| • brand leader |

## 17.4 Consumer marketing and industrial marketing

1   Explain **three** key ways in which selling to consumers (B2C) differs from selling to producers (B2B).

| UNDERSTAND THESE TERMS |
| --- |
| • consumer products |
| • industrial products |

### ≪ RECALL AND CONNECT 3 ≪

Explain four factors that can influence the number of workers needed by a business.

## 17.5 Mass marketing and niche marketing

| UNDERSTAND THESE TERMS |
| --- |
| • mass marketing |
| • niche marketing |

1   'Mass marketing is always better than niche marketing.' Evaluate this view.

**2**

> **Eco Travellers (ET)**
>
> ET specialises in offering holiday packages for ecotourists. Ecotourism is a form of travel that involves travelling to non-tourist hot spots with an element of conservation or just spending time with nature. While this has been a travel option since the 1980s, it has seen a real increase in demand over the last few years, with a significant growth in internet searches for 'ecommodation' and sustainable travel. ET takes groups of people to areas of natural beauty around the world and offers plastic-free holidays in accommodation that uses renewable energy.

Evaluate whether niche marketing would benefit ET.                              [12]

Copy and complete the balance grid in Table 17.4 with two points that you would like to discuss in your answer. Place these in the Factor column and then find reasons why they may and may not be benefits of niche marketing to ET.

| Why is this a benefit to ET? | Factor | How might it not benefit ET? |
|---|---|---|
|  |  |  |
|  |  |  |

**Table 17.4:** Balance grid for ET niche marketing

Now you should write an answer to Question 2.

**REFLECTION**

How did you feel using the balance grid to help you plan your answer before writing? Do you think it helped you understand what points you were going to write? How could you adapt this technique to support you in the future?

## 17.6 Market segmentation

1   Why is market segmentation important to a business?

2   Create a mind map to show the different ways a business can segment a market.

**UNDERSTAND THIS TERM**

- market segmentation

It is very useful to know which skills are being assessed in a question you are being asked and how many marks are allocated for these in the exam. This can help you understand what you need to show in your answer and how the mark scheme will be applied.

3

> **Pen Pals (PP)**
>
> PP is a national business which operates 150 retail stores in Country B that sell stationery and office supplies to the mass market. Market segmentation has been vital to the success of the business and the wide product range it offers to the market.

   a   Define the term 'market segmentation'.    [2]

   b   Explain **one** benefit to PP of market segmentation.    [3]

   c   Evaluate whether PP would benefit from using market segmentation.    [12]

Copy and complete Table 17.5 to indicate what exam skills are required for Questions 3(a), (b) and (c) and how many marks are available for each of these. You may need to refer to the specification for your course to help you (available from the Cambridge Assessment International Education website).

| | AO1 | | AO2 | | AO3 | | AO4 | |
|---|---|---|---|---|---|---|---|---|
| | Required? | Marks allocated | Required? | Marks allocated | Required? | Marks allocated | Required? | Marks allocated |
| 3(a) | | | | | | | | |
| 3(b) | | | | | | | | |
| 3(c) | | | | | | | | |

**Table 17.5:** Exam skills that are required

# 17.7 Customer relationship marketing

1   Do you think customer relationship marketing (CRM) is important for a business? Write a short report to a business that is considering increasing its annual spend on CRM, highlighting the benefits and costs of this marketing activity.

## 《 RECALL AND CONNECT 4 《

Which motivational theorist created Two-factor theory? What are the main implications of this theory on business practice today?

## REFLECTION

How confident are you that you understand the nature of marketing for a business? What can you do to improve your understanding of this concept?

## SELF-ASSESSMENT CHECKLIST

Let's revisit the Knowledge focus and Exam skills focus for this chapter.
Decide how confident you are with each statement.

| Now I can | Show it | Needs more work | Almost there | Confident to move on |
|---|---|---|---|---|
| analyse the role of marketing | Write a 300-word report on the role of marketing for a business that could explain the concept to someone with no knowledge of marketing. | | | |
| analyse the relationship between marketing objectives and corporate objectives | Give an example of each type of objective and explain how they work together. | | | |
| understand the distinction between consumer and industrial markets | Look at the definitions for these two terms and select two differences that might exist between these markets. | | | |
| understand the relationship between demand, supply and price | Over the next week, find a selection of news articles displaying changes in the business environment and create supply and demand diagrams to show what might happen because of the changes. | | | |
| analyse the difference between market orientation and product orientation | Create a mind map outlining the advantages and disadvantages of mass and niche marketing. | | | |
| measure market growth and market share | Create a revision card to show the formulas to measure market growth and market share. | | | |
| evaluate the relative advantages of mass marketing and niche marketing | Use your answer from Question 1 in Section 17.5 to help you demonstrate your understanding of this learning intention. | | | |

## CONTINUED

| | | | | |
|---|---|---|---|---|
| assess the significance of market segmentation and how this might be achieved | Take three different products made by the same company in the same industry and explain how they each use market segmentation. | | | |
| understand the importance of customer relationship marketing | Using your report from Question 1 in Section 17.7, identify any points from the suggested answers that you could add to your report improve your answer. | | | |
| learn how to use a balance grid to help plan AO4 evaluative exam answers to develop metacognition | Think about the many decisions you make in a day and use a balance grid to help you with these (e.g. deciding between two differently coloured jumpers). This will help you develop your thinking skills. | | | |
| develop my understanding of how the marks are allocated for a selection of questions, to gain a greater understanding of how the mark scheme is applied to answers | Look through a selection of past papers and mark schemes on the Cambridge Assessment International Education website and create a brief factsheet detailing how marks are allocated for three different types of question. | | | |

# 18 Market research

## EXAM SKILLS FOCUS

In this chapter you will:

- begin to learn how to approach numerical data provided in a case study

- start to develop an approach to metacognitive practice when answering questions with a focus on monitoring progress.

In exams, you will be presented with data not only in written form as a case study but also numerical data presented through charts and tables. It can be challenging to identify the actual numerical data that may be needed for an answer. You need to become familiar with different methods of displaying data and gain confidence in selecting relevant data from case studies.

Throughout this chapter, you will be presented with a selection of reflection tasks that will allow you to consider how you approach different questions. These tasks will encourage you to critically assess your conscious and unconscious thought processes so you can get a better idea of how you approach questions. By understanding what you already do, and how you work, you should be able to get a better idea of areas that you might need to develop further to develop your thinking skills.

# 18.1 Market research

1  What are the main purposes of a business undertaking market research?
   Try to identify and explain at least **three** different purposes.

2  How does market research support new product development?

## « RECALL AND CONNECT 1 «

What is the purpose of business activity?

# 18.2 Primary research and secondary research

## UNDERSTAND THESE TERMS

- primary research
- secondary research
- qualitative data
- quantitative data

1  Secondary research is the use of existing data that was originally collected
   for another purpose. Explain the reasons why secondary research data might
   be useful to a business.

2  What are the main sources of secondary data for a business?

3  Primary research is the collection of first-hand data, specifically for the needs of
   the business. Explain the reasons why primary research data might **not** be useful
   to a business.

4  Copy out and complete Table 18.1, explaining **one** benefit and **one** cost of each
   primary data collection method that could be used by a business.

| Primary data collection method | Benefit of its use | Cost of its use |
|---|---|---|
| Questionnaire: postal, in-store, online, mobile (cell) phone | | |
| Interview: face-to-face or mobile (cell) phone | | |
| Observation (e.g., in a large shop to see which displays and promotions attract shoppers) | | |
| Test marketing: in a specific geographical area | | |
| Focus groups: discussions with potential or existing consumers, with the aim of gaining qualitative data | | |

**Table 18.1:** Primary data collection methods

5   Businesses are increasingly using electronic means to gather necessary data before deciding on their marketing strategies. Explain how developments in technology can affect how businesses can conduct their market research.

Being aware of how you think is a really important skill to master. Look at Question 6. Before you write an answer to the question, you should reflect on what the question is making you think, how you are considering approaching the question, how you are deciding what to include in the answer and any other thoughts that come to your mind. You should make notes on any thoughts you become aware of as you go through the stages from reading the question to being prepared to write an answer.

Think about how you are planning your answer. Would you prefer to create visual aids, such as mind maps, or written notes? Are you someone who feels confident writing this answer based on facts in your memory or would you prefer to do lots of research?

You should now write an answer to Question 6.

6
> **Funtime Water World (FWW)**
>
> FWW is a water park located in City B. The site is set across three acres of land, containing a variety of water slides and swimming pools to meet the needs of the whole family. It is currently considering opening a new water park in either City H, located 250 kilometres away, or City M, located 175 kilometres away.

Evaluate how FWW could research the market to help it decide which city to expand into.                                                                 [12]

## REFLECTION

Consider Question 6. How did you write the answer to this question? Did you plan before you wrote an answer, or did you just start writing? Were you aware of how you were thinking as you were writing the answer? Make some notes to reflect on how you approached writing the answer. Are there things you did that you were not aware of at the time? Are there aspects of your approach you would like to change next time you write an answer? It is challenging to be reflective on your own learning, but it is a valuable task to complete to support yourself in making improvements.

# 18.3 Sampling

1   Outline **two** limitations for a business using sampling when collecting market research data.

## « RECALL AND CONNECT 2 «

What does 'limited liability' mean?

**UNDERSTAND THESE TERMS**

- sampling bias
- sample

## 18.4 Market research data

**1**

**The Shoe Place (TSP)**

TSP is a very popular retail chain that sells a variety of shoes for all occasions. Recently, it decided to learn more about its market, so it gathered some data on the ages of its customers, which is displayed in Table 18.2.

| | Age of customers |
|---|---|
| Last month | 21, 25, 30, 23, 30, 33, 24, 27, 39, 55, 68, 73, 81, 67, 54, 35, 32, 34, 56, 45 |
| This month | 33, 41, 55, 63, 71, 22, 27, 29, 40, 44, 58, 44, 71, 32, 63, 56, 51, 22, 45, 22 |

**Table 18.2:** Ages of TSP's customers

**UNDERSTAND THESE TERMS**

- arithmetic mean
- mode
- median
- coding

Using the market research data in Table 18.2, calculate the following for this month and last month:

**a** the mean

**b** the mode

**c** the median

**d** the range of the data.

**2** Explain the advantages and disadvantages of using each of the three main measures of averages: the mean, the median and the mode.

**3** You can use relevant software to support you with this question if preferred.

**a** Take the data in Table 18.2 and display the information in each of the following forms: pie graph, line graph, bar chart.

You will need to refer to your work from Question 3(a) for the following questions.

**b** Which was the most suitable method use to display your data? Explain your answer.

**c** Which was the least suitable method used to display your data? Explain your answer.

**d** Do you think there is a better type of graph that could be used to display the data in Table 18.2?

### « RECALL AND CONNECT 3 «

The total sales in a market are $500 000 and Business T has sales of $45 000. What is the market share of Business T?

There are some sections of this course that require numeracy skills. The most frequently used ones are:

- calculating and interpreting percentages and percentage changes

- calculating and interpreting ratios

- interpreting tables of data, pie graphs, line graphs and bar charts

- drawing or completing simple line graphs

- reading off data from a line graph

- addition, subtraction and multiplication.

In exams, you might be faced with data shown in different numerical forms, such as those mentioned earlier, so it is very important you become confident when handling different forms of displaying numerical data.

4

### Strawberry Fields (SF)

SF is a fruit farm located in Country A. The fruit is collected by workers who then clean, prepare and sell it in the farm shop on the farm site. The farm is open to visitors who can pay a small amount to enter and pick their own fruit, which they then pay for before they go home. SF is considering expanding its operations to include a wider range of fruit. It wants to learn more about its market so has conducted some primary market research.

#### Primary research method 1

Primary research method 1 was conducted using a questionnaire placed on its social media accounts asking: Which fruits would you like to purchase from the farm shop? You may only select one.

| Age | 18–30 | 31–50 | 51+ |
|---|---|---|---|
| Bananas | 15 | 35 | 40 |
| Raspberries | 20 | 15 | 30 |
| Apples | 45 | 5 | 20 |

**Table 18.3:** Primary research completed by SF (questionnaire data show the number of respondents)

#### Primary research method 2

Primary research method 2 was conducted by asking random customers who visited the farm the following question and recording their answers via survey: Would you prefer to pick you own fruit or just buy it from the shop (you may only select one option)? Each option received 100 responses.

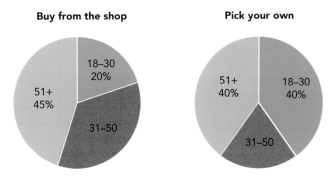

**Buy from the shop**  **Pick your own**

**Figure 18.1:** Primary research completed by SF (survey data show the number of respondents)

a    Refer to primary research method 1. Identify the age group that would most prefer to see bananas in the farm shop.    [1]

b    Refer to primary research method 1. Calculate the percentage of the whole sample who would prefer the farm shop to sell apples.    [2]

c    Explain **one** advantage of SF using a questionnaire on its social media to gather market research data.    [3]

d    Refer to primary research method 2. Calculate the total number of people who responded to the research who were in the 31–50 age category.    [2]

e    SF used sampling in its market research when gathering data. Explain **one** disadvantage to SF of using sampling when gathering market research data.    [3]

## REFLECTION

How confident do you feel when dealing with the numerical skills encountered within this chapter? Give yourself a mark from one (not confident) to ten (very confident). If you scored less than ten, what can you do to improve your level of confidence and understanding when presented with numerical data?

## SELF-ASSESSMENT CHECKLIST

Let's revisit the Knowledge focus and Exam skills focus for this chapter. Decide how confident you are with each statement.

| Now I can | Show it | Needs more work | Almost there | Confident to move on |
|---|---|---|---|---|
| analyse what market research is and the purpose of it | Create a leaflet to highlight the purpose of market research to a new business opening in your area. | | | |
| differentiate between the main sources of data | Develop a revision card to explain the difference between primary and secondary sources of data. | | | |
| evaluate the usefulness of data collected from primary research and secondary research | Create a mind map showing the advantages and disadvantages of at least four methods of collecting primary data and four methods of collecting secondary data. | | | |
| explain the need for sampling | Write a one-minute talk to present to a friend on the purpose of sampling. | | | |

| | | | | |
|---|---|---|---|---|
| assess the reliability of market research data | Add some information on the reliability of the market research methods used to gather data to your mind map. | | | |
| analyse and interpret qualitative and quantitative data | Create a questionnaire that contains questions that gather a mix of quantitative and qualitative data, then analyse your results. | | | |
| begin to learn how to approach numerical data provided in a case study | Look back at Table 18.3. You should use two different methods to display this information. These could include a bar chart, pie chart or another method of your choice. | | | |
| start to develop an approach to metacognitive practice when answering questions with a focus on monitoring progress | Write a 200-word diary entry to yourself to reflect on your own thinking and learning processes in this chapter. | | | |

# 19 The marketing mix: Product and price

## KNOWLEDGE FOCUS

You will answer questions on:

**19.1** The elements of the marketing mix

**19.2** Product: Why is this a key part of the marketing mix?

**19.3** Product portfolio analysis

**19.4** Price is a key part of the marketing mix

## EXAM SKILLS FOCUS

In this chapter you will:

- develop your skills of metacognition using the 'know it, need it' technique

- use multiple-choice questions as a revision tool to develop your knowledge and understanding.

It is important to try different methods of developing your thinking skills as you move through your studies. Some will work better for you than others, so spending time trialling different methods until you find the ones that work for you is a valuable use of your time. In this chapter you will be introduced to the 'know it, need it' technique. This is an activity to help you discover what you already 'know' about a topic and what you 'need' to revise further. By doing this, you should be able to focus your studies more on the areas you need to develop.

Another technique to develop your thinking skills is to use multiple-choice questions, such as the digital multiple-choice question provided as part of this resource, as a way to support your revision. While there is not a multiple-choice element on any of the AS or A Level Business papers, learning how to identify the distractors in a set of multiple-choice question answers can help you practise your own knowledge and understanding of a subject.

## 19.1 The elements of the marketing mix

1   What are the **four** elements of the marketing mix?
    How are they also collectively known?

### ≪ RECALL AND CONNECT 1 ≪

Explain the difference between adding value and added value.

## 19.2 Product: Why is this a key part of the marketing mix?

### UNDERSTAND THESE TERMS

- product differentiation
- unique selling point (USP)

1   Explain the difference between goods and services.

'Know it, need it' is a technique that encourages you to identify what you already know and what you need to revise further. A good way of doing this is by using past exam questions, which you can find on the Cambridge Assessment International Education website.

Step 1: Read the question you are being asked.

Step 2: Identify the topic on the syllabus you are being assessed on in the question.

Step 3: Allow yourself five minutes to write down any knowledge or key terms that you can remember about the topic being assessed in the 'know it' column. Do this without using notes or your coursebook.

| Know it | Need it |
| --- | --- |
| You can identify this information about the topic without using notes or your coursebook. | This is information on the topic you learn after the activity. |

**Table 19.1:** The 'know it, need it' technique

Use the 'know it, need it' technique for Question 2. Copy Table 19.2 and, using your notes and your coursebook, add in any missing information into the 'need it' column.

**2** Evaluate whether developing a new product is beneficial to a business. [12]

| Know it | Need it |
|---|---|
|  |  |

**Table 19.2:** 'Know it, need it' in practice

### REFLECTION

How confident did you feel doing the 'know it, need it' activity? Did you have more points in your 'know it' or 'need it' column at the end of the task? What are you going to do next to make sure you learn all the 'need it' points?

**3** What are intangible and tangible attributes of products?

### « RECALL AND CONNECT 2 «

What are the advantages and disadvantages of being a private limited company?

## 19.3 Product portfolio analysis

**1** How can having knowledge of a product's life cycle help a business?

**2** Outline **one** limitation of using the product life cycle for marketing decisions.

**3** For each of the following statements, identify which stage of the product life cycle it would apply to, as well as which aspect of the marketing mix it is explaining.

   **a** The product is found in restricted outlets, possibly high-class outlets if a skimming strategy is adopted.

   **b** New models and accessories may start to be introduced.

   **c** Spend on this area is likely to be reduced and it might just be used to inform customers of the low prices for any remaining stock.

   **d** Any initial use of a penetration pricing strategy will start to be replaced by an increase in prices.

A good way to practise your knowledge and understanding is through the use of multiple-choice questions. In Question 4, you should read through each option in turn. Copy and complete Table 19.3, and ask yourself if you think each option is correct or incorrect. You should then explain why you think so. Doing this will allow you to explore your own knowledge and provide a rationale for your selection. The first one has been done for you as an example.

4   The two stages of the product life cycle where cash flows are most likely to **not** be positive are as follows.

| Potential answers | Correct answer (✓) or incorrect answer (✗)? | Explanation |
|---|---|---|
| **a** Growth and decline | ✗ | In growth, the firm is likely to make lots of sales, so cash flow should be positive. In decline, sales are falling and not much revenue is coming in, so cash flow is not likely to be positive. This is an incorrect answer as both stages are not going to lead to cash flow not being positive. |
| **b** Maturity and decline | | |
| **c** Introduction and maturity | | |
| **d** Introduction and decline | | |

**Table 19.3:** Cash flows

5   A Boston matrix is an analytical tool that can be used when making marketing decisions. The corrective actions that can arise from issues with the Boston matrix are building, holding, milking and divesting. Explain what each of these actions means.

## 19.4 Price is a key part of the marketing mix

1   There are many determinants of the pricing decision for any product. Explain at least **four** different things that need to be taken into consideration when deciding on the most appropriate price for a good or service.

2  A business produces a single product that has a variable cost of $3 per unit. The total fixed costs of the firm are $50 000 per year. The business sells its products for $6 per unit. If it sells 70 000 units, how much profit will the business make? Copy and complete Table 19.4, inserting your answers.

| Potential answers | Correct answer (✓) or incorrect answer (✗)? | For incorrect answers, can you explain what error has been made to get this answer? |
|---|---|---|
| a $210 000 | | |
| b $420 000 | | |
| c $160 000 | | |
| d $369 997 | | |

Table 19.4: Profit

3  Copy and complete Table 19.5 to show your knowledge of pricing strategies.

| Pricing strategy | How the pricing strategy works | Advantage of the pricing strategy | Disadvantage of the pricing strategy |
|---|---|---|---|
| Cost-based pricing | | | |
| Competitive pricing | | | |
| Price discrimination | | | |
| Dynamic pricing | | | |
| Penetration pricing | | | |
| Market skimming | | | |
| Psychological pricing | | | |

Table 19.5: Pricing strategies

## « RECALL AND CONNECT 3 «

What is the difference between qualitative data and quantitative data?

## REFLECTION

How useful have you found the multiple-choice tasks in this chapter as a way of checking your understanding of topics? Are there any ways you can adapt this approach to develop your thinking and knowledge further?

## SELF-ASSESSMENT CHECKLIST

Let's revisit the Knowledge focus and Exam skills focus for this chapter.
Decide how confident you are with each statement.

| Now I can | Show it | Needs more work | Almost there | Confident to move on |
|---|---|---|---|---|
| analyse what the marketing mix means and what its key components are | Explain the four components of the marketing mix. | | | |
| evaluate the importance of product decisions to a marketing mix | Create a revision card detailing how the elements of the marketing mix link to stages of the product life cycle. | | | |
| use and apply product portfolio analysis | Find two examples of products that are in each of the four stages of the product life cycle. | | | |
| analyse the stages of the product life cycle and evaluate its usefulness for marketing decisions | Describe three ways a product is useful for a business when developing its marketing decisions. | | | |
| apply the Boston matrix analysis and evaluate the usefulness of it for marketing decisions | Create a Boston matrix for a business of your choice to evaluate its product portfolio. | | | |
| understand and analyse different pricing methods and evaluate their relevance in different business situations | Find real-world examples of each pricing strategy in the chapter being used. | | | |
| understand and evaluate the importance of pricing decisions to a marketing mix | For each of the examples you have found for your pricing strategies, explain how these link to the other elements of the marketing mix for the business. | | | |

**CONTINUED**

| | | | | |
|---|---|---|---|---|
| develop my skills of metacognition using the 'know it, need it' technique | Select a longer-response question from the Chapter 19 Exam style questions in the coursebook and use the 'know it, need it' technique to assess your understanding. | | | |
| use multiple-choice questions as a revision tool to develop my knowledge and understanding | Create a multiple-choice question for another student based on a topic in this chapter. Try to give them challenging distractors. | | | |

# 20 The marketing mix: Promotion and place

## EXAM SKILLS FOCUS

In this chapter you will:

- make links between concepts, focusing on the marketing mix and business and its environment

- start to develop an approach to metacognitive practice when answering exam questions with a focus on monitoring progress.

It is important to make links between new and previous learning points to help you master the synoptic nature of your Cambridge International AS & A Level Business course. As an example of this, the Recall and connect features in this chapter will support you in making links between elements in the marketing mix and topics from Chapters 1–5 relating to the concept of business and its environment.

How do you know if you are doing well when answering exam questions? Some might say you do well if you get a good mark, which is only partially correct. As you revise and prepare for exams, you need to be able to assess the progress that you are making as you go along so that when you sit the real exams you have reviewed yourself on a number of different skills. Just as businesses set objectives, you can measure yourself against your own objectives when faced with exam questions. You can then assess yourself against these objectives to help you monitor your own progress.

# 20.1 Promotion methods

**1** **a** What are the main objectives of promotion campaigns?

    **b** How can the success of promotion campaigns be measured?

**2** Copy and complete Table 20.1 on examples of the different methods of advertising and promotion.

| Advertising methods | Example of use | Explanation of method | Benefits | Limitations |
|---|---|---|---|---|
| Advertising promotion | Print advertising | | | |
| | Broadcast advertising | | | |
| | Outdoor advertising | | | |
| Sales promotion | Price offers | | | |
| | Customer loyalty schemes | | | |
| | Point-of-sale displays | | | |
| Direct promotion | Direct mail | | | |
| | Telemarketing | | | |
| | Personal selling | | | |

**Table 20.1:** Methods of advertising and promotion

**3** **a** Explain how each of the following methods of digital promotion work.

      **i** social media marketing

      **ii** email marketing

      **iii** online advertising

      **iv** smartphone marketing

      **v** viral marketing

      **vi** search engine optimisation.

    **b** What are the benefits and limitations to a business of using digital promotion?

> **UNDERSTAND THESE TERMS**
>
> - promotion
> - advertising
> - direct promotion
> - sales promotion
> - promotion mix
> - digital promotion

## « RECALL AND CONNECT 1 «

**a** Explain **three** reasons why some businesses fail.

**b** Explain how the marketing mix can be linked to reasons for business failure.

# 20.2 Place: An important part of the marketing mix

1 Explain the advantages and disadvantages of each of the following channels of distribution:

 a direct selling

 b single-intermediary channel

 c two-intermediary channel.

Look at Question 2 and set yourself an objective for each part: what you would like to achieve from each answer. These objectives could be related to how many marks you want to achieve on a question, what skills you want to demonstrate or assessing your current knowledge of a topic before revising. Once you have done this, you can answer the questions.

2

> **GB Magazines**
>
> GB Magazines is a magazine publisher who have been operating for 30 years. They specialise in the production and printing of magazines. They sell their magazines through shops owned by other people in Country A, as well as through their own website. George, the owner of GB Magazines likes the traditional nature of holding a physical copy of a magazine to read, however, the company has received some requests from customers asking for the magazines to be available as digital downloads so that they can be accessed on smart phones and laptops.

 a Explain the term 'channels of distribution'. [3]

 b Explain **one** way that GB Magazines can use the place element of the marketing mix. [3]

 c Analyse **one** advantage and **one** disadvantage to GB Magazines of using digital distribution. [8]

## REFLECTION

Look at the answers to Question 2 and mark your own work (you may be able to get another student or a teacher to help with this). Once you have done this, look back at the objectives you set yourself before you answered Question 2. Have you met your objectives? If so, do you think your objectives were challenging enough? If you have not met your objectives, reflect on why. What could you do differently next time?

## « RECALL AND CONNECT 2 «

**a** Outline the main features of a social enterprise.

**b** Explain how the marketing mix might differ when applied to a social enterprise compared to a standard business model.

**3** Joe has always been passionate about cooking, and it has always been his dream to open up his own restaurant. He has recently graduated from catering college and is getting ready to do so. He did A Level Business as part of his studies in college, so he knows that he needs to do some market research to find out what types of cuisine his potential customers would like and has created his menu using this information. He knows he needs to have an integrated marketing mix and needs some advice on how to do this. Imagine Joe was setting up his restaurant in your town. Create a marketing mix for his new restaurant that you think would give him the best chance of survival among current competitors. You should write a report (of no more than 500 words) to Joe outlining the best marketing mix for his restaurant, justifying each of your points.

## « RECALL AND CONNECT 3 «

**a** Explain how a business can grow organically.

**b** Explain how the marketing mix might be affected by organic growth.

## REFLECTION

How do you monitor your own progress? How do you know if you are making progress or not? Spend some time considering the methods that you currently use to monitor your own progress, which might include feedback from teachers, assessment against marking criteria, traffic light evaluation, etc. Could these methods be improved or developed to allow you to monitor your progress more effectively?

### UNDERSTAND THESE TERMS

- channel of distribution
- online marketing (e-commerce)
- digital distribution
- physical distribution

## SELF-ASSESSMENT CHECKLIST

Let's revisit the Knowledge focus and Exam skills focus for this chapter.
Decide how confident you are with each statement.

| Now I can | Show it | Needs more work | Almost there | Confident to move on |
|---|---|---|---|---|
| identify the differences between sales promotion, advertising and direct promotion | Write a sentence that explains the difference between sales promotion, advertising and direct promotion. | | | |
| understand the different objectives of a promotion campaign | Look at your answer to Question 1(a) in Section 20.1 and explain why each objective might be selected by a business. | | | |
| analyse the factors to consider when making promotion-mix decisions | Choose a real-world business and note down the main features that would affect its choice of promotion mix if it were to launch a new product into the market. | | | |
| evaluate the methods used to measure the effectiveness of promotional spending | Go back to your answer for Question 1(b) in Section 20.1 and explain which of these measures you think is the most useful when measuring the effectiveness of promotional spending. | | | |
| evaluate the impact of developments in digital marketing | Write a report of no more than 500 words that explains the impact of developments in digital marketing on a business of your choice. | | | |
| recognise the importance of packaging in the marketing of a product | Find some product packaging for a product of your choice and explain three features of it that make it stand out from competitor products. | | | |

## CONTINUED

| | | | | |
|---|---|---|---|---|
| understand the importance of place in the marketing mix | Explain three impacts to a business of getting the place element of its marketing mix wrong. | | | |
| discuss different distribution channels and assess their appropriateness in different circumstances | Find a real-world example of each distribution channel being used. | | | |
| make links between concepts – focusing on the marketing mix and business and its environment | Look through your notes from Chapters 1–5 and identify places where you can make links with the concepts in these and the marketing mix. | | | |
| start to develop an approach to metacognitive practice when answering exam questions with a focus on monitoring progress | Speak to other students and find out what methods they use to monitor their progress, as well as sharing some of your methods with them. | | | |

# Exam practice 5

This section contains both past paper questions from previous Cambridge exams and practice questions. These questions draw together your knowledge on a range of topics that you have covered up to this point and will help you prepare for your assessment.

For Questions 1 and 2, read the questions, the example student responses and the commentaries provided. Then, in part (c) of each question, write an improved answer to the question.

**1  a** Define the term 'opportunity cost'.                                         [2]

*Cambridge International AS & A Level Business (9609) Paper 12 Q1a, March 2021*

| Example student response | Examiner comments |
|---|---|
| The next best alternative that is given up when making a decision. | This is an excellent definition of opportunity cost that clearly shows what is meant by the term. Awarded **two** marks. |

  **b** Explain **one** quality an entrepreneur is likely to need for success.      [3]

| Example student response | Examiner comments |
|---|---|
| Motivated to do well. | This answer states a quality of an entrepreneur but does not explain how being motivated leads to success. Awarded **one** mark. To improve, examples of the quality need to be given. |

  **c** Think of another quality that an entrepreneur may need for success and write your own answer to Question 1(b).

**2  a** Define the term 'demand'.                                                   [2]

*Cambridge International AS & A Level Business (9609) Paper 12 Q2a, March 2021*

| Example student response | Examiner comments |
|---|---|
| How much of something a customer buys. | This answer only refers to one element of demand (quantity); therefore, it is only awarded **one** mark. To improve this answer, there needs to be a more comprehensive definition of this term. For example, 'The quantity of a product a customer is willing to purchase at a given price'. |

**b** Explain **one** factor which might influence supply of a product. [3]

| Example student response | Examiner comments |
|---|---|
| One factor that may affect the supply of a product is the availability of resources. For example, if there is a snowstorm that blocks the roads, then raw material deliveries will not make it through to the factories. This means they will not have the raw materials they need to continue to produce, therefore lowering the level of supply. | This answer clearly understands how changes in the weather will affect supply. There is a good example provided (snowstorm that blocks the roads and raw materials) that provide examples that will affect the supply availability. Awarded *three* marks. |

**c** Think of another factor than might influence the supply of a product and write your own answer to Question 2(b).

Question 3 has example student responses and commentaries provided. For each part of the question, work through the question first, then compare your answer to the example student response and commentary.

**3 a** Analyse **two** benefits to a business of recruiting employees from outside the business. [8]

| Example student response | Examiner comments |
|---|---|
| One benefit of recruiting from outside the business is that it can bring in new ideas. The new employees may have experience of working in other organisations and can bring their experiences and understanding of other practices with them into the new organisation. These new ideas could make the business more efficient and productive, reducing its overall costs.<br><br>Another benefit of recruiting from outside the business is that it can lead to a wider pool of applicants being available. If the business only recruited from the employees within its organisation, it might not have the best person for the job already working within the firm, so it needs more people to choose from. | This answer contains clear knowledge and understanding of employees and external recruitment.<br><br>There is no application to a relevant business context in the answer. It is purely theoretical.<br><br>The first paragraph shows clear development of the impacts on the business of the external recruitment, leading to a measurable consequence. The second paragraph is less developed and does not clearly explain the implications on the business of being able to select from a larger pool of applicants. This needs to be developed.<br><br>*5/8 marks* |

**b** Evaluate whether the use of Herzberg's 'Two-Factor' theory could improve employee motivation in a school. [12]

| Example student response | Examiner comments |
|---|---|
| Herzberg's 'Two-Factor' theory involves the use of hygiene factors and motivators in the workplace. | The student starts with a good outline of Herzberg's theory. However, it would appear that the student has mistakenly suggested Herzberg meant 'hygiene' to refer to cleanliness. This statement could be given the benefit of the doubt. The cleanliness of the workplace might be a hygiene factor in the way it could demotivate employees if it is not present, but would not motivate if it is present. The remaining part of the answer shows excellent knowledge and understanding of the concept. |
| One way this theory could be used to improve motivation in a school is through the use of hygiene factors such as having a clean working environment. If the classrooms and corridors are kept clean, then the employees will be much happier and will work harder because they are motivated. | |
| Another use of the hygiene factors is through the relationships that exist between the employees. If the employees have good working relationships, then this will not result in job dissatisfaction, which Herzberg says will exist if the hygiene factor is not present. This should lead to employees feeling happy and motivated in the school. However, the use of hygiene factors does not by itself motivate workers. Just because there are good working relationships between teachers, support teachers and other staff does not mean that the employees will be any more motivated in their job; it just means that workers will not be de-motivated by their existence, showing that perhaps hygiene factors are not suitable to be used as a motivational tool in a school. | There is some good application to a school environment through the use of terms such as 'classrooms', 'grades' and 'students' as well as relevant examples that can be applied to a school environment. There could be more development of this skill in places. The knowledge of Herzberg is used well alongside this.

The discussion surrounding the use of relationships is well-developed. The student explains how this can affect levels of motivation, and further develops this by looking at how this may not work. The section relating to the 'awards' does not clearly explain how these can motivate workers, although some discussion about how they are not suitable is present, which provides analysis. |
| Alternatively, the school could use a motivating factor such as offering 'Teacher of the Month' awards to the teachers whose students get the best grades. However, this could be demotivating for some teachers who do not get given the award. They may be working really hard, but if only one teacher gets the award, then those not awarded may become sad and feel like a failure, which will be demotivating. There are also lots of other employees in a school, such as caretakers, so this award would not apply to them and would not motivate them to work harder. | |
| Overall, I think it can be very challenging to use Herzberg's 'Two-Factor' theory to improve motivation in a school. This is because there are lots of different types of employees. | There is a good judgement at the end of the section discussing relationships, where the student has provided a conclusion based on good analysis. At the end of the answer, there are excellent conclusions drawn relating to the suitability of Herzberg's theories, with alternatives suggested and justified. An improvement would be to have a little more reference to the dynamic nature of schools and/or the impact on different types of schools.

*11/12 marks* |

Now that you have read the example student responses to Question 3, here is a similar past paper question which you should attempt. Use the guidance in the commentaries to help you as you answer Question 4.

4    a    Analyse **two** reasons why a business might invest in market research.        [8]

     b    Evaluate whether an airline business might increase its profits by more effective market segmentation.        [12]

Question 5 has example student responses and commentaries provided for parts (a) to (c). For each part of the question, work through the question first, then compare your answer to the example student response and commentary. Part (d) provides a practice question for you to attempt. Use the guidance in the commentaries in this section to help you as you answer the question.

5

> ### Flora's Fitness (FF)
>
> Flora is a self-employed personal trainer and she trades as FF. She invested $10 000 as start-up capital. She has seen reports showing that keeping fit is becoming a trend in Country P. ABC is a national bank with a focus on corporate social responsibility (CSR). Flora thinks there is an opportunity to provide group fitness sessions to employees at ABC's head office. These sessions could include exercises and stretching techniques. She could also offer yoga and other fitness-related classes. These sessions would allow ABC to promote itself as a 'healthy employer'. Flora is keen to show the benefits of fitness sessions to ABC. A survey has shown that many employees do not currently visit gyms or fitness centres. High prices and lack of time are given as the most important reasons. She has arranged a meeting with John, the human resource director at ABC. He is interested in offering fitness sessions as a fringe benefit for employees. He has asked Flora to provide a business proposal for the meeting. She plans to provide one session before work and one session at lunchtime, five days per week. Flora proposed two pricing strategies (see Table 1).
>
> | Pricing strategy 1 | Pricing strategy 2 |
> | --- | --- |
> | Price per person: $5 | Total price per session: $75 |
> | Maximum 20 people per session | Maximum 20 people per session |
>
> **Table 1:** Proposed pricing strategies

   a    i    Define the term 'corporate social responsibility (CSR)'.        [2]

*Adapted from Cambridge International AS & A Level Business (9609) Paper 22 Q1a i, March 2021*

| Example student response | Examiner comments |
| --- | --- |
| It is when a business does good for society. | This answer would be awarded **zero** marks. It needs to explain what is meant by CSR (it is an aim/objective/strategy) and then provide some examples of the elements of CSR (people, planet, profit). |

ii  Explain the term 'start-up capital'. [3]

*Cambridge International AS & A Level Business (9609) Paper 22
Q1a ii, March 2021*

| Example student response | Examiner comments |
|---|---|
| This is money that is invested into equipment and premises that are needed for a new business | This is a very clear answer that shows good understanding of the term and provides relevant examples. Awarded **three** marks. |

b  i  Refer to Table 1 and any other relevant information.
Calculate the maximum weekly revenue for pricing strategy 1. [3]

*Cambridge International AS & A Level Business (9609) Paper 22
Q1b i, March 2021*

| Example student response | Examiner comments |
|---|---|
| $5 × 20 people = $100 per session<br><br>$100 × 2 sessions per day = $200<br><br>$200 a day × 7 days per week = $1400 | This answer has incorrectly multiplied the daily revenue by seven days. Awarded **two** marks for two correct steps. The case study states that FF will only operate five days a week. |

ii  Explain **one** advantage to FF of pricing strategy 2. [3]

*Cambridge International AS & A Level Business (9609) Paper 22
Q1b ii, March 2021*

| Example student response | Examiner comments |
|---|---|
| An advantage is that it will help FF with its cash flow. | This is an advantage to FF of the pricing strategy, but it has not been explained or applied to the case study. Awarded **one** mark. To improve the answer, there needs to be an explanation of the pricing strategy in context, e.g. it is a new business and this would guarantee $75 per session, no matter how many people attend. |

c   Analyse **two** sources of secondary information Flora could use
    to find out more about trends in the fitness market.          [8]

**Cambridge International AS & A Level Business (9609) Paper 22 Q1c,
    March 2021**

| Example student response | Examiner comments |
|---|---|
| One source could be a government census. This would provide lots of information on population of the country. Flora could use this to see how old people are because old people might not exercise or go to the gym so won't be interested in Flora's business. | There is clear knowledge and understanding of the sources of secondary information. |
| Another source of information could be through the use of market research reports. Flora could buy a report on the fitness industry in Country P that has all the data in that she might need to know such as who is doing exercise, what exercises they are doing, how much they pay for fitness classes etc. This information is easy to gain. However, it can be very expensive, which may be a problem for a new business as it may not have enough money to be able to invest into buying data. | The application in this answer is well applied to the fitness market and the second paragraph makes clear references to the data in the case study. However, the answer makes very stereotypical judgements about 'old people' which are not backed up by any data. These sorts of discriminatory comments should be avoided. |
| I think they best method for Flora to use is the census. This is because the data is free and will tell her information about the population which she can then use to help plan her new fitness business. | The first paragraph does not provide any relevant analysis of the use of a census to gather information on the fitness market. There is also no relevant impact on Flora's business of this data. The second paragraph is much stronger and provides a relevant two-sided argument on the use of market research reports. The student has attempted a judgement at the end of the answer. There are no marks for evaluation in this question, so this is an unnecessary addition to this answer. |
| | *7/8 marks* |

Try the following question for yourself.

d   Evaluate the benefits to ABC of offering employees fitness sessions.    [12]

# 21 Marketing analysis

The command word 'calculate' is often used in questions worth one to four marks, but can occasionally be seen with eight-mark questions, and requires mathematical calculations using the data provided by the exam question. 'Calculate' questions test AO1 Knowledge and understanding, and the best way to learn the skills required by this command word is by practice.

Twelve-mark questions require coverage of all four assessment objectives. Planning your responses to these questions is particularly important so that you can develop a chain of analysis, as well as areas of evaluation that provide an answer to the question, which must all be applied to the case material.

# 21.1 Elasticity of demand

| UNDERSTAND THESE TERMS |
|---|
| • price elasticity of demand (PED) |
| • income elasticity of demand (YED) |
| • inferior good |
| • promotional elasticity of demand |

1  Copy the information in Table 21.1, but adjust the rows so that each command word is matched with the correct definition.

| Command word | Definition |
|---|---|
| Analyse | Judge or calculate the quality, importance, amount or value of something |
| Advise | Set out purposes or reasons/make relationships between things evident/provide why and/or how and support with relevant evidence |
| Calculate | Write down a suggested course of action in a given situation |
| Evaluate | Work out from given facts, figures or information |
| Explain | Name/select/recognise |
| Identify | Give precise meaning |
| Define | Examine in detail to show meaning, identify elements and the relationship between them |

**Table 21.1:** Command words

Question 2 requires you to use the command word 'calculate'. 'Calculate' is a command word used in numerical questions and you will always be provided with all of the information you need to complete the task. Remember to always show your workings so that your thought process can be followed.

2

**American Ice Cream (AIC)**

AIC operates a number of ice cream cafés in five US states along the Gulf coast. The business was founded by Chi Peng in 2010. It now faces a critical decision: whether to continue exclusively in the current business model or expand its operations into other states, where there is considerable competition and the business is not currently known. The states that the business is considering expanding into are all wealthy regions and so Chi Peng is excited about the plan, believing that it offers growth potential for the business. The ice cream parlour offers three types of ice cream–Deluxe, Super and King Cone–and is experimenting with different prices: $4.00, $5.00 and $7.50. Average daily sales across all of the outlets at each price are shown in Table 21.2.

| Average ice cream price | Deluxe | Super | King Cone |
|---|---|---|---|
| $4.00 | 9464 | 6469 | 16500 |
| $5.00 | 8450 | 5175 | 11000 |
| $7.50 | 6760 | 3450 | 2200 |

**Table 21.2:** Average daily sales

Following more in-depth research into the revenue generated by the business, AIC also compiled the data shown in Table 21.3 and Table 21.4 on each of the three products.

| Average promotional spend | Deluxe, million | Super, million | King Cone, million |
|---|---|---|---|
| $50000 | 2500 | 3800 | 4125 |
| $75000 | 3750 | 6460 | 4640 |

**Table 21.3:** Average promotional spend and quantity demanded

| | Deluxe | Super | King Cone |
|---|---|---|---|
| Income elasticity of demand YED | 1.5 | 0.75 | −0.2 |

**Table 21.4:** Income elasticity of demand

Calculate the price elasticity of demand (PED) for each of the following products sold by AIC when the price rises from $5.00 to $7.50.

a   Delux                                                          [3]

b   Super                                                          [3]

c   King cone.                                                     [3]

**3** Calculate the promotional elasticity of demand for each of the following products sold by AIC when the advertising expenditure rises from $50 000 to $75 000.

   **a** Delux [3]

   **b** Super [3]

   **c** King cone. [3]

For Question 4, make sure you develop your response and use full sentences (rather than bullet points). You will need to use full sentences in an exam, so it is helpful to get into the habit of this when answering practice questions.

To show evaluation, you will need to include a substantiated judgement or recommendation which is clearly related to the context of the question. Remember to focus on the question to ensure your answer is in context, but you can also evaluate by explaining how your judgement will depend on other important factors. Finally, in the evaluation avoid simply writing a summary of what you have written earlier in the essay or basing your answer on opinions rather than reasoned argument or evidence.

**4** Evaluate how AIC might use income elasticity of demand (YED) analysis to increase its sales revenue. [12]

### REFLECTION

How can you remember the difference between PED and YED, and are there goods and services that are PED-elastic but YED-inelastic or vice versa? How do you remember the formulae for PED and YED? Students will sometimes forget which value is the denominator and which is the numerator. To get this right, remember that it is always quantity demanded on the top and then price or income on the bottom. Why not write out revision cards for both terms to highlight the difference?

### ≪ RECALL AND CONNECT 1 ≪

**a** How might a business use PED when deciding on the correct price to set for a product?

**b** Explain the role of promotional elasticity of demand in negotiating the marketing budget allocated for a good or service.

## 21.2 New product development

### UNDERSTAND THESE TERMS

- new product development
- research and development (R&D)
- test marketing

1 Copy and complete Figure 21.1 in order to explain the stages of the product development process.

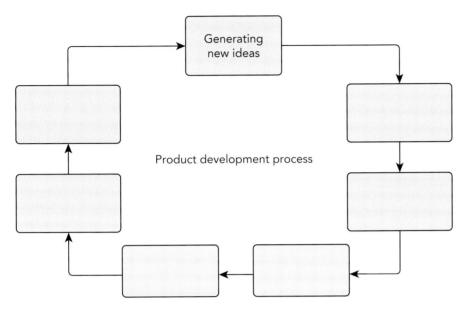

Figure 21.1: The product development process

2 a Describe five factors that influence the level of R&D expenditure by a firm.

b Investigate how much is spent on R&D by the world's largest businesses, for example, Apple or Microsoft.

**REFLECTION**

How did you go about researching these companies? Was it easy to find the information you needed? What advice could you share with another student carrying out this task?

3 Analyse **one** way that product development can increase sales within an organisation. [5]

**《 RECALL AND CONNECT 2 《**

Explain the relationship between the marketing of a new product and new product innovation.

# 21.3 Sales forecasting

## UNDERSTAND THESE TERMS

- sales forecasting
- trend
- seasonal fluctuations
- cyclical fluctuations
- random fluctuations
- qualitative sales forecasting

1

### American Ice Cream (AIC)

Further research of sales revenue generated by AIC illustrates the seasonal nature of the business, with revenue heavily weather-dependent, as the sale figures in Table 21.5 illustrate.

| Year | Quarter | Sales revenue (in $m) | Four-quarter moving total | Eight-quarter moving total | Quarterly moving average (trend) | Seasonal moving variation | Average seasonal variation |
|------|---------|-----------------------|---------------------------|----------------------------|----------------------------------|---------------------------|----------------------------|
| 2020 | 1 | $36 | | | | | |
| | 2 | $110 | | | | | |
| | 3 | $135 | | | | | |
| | 4 | $45 | | | | | |
| 2021 | 1 | $40 | | | | | |
| | 2 | $125 | | | | | |
| | 3 | $155 | | | | | |
| | 4 | $65 | | | | | |
| 2022 | 1 | $45 | | | | | |
| | 2 | $125 | | | | | |
| | 3 | $145 | | | | | |
| | 4 | $70 | | | | | |

**Table 21.5:** AIC sales figures

Copy and complete Table 21.5.

2   Evaluate the impact of using sales forecasting on AIC's business decisions.   [12]

## ≪ RECALL AND CONNECT 3 ≪

a   Identify the role of sales forecasting in the business strategy process.

b   Identify the role of sales forecasting in the budget allocation process.

## SELF-ASSESSMENT CHECKLIST

Let's revisit the Knowledge focus and Exam skills focus for this chapter.
Decide how confident you are with each statement.

| Now I can | Show it | Needs more work | Almost there | Confident to move on |
|---|---|---|---|---|
| measure and interpret elasticity of demand: price, income and promotional | Calculate the price and income elasticity of demand for a range of products. Explain why the demand for some products is more responsive to changes in price and income than for others. | | | |
| analyse the impact of elasticity results on business decisions | Research one business you know well and identify ways that the business might use elasticity theory to increase sales revenue. | | | |
| evaluate the importance of new product development and of research and development | Identify some products that have emerged in the last five years in the industries of smart phones, energy generation or social media. Which of these products use completely new/ invented technology and which were created using an adaption to existing technologies? | | | |
| analyse sales data using the moving-average method | Investigate the sales figures for a seasonal business, e.g., ice cream, sun cream, holidays, and calculate the following: sales revenue, four-quarter moving total, quarterly moving average (trend) and seasonal variation. | | | |
| evaluate the impact of sales forecasting on business decisions | Extrapolate the data collected to predict future sales figures for the business you investigated. Explain why sales forecasting figures might not always be accurate. | | | |

## CONTINUED

| | | | | |
|---|---|---|---|---|
| further develop my confidence answering 'calculate' questions | A firm produces plastic cups for a unit price of $5 per pack. Calculate the breakeven level of output required at the following prices: $7.50, $9.50, $12.00. The fixed costs of the business are $200 000. | | | |
| understand how to structure a 12-mark extended-response question | Practise writing answers to some of the 12-mark questions in the Exam practice section. This will expose you to different past paper question styles. | | | |

# 22 Marketing strategy

## EXAM SKILLS FOCUS

In this chapter you will:

- develop metacognitive practice by evaluating your progress in answering exam questions.

One aspect of metacognitive practice is evaluating your progress. Some tips for this include completing as many exam paper questions as possible, such as the ones included in this resource, as well as completing a self-evaluation of different questions. Review your answers, including comparing your work with the sample answers in the Answers for this resource. Ask your teacher for further feedback on those areas in which you can improve.

## 22.1 Planning the marketing strategy

1   Identify the **four** contents of a marketing plan.

2   Outline the advantages and disadvantages of marketing planning for a business.

### ≪ RECALL AND CONNECT 1 ≪

How do businesses use forcefield analysis to weigh up the strengths and weaknesses of any business idea?

### UNDERSTAND THIS TERM

* marketing plan

### ≪ RECALL AND CONNECT 2 ≪

a   Explain the role of human resources on marketing planning.

b   Explain the role of budgeting on marketing planning.

## 22.2 Approaches to marketing strategy

1   Describe the **three** issues that marketing managers must consider when discussing an effective marketing strategy.

2

### Belgium Chocolates (BC)

BC is a well-established business operating in the Netherlands, Belgium and Luxembourg. It is a brand famous for the quality of its product, which commands a premium price. As part of its market development approach it is planning to expand to other European nations. The benefits of expanding to neighbouring states are obvious, meaning an expansion of its customer base that allows the firm to benefit from increased profile and increased economies of scale. Sales in its existing outlets are going well and growing at 5% a year. Mark Peters, one of the partners, is reticent about the ambitious expansion plans, believing that with the current trajectory of the business positive, the business should not be taking risks expanding into new territories. His brother and business partner, Chris Peters, however, believes that any business must open new stores and has suggested accompanying their expansion plans with a significant rise in marketing spending.

Advise BC on how the organisation might use information technology (IT) to support its expansion plans.                                         [20]

Do you have a way of remembering the four Ps; for example, is there a mnemonic for remembering each P? Can you explain, using examples, the meaning of a coordinated marketing mix?

3   Evaluate how BC might use AI within the marketing mix.                [12]

**《 RECALL AND CONNECT 3 《**

Explain the role of the finance department in any marketing strategy.

# 22.3 Strategies for international marketing

**UNDERSTAND THESE TERMS**

- economic collaboration
- international marketing
- pan-global marketing

1
### Belgium Chocolates (BC)

A newly recruited director of marketing to plan and coordinate BC's marketing strategy, Michael, believes that the business should focus all of its marketing efforts on developing the brand across Europe.

Evaluate the likely impact of globalisation on BC's marketing.        [12]

2   Identify reasons why BC might want to export its products to overseas markets.

**REFLECTION**

How confident are you at approaching 'evaluate' questions? What can you do to help you remember to include the stakeholders for any business?

**《 RECALL AND CONNECT 4 《**

Explain the role strategic alliances and joint ventures might have on an international marketing strategy.

## SELF-ASSESSMENT CHECKLIST

Let's revisit the Knowledge focus and Exam skills focus for this chapter.
Decide how confident you are with each statement.

| Now I can | Show it | Needs more work | Almost there | Confident to move on |
|---|---|---|---|---|
| analyse the importance of planning marketing strategy | Investigate situations where businesses have launched a new product without an effective marketing strategy. What problems did they encounter and how might these have been resolved/mitigated by a more effective strategy? | | | |
| analyse the need for a coordinated and consistent marketing strategy | Investigate a successful marketing campaign that you are familiar with. Identify ways that all aspects of the marketing mix (the four Ps) are consistent with each other and with the target market. | | | |
| analyse the need to link marketing strategy to marketing objectives | Investigate and then write out the marketing objectives for a business that you know well. Then write a strategy, including a realistic time frame for completion, to complete the objectives. | | | |
| evaluate the changing role of IT and AI in marketing | If possible investigate a business that you know well (ideally by interviewing a friend or family member) and write out examples of how both IT and AI are used in the marketing of the firm's products. | | | |

| CONTINUED | | | | |
|---|---|---|---|---|
| evaluate and select appropriate strategies for entering international markets | Select a multinational business and suggest different strategies that the business could use to enter international markets. Do businesses need to change their strategy for each country they enter, depending on that country's unique characteristics/culture? | | | |
| develop metacognitive practice by evaluating my progress in answering exam questions | Create a self-assessment for the exam skills questions in this chapter. | | | |

# Exam practice 6

This section contains both past paper questions from previous Cambridge exams and practice questions. These questions draw together your knowledge on a range of topics that you have covered up to this point and will help you prepare for your assessment.

For Question 1, read the case study, questions, example student responses and commentaries provided. Then, in part (d), write an improved answer to Question 1(c), but for a different organisation.

1

---

### Southwest Farming (SWF)

SWF is a family-controlled private limited company based in Country Q. The current managing director, Lee Tae-woo, is the grandson of the founder of this farming business. The core focus of SWF changed in the 1980s. Lee recognised an opportunity to increase profitability by shifting production from cereal products to milk from cows, in response to changing tastes in Country Q. Sales of fresh milk now account for 70% of SWF's revenue. Other milk-based products have also been introduced to increase sales and include cheese, butter and ice cream. Using the SWF brand, products are sold direct to retailers, including a national supermarket group. SWF also supplies the government with milk for consumption in schools. SWF has established a reputation for high-quality products and its mission statement is to:

- 'bring health to all our customers naturally'

- 'ensure that our customers' needs and expectations are the starting point for everything we do'

- 'maintain excellent long-term relationships with employees, retailers and customers'.

Lee has transformed the business from being a small single farm to owning 20 large farms spread throughout Country Q. The business has grown through acquisition.

### Strategic options for growth

Lee wants SWF to grow. As a result of the demand changes already experienced and future anticipated changes, Lee commissioned reports into two strategic options.

### Option 1

Demand for organic food products is increasing in Country Q. This is a consequence of rising incomes, greater awareness of the environmental impact of non-organic farming and the possible health benefits of organic produce. Certification of organic standards takes at least five years for

---

**CONTINUED**

a farm to achieve. There would be medium-term costs to SWF as a result of lower milk yields before organic status is achieved. The reduction in profit is estimated to be $10 000 000. However, this market segment is predicted to grow at 10% per year and organic products can be sold at higher prices. Currently 90% of organic milk products sold in Country Q are imported.

*Option 2*

Market research indicates increasing demand for frozen yoghurt products. A successful entry into this market could compensate for the falling demand for fresh milk and increase SWF's product portfolio. Research would be required to develop new products. The production of frozen yoghurt is similar to ice cream manufacture. Capital investment of $3 000 000 would be required but the production of frozen yoghurts would increase capacity utilisation in the ice cream factory.

**Appendix 1: Ice cream sales data by volume (thousand litres)**

| Year | Quarter | Sales volume | Centred quarterly moving average | Seasonal variation | Average seasonal variation |
|---|---|---|---|---|---|
| 2014 | 2 | 25 | | | |
| | 3 | 35 | | | |
| | 4 | 25 | 25.88 | −0.88 | 0.22 |
| 2015 | 1 | 16 | 27.13 | −11.13 | −12.09 |
| | 2 | 30 | 28.63 | 1.38 | 0.34 |
| | 3 | 40 | 30.00 | See Question 1(a)(ii) | 11.97 |
| | 4 | 32 | 30.88 | 1.13 | 0.22 |
| 2016 | 1 | 20 | 31.88 | −11.88 | −12.09 |
| | 2 | 33 | 32.75 | 0.25 | 0.34 |
| | 3 | 45 | 33.25 | 11.75 | 11.97 |
| | 4 | 34 | 33.75 | 0.25 | 0.22 |
| 2017 | 1 | 22 | 34.38 | −12.38 | −12.09 |
| | 2 | 35 | 35.00 | 0.00 | 0.34 |
| | 3 | 48 | 35.38 | 12.63 | 11.97 |
| | 4 | 36 | 35.63 | 0.38 | 0.22 |
| 2018 | 1 | 23 | 36.00 | −13.00 | −12.09 |
| | 2 | 36 | 36.25 | −0.25 | 0.34 |
| | 3 | 50 | See Question 1(a)(i) | | 11.97 |
| | 4 | 36 | | | |
| 2019 | 1 | 25 | | | |

## CONTINUED

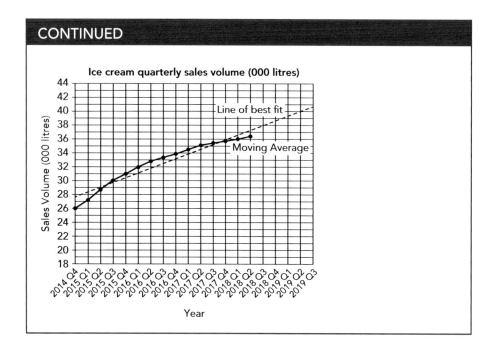

**a** Refer to the table in Appendix 1. Calculate:

**i** the centred quarterly moving average for quarter 3, 2018 [3]

*Cambridge International AS & A Level Business (9609)*
*Paper 32 Q4a i, June 2019*

| Example student response | Examiner comments |
|---|---|
| The centred quarterly moving average is calculated by the 8-period moving total of (23 + 36 + 50 + 36 + 36 + 50 + 36 + 25)/8 = 292/8 = 36 500 litres or 36.5 thousand litres. | The student has correctly calculated the centred quarterly moving average. Awarded **three** marks. |

**ii** the seasonal variation for Quarter 3, 2015. [2]

*Cambridge International AS & A Level Business (9609)*
*Paper 32 Q4a ii, June 2019*

| Example student response | Examiner comments |
|---|---|
| Sales for Q3 of 2015 of 40 – four-period moving average trend of 30 = 10 000 litres | The student has correctly calculated the seasonal variation. Awarded **two** marks. |

**b** Refer to the table and graph in Appendix 1. Calculate SWF's forecast sales for Quarter 3 in 2019. [3]

*Cambridge International AS & A Level Business (9609) Paper 32 Q4b, June 2019*

| Example student response | Examiner comments |
|---|---|
| The predicted trend from inspection of the graph is 40.8, plus the average seasonal variation for Q3 = 11.97. Therefore, the forecast sales = 527.700 or 527.7 thousand litres | This response receives full marks for the correct response, with working clearly identified. Awarded *three* marks. Note that, due to possible differences in the reading of the diagram, an answer between 527570 and 527970 would be accepted. |

**c** Refer to your result from 1(b). Evaluate the usefulness of sales forecasts to SWF when making marketing and operational decisions. [12]

*Adapted from Cambridge International AS & A Level Business (9609) Paper 32 Q4c, June 2019*

| Example student response | Examiner comments |
|---|---|
| SWF, like all businesses, make use of sales forecasts to help make marketing and operational decisions. SWF could use a range of different methods for forecasting sales. One example might be TSA which bases sales forecasts on extrapolating from past sales data. This is a popular method of sales forecasting because it uses real world data and presumes that previous periods of trend growth will be maintained and so this process involves a simple mathematical extrapolation process. A second method that SWF might employ is the Delphi technique-based estimates of a panel of experts. This method is more subjective than the use of simple time series analysis data. Sales forecasting using Time Series Analysis takes account of seasonal variations and gives a realistic prediction. Sales forecasts are then used as the basis for marketing decisions/marketing strategy, as well as operational decisions relating to production e.g. stock control, capacity utilisation etc. SWF will use the forecast sales data to decide how and where resources are allocated such as the potential decision to increase profitability by shifting production from cereal products to milk from cows. | Both time series analysis and the Delphi technique are well explained. However, there is far too much information provided in the first paragraph that is not applied to the business context and or the question.<br><br>Later in the response, knowledge is applied well to the text with sales trends from the case study skilfully used within the answer, and a note about seasonal variations included. |

| Example student response | Examiner comments |
|---|---|
| Using the time series analysis method of forecasting the trend for SWF clearly shows that sales of ice cream are increasing, shown by the rising quarterly moving average. This forecast enables planning and fits the ice cream sales pattern well. In other words SWF faces clear seasonal variation, with milk sales highest in the summer months, and has consistent past trends. As such it is reasonable to assume that the future will be similar, making forecasting valuable for planning e.g. the volume of milk required to meet production requirements. The combined forecasting sales of milk and milk products will inform SWF's decisions regarding purchase of animal feed and herd size required – decisions which require relatively long-term planning as herd size may take time to alter.<br><br>The sales analysis will also help ensure a more efficient use of labour and machinery, helping to control costs of production and therefore ensure profitability. Marketing decisions regarding pricing will also be influenced by many other factors such as PED and costs of production.<br><br>Sales forecasting using TSA or the Delphi method will add credibility and accuracy to any sales forecasting predictions, making them more reliable than simple forecasting or just projecting a trend. The method is not without critics. The data relies on future events behaving as in the past so may not be reliable and it is generally believed that they need to be used alongside other evidence e.g. a prediction of competitors' behaviour, likely future government actions, and/or economic changes. | The response also included analysis, although this area was a little general. For example, comments such as 'advertising spends are also likely to be influenced by overall sales' were accurate but not applied to SWF. One clear chain of developed analysis is provided in the answer shown through the impact of the seasonal variations in sales data and the effect they are likely to have on decision-making.<br><br>To gain marks for evaluation, the answer needs to provide a judgement. The answer does not explicitly make a judgement on the suitability of sales forecasting using TSA or the Delphi technique on operational decisions. The attempt at a conclusion at the end does not address the question or make any reference to the usefulness of using TSA or the Delphi technique.<br><br>*7/12 marks* |

d   Now write your own answer to Question 1(c) for a different organisation, evaluating the usefulness of sales forecasts to a business when making marketing decisions. [12]

The following question has an example student response and commentary provided. Work through the question first, then compare your answer to the example student response and commentary.

**2**  Advise SWF on a marketing strategy to use if they select strategic Option 2 for growth.                                                        [20]

| Example student response | Examiner comments |
|---|---|
| A marketing strategy includes the use of the 4Ps (price, product, promotion and place) to support marketing objectives. | The answer demonstrates a clear understanding of the elements of a marketing strategy including the 4Ps and market research. Points of knowledge are present throughout the answer showing the student has a good appreciation of what might be involved in the development of a marketing strategy. |
| The first thing that SWF needs to consider is their product. Currently, SWF produces milk from cows, but if they select Option 2, this will involve the business moving into a new market for frozen yoghurt. SWF does not produce yoghurt as part of their portfolio, so may have limited knowledge about their market. The data in Appendix 1 shows that there has been an increase in demand for ice cream, but this does not mean that the demand for frozen yoghurt will be the same. If the trend for ice cream does continue, and the frozen yoghurt market also follows the same trend then the frozen yoghurt market might be very profitable for SWF to enter. Additionally, SWF will need to do market research into the market to find out what flavours of frozen yoghurt the customers want to buy. The market research is really important as SWF is taking a huge risk by diversifying into a new market because 70% of their sales are in the fresh milk market, and to enter a new market, they may have to take some focus away from the milk market to focus on the production of frozen yoghurt. | |
| Another thing that SWF needs to consider is the price they charge for the frozen ice cream. They will need to spend $3,000,000 to upgrade their factory to be able to produce the new product, so they need to set a price that allows them to cover this initial cost. As well as this, they will need to research the market to find out how much other firms are charging for their frozen yoghurt so that SWF can decide where they are going to place themselves in the market. | Throughout the answer, there is a strong use of the case study material; both quantitative and qualitative information have been used and have generally been applied to the answer well. However, it should be noted that for application skills to be awarded, the case study material has to be used to answer the specific question being asked. For example, in the middle of the second paragraph, the answer drifts from the question by commenting on SWF's likely success or failure in entering the market for frozen yoghurt. While this might appear to be good knowledge, understanding and application, it is not directly answering the question being asked. It is commenting on SWF's likely success or failure of entering the market for frozen yoghurt rather than an appropriate marketing strategy to use when entering the market. This means it would be classified as 'NAQ' (not answering the question) and therefore cannot be rewarded. |
| SWF will need to develop a new strategy for the promotion of the frozen yoghurt. Although SWF has experience of producing ice cream and are known in that market, they are not established in the frozen yoghurt market. SWF will need to create a promotional campaign to let potential customers know that they have diversified into the frozen yoghurt market. SWF have an excellent relationship with their customers, so it would be important to make sure that the customers are fully informed about this change in business strategy. This should involve the use of email communications to their current buyers in the business-to-business market to see if they are interested in the new product to stock in their supermarkets and schools. Although this will take a long time to do, this is the easiest way to get their message to their customers about the new product that is available. | |

| Example student response | Examiner comments |
|---|---|
| It is essential that SWF plans their marketing strategy before they move into the frozen yoghurt market. They need to set clear marketing objectives that cover the 4Ps so they know what they are aiming to achieve throughout this new venture. It might be helpful for SWF to use an Ansoff Matrix to help them plan their growth strategy.<br><br>The most important part of the marketing strategy that SWF need to plan for is the product. Although they are experienced in many parts of the dairy market, moving into the frozen yoghurt market is still a risk for them. | There is analysis present throughout the answer but is it not particularly strong as there are no developed chains of argument focused on marketing strategy or parts of the strategy. In the third paragraph, there is some analysis stating that SWF needs to do some market research to see where they will place themselves, but this is not developed any further or linked to the impact(s) it may have on the development of a future marketing strategy. A similar issue can be identified in the middle of the fourth paragraph where there is the acknowledgement that customers need to be informed about the change but there is no further development of the impact/implications of this for SWF.<br><br>The final two paragraphs include some application/use of context as well as evaluative statements, but the development of these into evaluative comments is not of a strong enough standard to be awarded. The final statement is unsupported; there is no justification why the product is the most important part of the marketing strategy for SWF. There is no evidence of a developed evaluative comment that balances the key points made throughout the answer. Additionally, more focus on the overall development of the marketing strategy needs to be considered in any evaluation.<br><br>*9/20 marks* |

For Question 3(a) read the case study, question, example student response and commentary provided. Then, in Question 3(b), write an improved answer to the question, using the guidance in the commentary to help you.

**3**

### Quality Fencing (QF)

Quality Fencing is owned by Seojun. Seojun is a sole trader who repairs and builds wooden fences. Most of his customers own houses with gardens in Country X. Seojun is an entrepreneur who has an aim to be rich. He set up QF two years ago to fulfil his aim and he set himself the objectives of:

- making $1 000 000 profit within five years

- having a 20% market share in City X within five years.

Seojun has made some progress towards his objectives (see Table 1).

| | Year 1 | Year 2 | Year 3 (forecast) |
|---|---|---|---|
| Total revenue | $120 000 | $240 000 | $480 000 |
| Direct costs | $70 000 | $110 000 | $150 000 |
| Indirect costs | $20 000 | $40 000 | $80 000 |
| Market share in City X | 2% | 4% | 8% |

**Table 1:** Financial and market share data for QF

Seojun's target market is house owners with medium to large gardens. Most houses in City X have a garden. Promotion is important to Seojun, because the market for fence building and repairs is very competitive in City X. Most customers book QF's services by telephone, but there is a growing need for online bookings. The business is forecast to continue to grow. Seojun has decided to employ two new workers. He has written a job description (see Table 2).

---

**Job title:** Fence builder

**Required:** As soon as possible

**Salary:** Based on age

**Qualifications:** A Levels are desirable but not essential

A workman is required to build and repair fences for a growing local business called QF. Full training will be provided. Experience of building and repairing fences is essential. Must be fully physically fit and under the age of 25.

---

**Table 2:** Job description

**a** Evaluate a suitable promotion method which would help Seojun to achieve his objectives. [12]

| Example student response | Examiner comments |
|---|---|
| By using newspaper advertising Seojun can target higher-income people in City X, who are more likely to own houses with gardens. This would be an efficient way to target his customers which reduces the costs for QF. Another advantage of newspaper advertising is that it typically costs less per thousand readers than television, radio and direct mail advertising. In addition, newspaper staff members will work directly with advertisers to create ads at no additional costs. Newspaper advertising can also be customised to meet any budget. | The response shows knowledge and understanding of newspaper advertising as a method of promotion, as well as other methods (television, radio and direct mail). |
| Overall, newspaper advertising is most likely to target Seojun's current target customers because he can advertise his telephone number and that is how most customers book; however, if he really wants to develop his online bookings, another method may be best. | The response notes that by using newspaper advertising Seojun can target higher-income people in city X, who are more likely to own houses with gardens. This is the only example of application in the answer. Much of this is due to the fact only one paragraph has been provided as a discussion of a suitable method. There are two good points raised in the first paragraph and each of these could have been discussed in more depth as separate paragraphs. |
| | There is an appreciation that a strength of newspaper advertising is that it may allow Seojun to target higher-income people in city X, who are more likely to own houses with gardens. However, this is not developed. The impact of the use of newspapers is quite superficial (reduce costs) but this does not go any further. |
| | The response makes an attempt at an overall judgement that newspaper advertising is suitable as a phone number can be printed and this is how most customers book with Seojun. There is no evaluative comment in the answer. |
| | *7/12 marks* |

**b** Now write an improved answer to Question 3(a).

The following question has an example student response and commentary provided. Work through the question first, then compare your answer to the example student response and commentary.

**4**

### Benjamin's Beds (BB)

Benjamin's Beds is a large manufacturer of beds and has a strong brand image for quality. Its main channel of distribution is through the producer market (B2B) to national hotel chains. Recently, BB has also entered the consumer market (B2C) by selling online direct to customers. BB uses flow production. BB's existing machinery is old and cannot satisfy the increased demand. The directors of BB have decided its existing machinery needs replacing. Table 1 shows data for existing and proposed new machinery.

|  | Variable cost per unit | Output per year |
|---|---|---|
| Existing machinery | $50 | 5000 |
| New machinery | $40 | 7500 |

**Table 1:** Data for existing and proposed new machinery

Fixed costs are $500 000 per year. Using new machinery would reduce this by 10%. BB sales data suggests that its market share is growing rapidly. The consumer market (B2C) is becoming more important to BB because online orders are increasing. However, online demand is for a wide range of bed styles. The consumer market requires a substantial marketing budget and some retraining of employees. Orders from national hotel chains in the producer market (B2B) are for a more limited range of bed styles. These orders remain constant, with low marketing costs. However, BB is increasingly under pressure to reduce prices to hotels. BB uses non-financial motivators and until recently had a motivated workforce. Efficiency is falling due to employees having to work longer hours because of increased demand. This is decreasing staff morale and welfare.

Evaluate whether BB should focus on the producer market (B2B) or the consumer market (B2C).                                                                  [12]

| Example student response | Examiner comments |
|---|---|
| The B2B market is directed at people who will purchase a product on behalf of a business, typically a key decision-maker. This type of marketing is primarily concerned with the people who will be using the product, the business goals the product will enable or the return on investment (ROI) that the purchase will deliver. Therefore, the most effective marketing strategies will focus on the results BB's products will deliver, how the product helps the buyer, or what benefits it will bring to them personally. | There is a good explanation of the difference between the two markets detailed at the beginning of the response. The answer clearly shows the difference between B2B and B2C markets. |
| Through its B2C sales BB sells directly to consumers and through retailers and online. Purchased by the end user the BB brand is important in attracting customers in a competitive market. Sales of its beds are likely to be primarily in single units. Through its B2B sales, BB sells directly to hotels who uses the product to deliver their own product/service. When selling to hotels, the most important selling points are price, added value and durability. | The response also includes a significant amount of application to BB. For example, the response addresses the historical role of the B2B market, the growing importance of the B2C market as well as the importance of raising revenues to finance the new machinery. |
| BB, as a large manufacturer of beds, has a strong brand image for quality, which is likely to be important if they choose to focus more on the consumer market. Historically, their main sales have always been through direct channels to hotels, but the B2C market is becoming more important as online orders are increasing. Much will depend on the proposition to introduce new machinery (at a cost), as this will require additional sales to justify the investment. | There is a lack of analysis and development in the points made. There is good use of theory, but the overall impact on BB is lacking throughout. It can be helpful to bring the points being made back to a measurable impact for example – the level of potential revenue, market share or rising costs of entering a new market. |
| On balance, I believe that BB should focus on both markets, perhaps putting slightly more emphasis on the B2C market moving forward, while maintaining its current production of beds for the hotel market. The hotel market is stable and requires fewer operating costs than selling directly to customers and so I believe it would be foolish to ignore this market completely. This sector can continue to provide BB with a steady, if relatively small, income and buy the business time to focus expansion plans on the B2C market, with the new machinery driving higher product quality that will be crucial for it to grow in this market. | The response included a suitable recommendation about whether BB should focus on the consumer (B2C) or producer (B2B) market. A judgement about the relative suitability of each market was also made, including the advantages/disadvantages of each market. There is really good use of context within the judgement, to put the final paragraph into context. |
| | *9/12 marks* |

Here is another practice question which you should attempt. Use the guidance in the commentaries in this section to help you as you answer the question.

5    'The most effective way for a loss-making retail clothing business to survive is to change the price element of its marketing mix.'
Evaluate this view.                                                                                      [12]

# 23 The nature of operations

As part of your Cambridge International AS & A Level Business course, you are expected to develop a critical understanding of business organisations. To do this, as well as needing an in-depth level of knowledge about all the different factors that go into running a business organisation, you also need to understand how all these factors work together. You may have found that when learning about a topic, you can make links to other topic areas that you have already studied, and this is an excellent skill to focus on. Business functions do not operate in isolation; they all need to work together for business organisations to be successful. In this chapter you will consider links between the operations and marketing functions.

In Chapter 11 you were introduced to the STEPS technique to support you in developing the skills needed to enhance the level of application in your answers. Remember, in longer-response answers, if there is no application of your answer to the case study, then you cannot access any of the higher levels of the mark scheme. Good application is the key to developing your exam performance.

## 23.1 The production (transformational) process

1   Copy and complete the transformational process diagram in Figure 23.1.

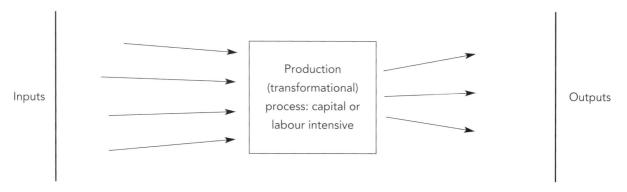

**Figure 23.1:** The transformational process

2   Explain how each of the factor inputs is used in the production process.

### ≪ RECALL AND CONNECT 1 ≪

There are many barriers that every entrepreneur must overcome to turn their business ideas into reality. Identify at least **three** potential barriers for an entrepreneur.

### UNDERSTAND THIS TERM

*   transformational process

## 23.2 Efficiency, effectiveness, productivity and sustainability

1   Outline **four** ways a business can increase its productivity.

2   A business has an annual output of 10 000 units and it has 25 workers. Calculate the labour productivity rate of the business.

In Chapter 11, you were introduced to the STEPS technique to help you gain a better understanding of a case study and its business context to support your application skills. Here is an opportunity for you to revisit this technique in order to help you gain more confidence in using it. Before you write your answer to Question 3, read the case study on CD Footwear and make notes on some elements of STEPS for this case study. You may not be able to do all element of STEPS as there is limited information. Go back to Chapter 11 to remind yourself about this technique if you need to, then answer Question 3.

3

**CD Footwear**

CD Footwear was founded by friends Carlos and Dani ten years ago. They both have an interest in hiking and outdoor pursuits and were unable to find suitable footwear that was both comfortable and fashionable. They decided to create their own range of footwear and have steadily developed a large customer base due to their ability to sell via their own website and deliver their products internationally through the postal system. Recently, CD Footwear has started to look at the sustainability of its operations as it feels its current production methods and wide range of available designs create too much waste. It is also concerned by the number of non-recyclable materials it uses in its products and whether recyclable alternatives would be durable enough to use in its footwear.

> **UNDERSTAND THESE TERMS**
> * productivity
> * efficiency
> * effectiveness

Evaluate the impact on CD Footwear of increasing the sustainability of its operations. [12]

# 23.3 Labour-intensive and capital-intensive operations

1　Copy and complete Table 23.1. Identify whether the statement refers to labour-intensive production or capital-intensive production and whether it is a benefit or a cost of that method of production.

| | Labour-intensive | Capital-intensive | Benefit | Cost |
|---|---|---|---|---|
| Interesting and varied work | | | | |
| High fixed costs | | | | |
| Low machine costs | | | | |
| Consistent quality | | | | |
| Economies of scale | | | | |
| Low output levels | | | | |
| High maintenance cost | | | | |

**Table 23.1:** Labour-intensive and capital-intensive production

**2** In which type of industries are you more likely to find labour-intensive production techniques being used rather than capital-intensive methods?

## ≪ RECALL AND CONNECT 2 ≪

Explain what a cooperative is and outline the key features of this type of business organisation.

# 23.4 Operations (production) methods

**1** Copy Table 23.1. Match the definition to the correct method of production.

| Method of production | Definition |
|---|---|
| Job production | The production of items in a continually moving process |
| Batch production | The production of a one-off item specially designed for the customer |
| Flow production | The production of a limited number of identical products – each item in the batch passes through one stage of production before passing on to the next stage |
| Mass customisation | The use of flexible computer-aided technology on production lines to make products that meet individual customers' requirements for customised products |

**Table 23.2:** Methods of production

**2 a** What are **two** advantages and **two** disadvantages of using job production?

**b** Give **two** examples of when using job production would be most suitable.

**3 a** What are **two** advantages and **two** disadvantages of using batch production?

**b** Give **two** examples of when using batch production would be most suitable.

**4 a** What are **two** advantages and **two** disadvantages of using flow production?

**b** Give **two** examples of when using flow production would be most suitable.

**5** Explain **three** factors that may be used to determine the production method chosen by a business.

Some exam questions will not make it obvious what areas of this course you need to refer to in order to answer them. You need to be prepared to use your knowledge from across more than one of the business functional areas (marketing, operations, finance and human resources) to help you develop answers to these types of questions.

For the following question, you could use knowledge from many different areas of this course. However, for this activity you should only use knowledge from the operations and marketing functions as a way of practising your application of these two functional areas.

6

**Serenity Scents (SS)**

SS is a small business start-up that has been operating for six months. It was started by Jonathan and his sister Candy as a way of earning some money after they left school. They have created a range of four different candles with fragrances that help promote positive mental wellbeing, including lavender and camomile. Currently, the candles are made in a spare room in their family home, with Jonathan and Candy sharing all responsibilities and workload evenly. Recently, they took their candles to a local market where they set up a small stall and their candles sold out quickly. Jonathan and Candy received really positive feedback from their customers, asking for more of their products and more fragrances. Jonathan and Candy are considering increasing the scale of candle production and introducing new fragrances as a way of growing SS.

Evaluate the factors Jonathan and Candy need to consider as Serenity Scents grows. [12]

Before you answer Question 6, copy and complete Table 23.3. Try to complete two more rows to show how areas of operations link to marketing.

| Operation factor | How this links to a marketing factor |
|---|---|
| Costs: will costs increase with increased number of fragrances? | Prices: SS may need to change its prices to cover the increased costs, which could put off some customers. |
| | |
| | |

**Table 23.3:** Linking operations with marketing

Now you should answer Question 6. Try to include links between the factors relating to operations and the factors relating to marketing.

**≪ RECALL AND CONNECT 3 ≪**

What is meant by the terms 'redundancy' and 'dismissal'?

**REFLECTION**

How confident do you feel when linking your knowledge from this chapter to areas of the marketing mix? Think about what you can do to improve your confidence in this area.

**UNDERSTAND THESE TERMS**

- job production
- batch production
- flow production
- mass customisation

## SELF-ASSESSMENT CHECKLIST

Let's revisit the Knowledge focus and Exam skills focus for this chapter.
Decide how confident you are with each statement.

| Now I can | Show it | Needs more work | Almost there | Confident to move on |
|---|---|---|---|---|
| explain what is meant by operations management | Write a definition of the term 'operations management'. | | | |
| analyse the nature of the production process and how value can be added | Look at the completed answer for Figure 23.1 and explain in words what is being shown in this diagram. | | | |
| differentiate between production and productivity, efficiency and effectiveness | Write a sentence that shows the difference between each set of words. | | | |
| analyse how a business could increase the sustainability of its operations | Create a mind map to show the methods a business could use to increase the sustainability of its operations. | | | |
| evaluate labour-intensive and capital-intensive operations | Find an example of each operation method being used and explain why the business has made that production decision. | | | |
| evaluate the advantages and disadvantages of different operations methods | Create a table that shows the advantages and disadvantages of the four operations methods covered in Section 23.4. | | | |
| develop links between the operations function and the marketing function | Look through your notes from Chapters 17–20 and identify places where you can make links with the concepts in these and the operations function. | | | |
| practise the use of the STEPS technique to improve application skills | Find some news articles about four different businesses and apply the STEPS technique to these based on the information you find as well as your own knowledge. | | | |

# 24 Inventory management

## EXAM SKILLS FOCUS

In this chapter you will:

- understand how to manage your time across AS Level Paper 1 – Business Concepts 1

- be familiar with the breakdown of marks across AS Level Paper 1 – Business Concepts 1.

You can help yourself to prepare for assessment by gaining an understanding of the exams. By preparing yourself thoroughly, you can look forward to this important stage of your course with a good level of confidence. In this chapter you will look at AS Level Paper 1 – Business Concepts 1 in more detail, focusing on how to manage your time and gaining an understanding of how the marks are allocated across the paper.

# 24.1 Managing inventory

1   Businesses hold three types of inventories: raw materials and components, work in progress and finished goods. Explain what is meant by each of these types of inventories.

2   a   What are the benefits to a business of holding inventory?

    b   What could happen if a business does not manage its inventory effectively?

3   What is meant by supply chain management? How can effective supply chain management reduce the time it takes to convert raw materials into completed products?

What do you know about the AS Level Business Paper 1 exam?

4   The following questions are all about Paper 1.

    a   How long do you have to complete Paper 1?

    b   How many marks are available on Paper 1?

    c   What question types will you find in Section A of Paper 1?

    d   What question types will you find in Section B of Paper 1?

    e   What assessment objectives does Paper 1 assess?
        What percentage does each assessment hold on the paper?

    f   What percentage of the does Paper 1 make up?

5   Let's look at AS Level Paper 1 in more detail.

    Table 24.1 shows an example of how the questions on Paper 1 might look with the marks allocated. How would you divide the available exam time across each question?

|  | Question | Command word | Number of marks | Time allocated (in minutes) |
|---|---|---|---|---|
| Section A | 1(a) | Define | 2 | |
| | 1(b) | Explain | 3 | |
| | 2(a) | Define | 2 | |
| | 2(b) | Explain | 3 | |
| | 3(a) | Define | 2 | |
| | 3(b) | Explain | 3 | |
| | 4 | Analyse | 5 | |
| Section B | (a) | Analyse | 8 | |
| | (b) | Evaluate | 12 | |
| | | Remaining time for checking answers, planning, etc. | | |
| | | **Total** | | |

**Table 24.1:** Allocation of time for AS Level Paper 1 questions

## REFLECTION

Now you have a better indication of how you should allocate your time across an AS Level paper, think about the time you were spending when answering questions. Was this more or less than the time you decided to allocate in Question 5(b)? What can you do to try to manage your time in exams more effectively?

## UNDERSTAND THESE TERMS

- inventory management
- buffer inventory
- re-order level
- lead time
- supply chain

## ≪ RECALL AND CONNECT 1 ≪

Explain the role of intrapreneurship.

Based on your knowledge of how to allocate your available time in exams based on the marks being awarded, set yourself a time to complete Question 6 before you start to plan and write your answer.

6

> ### Fashion Boutique (FB)
>
> FB is a small fashion retailer located in a busy city in Country D. FB has been operating for four years and has built up a small, but loyal, customer base over this time. Once a year the owner, Sandra Garcia, takes two months off to travel to multiple fashion events around the world to learn about the latest catwalk trends. Following this, she places orders with her suppliers for clothing items she believes reflect current fashions and trends. The customers of FB like to wear the most up-to-date fashions, but they also care about them being affordable. Sandra needs to carefully plan what stock she needs to order so that she has a variety of colours and sizes available for her customers to purchase. Due to her lack of experience, she does not always get this right and currently has a stock room full of clothing from the last two years that she has been unable to sell.

Evaluate the costs to FB of holding inventory. [12]

In Question 6 you set yourself time to complete this answer. How did you use this time? Did you manage to complete the answer in the time you set yourself? Consider whether you need to reassess how many minutes you allocate to questions or what you need to do to manage your time better.

## 24.2 JIT inventory management

1   The principle of JIT is easy to understand but less easy to put into practice. For JIT to be introduced successfully, there are certain important requirements that a business must meet. Explain at least three factors that can affect the effectiveness of using JIT for inventory management.

2   What are the advantages and disadvantages to a business of using JIT for inventory management?

### UNDERSTAND THESE TERMS

- just-in-time (JIT) inventory management
- just-in-case (JIC) inventory management

### « RECALL AND CONNECT 2 «

Outline **three** methods of employee participation.

### SELF-ASSESSMENT CHECKLIST

Let's revisit the Knowledge focus and Exam skills focus for this chapter. Decide how confident you are with each statement.

| Now I can | Show it | Needs more work | Almost there | Confident to move on |
|---|---|---|---|---|
| analyse why businesses hold inventories and the costs of inventory holding | Outline three benefits and three costs to a business of holding inventory. | | | |
| analyse the advantages and disadvantages of traditional inventory management systems | Create a table to show the advantages and disadvantages of using inventory control charts and supply chain management. | | | |

CONTINUED

| | | | | |
|---|---|---|---|---|
| evaluate the JIT inventory management system and compare it with JIC inventory management | Create a revision card to show how both JIT and JIC inventory management systems work. | | | |
| understand how to manage my time across AS Level Paper 1 – Business Concepts 1 | Select three questions from the specimen papers available on the Cambridge Assessment International Education website and answer these using the time allocation you identified in Question 5 in Section 24.1. | | | |
| be familiar of the breakdown of marks across AS Paper Level 1 – Business Concepts 1 | Create an information guide for someone who is sitting AS Level Paper 1 – Business Concepts 1 next year to explain how the marks are allocated across the paper. | | | |

# 25 Capacity utilisation and outsourcing

In Chapter 24 you looked at the requirements of AS Level Paper 1 – Business Concepts 1. In this chapter you will look at AS Level Paper 2 – Business Concepts 2 in more detail, focusing on how to manage your time and gaining an understanding of how the marks are allocated across the paper. Spending time doing this will help you prepare for your exam and hopefully will help reduce some anxiety that might arise from external exams.

# 25.1 Measurement and significance of capacity utilisation

1   What are the disadvantages to a business of operating at over maximum capacity for a long period of time?

2   How can a business deal with excess capacity:

   a   In the short term?

   b   In the long term?

---

**≪ RECALL AND CONNECT 1 ≪**

What are the benefits and costs of a business plan?

---

3

> **Paterson Agriculture (PA)**
>
> PA is a large manufacturer of agricultural vehicles such as tractors and harvesting equipment. It has been operating for over 50 years. It was founded by Olaf Paterson, who is a farmer in Country D. He has built up an excellent reputation for the customer service and personal design service he offers to those who want to buy agricultural vehicles from him. His current output level is 120 vehicles per year and he has the capacity to produce 150 vehicles. Olaf has seen a steady increase in the demand for his agricultural vehicles over the last few years and has started to become concerned by his ability to increase his capacity to cope with further increases in demand in the long term.

   a   Explain the term 'capacity utilisation'. [3]

   b   Calculate the rate of capacity utilisation for PA. [3]

   c   Explain **one** impact on PA of operating under capacity. [3]

   d   Evaluate how PA could improve its capacity utilisation. [12]

---

**REFLECTION**

When you were answering Question 3, how did you decide which was the best method for PA to improve its capacity utilisation? Did you think that one factor was more important than another in your decision-making? Can you explain to another student how you made your decision? Would your decision have been different if the question had been related to a different case study?

**UNDERSTAND THESE TERMS**

- maximum (full) capacity
- capacity utilisation

---

**≪ RECALL AND CONNECT 2 ≪**

Explain what an employment contract is and outline its main features.

---

# 25.2 Outsourcing

1   What are the main reasons for a business to use outsourcing?

2   What issues might occur if a business outsources operations to another firm?

3   Let's take a look at the requirements for AS Level Paper 2 – Business Concepts 2.

  a   How long do you have to complete Paper 2?

  b   How many marks are available on Paper 2?

  c   How does the layout of Paper 2 differ from Paper 1?

  d   What question types will you find in Paper 2?

  e   What assessment objectives does Paper 2 assess?
      What percentage does each assessment hold on the paper?

  f   What percentage of the AS Level does Paper 2 make up?

4   Now let's look at Paper 2 in more detail.

Table 25.1 shows an example of how the questions on Paper 2 might look with the marks allocated. How would you divide the available exam time across each question? Do not forget to allocate some time to read the case studies and check your answers.

| | Question | Command word | Number of marks | Time allocated (in minutes) |
|---|---|---|---|---|
| Question 1 | 1(a)(i) | Identify | 1 | |
| | 1(a)(ii) | Explain | 3 | |
| | 1(b)(i) | Calculate | 3 | |
| | 1(b)(ii) | Explain | 3 | |
| | 1(c) | Analyse | 8 | |
| | 1(d) | Evaluate | 12 | |
| Question 2 | 2(a)(i) | Identify | 1 | |
| | 2(a)(ii) | Explain | 3 | |
| | 2(b)(i) | Calculate | 3 | |
| | 2(b)(ii) | Explain | 3 | |
| | 2(c) | Analyse | 8 | |
| | 2(d) | Evaluate | 12 | |
| | | Remaining time for checking answers, planning, reading the case studies, etc. | | |
| | | **Total** | | |

**Table 25.1:** Allocation of time for AS Level Paper 2 questions

## ≪ RECALL AND CONNECT 3 ≪

What is meant by the term 'marketing mix'?

## SELF-ASSESSMENT CHECKLIST

Let's revisit the Knowledge focus and Exam skills focus for this chapter.
Decide how confident you are with each statement.

| Now I can | Show it | Needs more work | Almost there | Confident to move on |
|---|---|---|---|---|
| evaluate the benefits and limitations of high capacity utilisation | Create a poster to highlight the benefits and limitations of high capacity utilisation to a business. | | | |
| analyse the impact of low capacity utilisation | State three impacts to a business of having low capacity utilization. | | | |
| evaluate the different approaches to excess capacity or capacity shortage | Outline two approaches to deal with excess capacity and two approaches to deal with capacity shortage. | | | |
| assess the reasons for the rapid growth of outsourcing | Conduct research and find an article that discusses the reasons behind the growth in outsourcing. | | | |
| evaluate the benefits and limitations of outsourcing | State two benefits and two limitations of outsourcing for a business. | | | |
| understand how to manage my time across AS Level Paper 2 – Business Concepts 2 | Select three questions from the specimen paper available on the Cambridge Assessment International Education website and answer these using the time allocation you identified in Question 4 in Section 25.2. | | | |
| be familiar of the breakdown of marks across AS paper 2 – Business Concepts 2 | Create an information guide for someone who is sitting AS Level Paper 2 – Business Concepts 2 to explain how the marks are allocated across the paper. | | | |

# Exam practice 7

This section contains both past paper questions from previous Cambridge exams and practice questions. These questions draw together your knowledge on a range of topics that you have covered up to this point and will help you prepare for your assessment.

Questions 1 and 2 have example student responses and commentaries provided. For each question, work through the question first, then compare your answer to the example student response and commentary.

**1  a**  Define the term 'laissez-faire leadership'.                                              [2]

*Cambridge International AS & A Level Business (9609) Paper 11 Q1a, June 2021*

| Example student response | Examiner comments |
|---|---|
| The manager provides minimal supervision to the workers, allowing them to work autonomously and make decisions themselves. | This is an excellent definition of the term that provides two rewardable points about laissez-faire leadership (supervision/autonomy and decision-making). Awarded **two** marks. |

**b**  Explain **one** disadvantage to employees of autocratic leadership.                         [3]

| Example student response | Examiner comments |
|---|---|
| One disadvantage of autocratic leadership is that it might be demotivating. | A basic understanding of a disadvantage of autocratic leadership to an employee is provided, but this has not been explained. Awarded **one** mark. To improve this answer there needs to be some application to a business context to show how autocratic leadership is demotivating. |

**2  a**  Define the term 'market segmentation'.                                                   [2]

*Cambridge International AS & A Level Business (9609) Paper 11 Q2a, June 2021*

| Example student response | Examiner comments |
|---|---|
| Market segmentation is the identification of different groups of customers with common needs within a market and the marketing of different products or services to those customer groups. | This is an excellent definition of the term, showing a superb level of knowledge and understanding, and is awarded **two** marks (different groups and customers with common needs). |

**b** Explain **one** benefit to a business of market segmentation. [3]

| Example student response | Examiner comments |
|---|---|
| One benefit to a business of market segmentation is that if a business can define its market, then it will sell more. | This answer is awarded **zero** marks. The ability to define your market is not a benefit of segmentation (it is a feature of segmentation). There is also no application to a business context in the answer. |

For Question 3(a) and (b) read the question, the example student responses and the commentaries provided. Then, in part (c), write an improved answer to the question, using the guidance in the commentary to help you.

**3 a** Define the term 'inventory reorder level'. [2]

*Cambridge International AS & A Level Business (9609) Paper 11 Q4a, June 2021*

| Example student response | Examiner comments |
|---|---|
| This is when a business reorders inventory. | This answer does little more than just rewrite the question. No knowledge of the term is shown. Awarded **zero** marks. |

**b** Explain **one** advantage to a business of holding buffer inventory. [3]

| Example student response | Examiner comments |
|---|---|
| It means the business is able to continue making products while it is waiting for new stock to arrive, which will allow it to continue to have goods to sell. | This answer provides a clear advantage of holding buffer inventory. For the remaining marks, there needs to be application so a relevant business example needs to be provided: for example, a restaurant may keep some buffer stock in the form of frozen vegetables in case they are unable to get a delivery from their supplier. Awarded **one** mark. |

**c** Think of another advantage to a business of holding buffer inventory and write your own answer to Question 3(b).

The following question has an example student response and commentary provided. Work through the question first, then compare your answer to the example student responses and commentaries.

4  a  Analyse **two** roles of small businesses in a country's economy.          [8]

| Example student response | Examiner comments |
|---|---|
| Small businesses can provide jobs for people. This is good for the economy because if people have jobs, then they can spend their income in other businesses, creating a multiplier effect. This then means there will be less unemployment and increased spending within the economy, which will make the country's economy look good. | The student shows good knowledge throughout of the role of small businesses to a country's economy. There is some explanation of the role small businesses can have in a country's economy. |
| Another role of a small business in a country's economy is that it provides goods and services that can be used by other businesses. This means that the business will be able to make more revenue, which will mean more profits that can be invested into growing the business to make it a big business. | The first paragraph could be talking about any size of business, so an example might have helped here. The second point is slightly more developed and linked specifically to 'small' businesses through the use of the word 'niche', showing some application to a business context. |
| | There are good links in both points to the impacts that will be felt by the country's economy by both the stated roles. The impacts are a little superficial and undeveloped in the first paragraph, e.g. what is meant by making a country's economy look good? |
| | *7/8 marks* |

b  Evaluate the importance to an expanding business of effectively communicating its objectives to its workforce.          [12]

| Example student response | Examiner comments |
|---|---|
| It is important that objectives are communicated effectively to the workforce so that it knows what is going on. During times of expansion, workers may feel worried or scared about what is happening and how it might affect them and their job, so it is important that there is clear communication between the workers and the managers so that workers' fears are discussed and resolved. | The answer shows good knowledge of objectives, as well as business expansion. |
| | Throughout the answer the student is clearly talking about an expanding business, and not just any business effectively communicating its objectives. This provides excellent application to a specific and focused business context. |

| Example student response | Examiner comments |
|---|---|
| This should mean that the workers' motivation levels will not fall as they understand the business's objectives through this period of growth and how they will affect them. However, this communication may not be very important if the business is a large global business. For example, if the business is growing through opening more stores in America, then the current workers in France may not be affected by this in any way at all so there is no reason to communicate the growth objectives to them.<br><br>Another benefit of communicating objectives with the workforce is that the employees may be involved in the growth and will need to know what their role is within this. For example, if the firm is growing through increased levels of production due to increased demand, it may find that the workplace itself is having to expand to deal with this new level of capacity. As a result, workers would need to know about this so that they are prepared for changes in their working environment. Workers who do not know about changes that happening are less likely to help a business when working towards that goal, which means that the business is less likely to be successful.<br><br>Overall, when a business is expanding it is important that it effectively communicates its objectives with its workforce. This is so that everybody involved in the workplace knows what is happening and what is expected of them, which means that the objectives are more likely to be met and be more successful. However, the level of importance of this communication does depend on how directly impacted the workforce is. The more impacted the workforce is by the potential growth, the more important it actually is to make sure that it is fully aware of the business decisions if it is going to be affected directly by these. | The answer clearly discusses how and why effective communication of objectives is important during periods of growth. There are clear chains of analysis, showing links between the points and the effects of what will happen if objectives are not clearly communicated with the workforce.<br><br>Attempts to evaluate throughout this answer are missed in places. For example, at the end of the first paragraph, the student could have actually included a judgement here as to whether the communication of the objectives is essential or not. The final paragraph provides a good level of evaluation explaining why they believe communication is effective and the impacts on the level of importance. However, the main issue affecting the quality of evaluation in this answer is the lack of application to a business context (an expanding business specifically).<br><br>*10/12 marks* |

Now that you have read the example student response to the previous question, here is a similar practice question which you should attempt. Use the guidance in the commentary to help you as you answer the question.

5   a   Analyse **two** likely benefits to a car manufacturing company of using capital-intensive processes. [8]

   b   Evaluate whether batch production is the best method of production for a small jewellery manufacturing business. [12]

Question 6 has example student responses and commentaries provided. For each part of the question, work through the question first, then compare your answer to the example student response and commentary.

**6**

> ### Ray's Taxis (RT)
>
> Ray is a sole trader providing a taxi service in City L. Recently, demand for Ray's Taxis has fallen due to an increase in the number of competitors. Ray is thinking of joining Summus, which offers a smartphone app (application) which connects passengers to taxi drivers. Ray would be the first taxi driver in City L to join Summus. The app uses dynamic pricing to set the fare (amount paid) for a journey. Summus takes 20% of the fare and the remaining 80% is revenue for the taxi driver. Summus has provided forecast data in Table 1.
>
> | Average fare | $15 |
> |---|---|
> | Average number of journeys per day | 16 |
> | Average distance travelled per journey | 5 km |
>
> **Table 1:** Forecast data about each taxi using the Summus app
>
> Ray has calculated costs, shown in Table 2.
>
> | Fixed cost per day | $42.00 |
> |---|---|
> | Variable cost per km | $0.50 |
>
> **Table 2:** Ray's costs
>
> Passengers like the Summus app as it is easy to use, quick and reliable. Taxi drivers like it as they can decide when and where to work and they can earn more revenue. However, a recent article on a taxi drivers' forum suggested there are problems with Summus.
>
> - It signs up too many taxi drivers.
>
> - Taxi drivers are not employed by Summus and are not guaranteed any revenue.
>
> - Customers have to wait longer for a taxi when fares are low.

a    i    Define the term 'competitors'.                                              [2]

*Cambridge International AS & A Level Business (9609) Paper 21 Q1a i, June 2021*

| Example student response | Examiner comments |
|---|---|
| Competitors are businesses that sell similar goods or services in the same market. | An excellent definition to explain what is meant by the term competitors, which covers two separate elements (similar product and similar market). Awarded **two** marks. |

ii   Explain the term 'dynamic pricing'.                                    [3]

**Cambridge International AS & A Level Business (9609) Paper 21**
**Q1a ii, June 2021**

| Example student response | Examiner comments |
|---|---|
| These are prices that are constantly changing. | The answer suggests that dynamic pricing is where prices are constantly changing. However, this is not clear enough as any pricing method can constantly change and therefore this does not differentiate dynamic pricing from other pricing methods enough. There needs to be more specific knowledge about dynamic pricing shown, and an example given, such as a market where dynamic pricing is a key feature. Awarded **zero** marks. |

b   i   Explain **one** way Ray could increase his profit margin.              [3]

**Cambridge International AS & A Level Business (9609) Paper 21**
**Q1b i, June 2021**

| Example student response | Examiner comments |
|---|---|
| One way that Ray could increase his profit margin is to increase the number of taxi journeys from 16 per day, therefore increasing his revenue. | This answer confuses the terms 'profit' and 'profit margin'. There is some understanding that increasing volume may increase profit margin, although the reason for this is somewhat implied (by undertaking more taxi journeys, the fixed costs are spread over more units, so the profit margin per journey will increase). This needs to be clearly explained in the answer, as marks can only be awarded for what is provided. There is some application to the case study, meaning some limited application has been shown. Awarded **two** marks. |

ii  Refer to Table 1. Calculate Ray's forecast average daily revenue
    if he joins Summus. [3]

*Adapted from Cambridge International AS & A Level Business
(9609) Paper 21 Q1b ii, June 2021*

| Example student response | Examiner comments |
|---|---|
| Revenue = price × quantity<br><br>$15 × 16 journeys = $240 | This answer has calculated the total revenue received from the journeys undertaken by Ray in day. However, we are told in the case study that Ray only gets to keep 80% of this, and this stage has not been calculated. Awarded **two** marks. |

c  Analyse **two** pricing methods, other than dynamic pricing,
   Summus could use to price taxi fares. [8]

*Cambridge International AS & A Level Business (9609) Paper 21 Q1c,
June 2021*

| Example student response | Examiner comments |
|---|---|
| One pricing method that Summus could use for its taxi fares is penetration pricing. We are told that there are lots of competitors within the market, so if Summus prices its taxi fares below the price charged by existing companies, it would allow it to attract customers from the other companies. This would allow it to increase its customer base as it is setting up, and hopefully these customers will remain with Summus into the long term.<br><br>Another pricing method that Summus could use is dynamic pricing. Taxis can be busy at different times of the day, so by using dynamic pricing on the new app it would mean that drivers could capitalise on the changing level of demand for their taxis, allowing them to maximise their revenues for their journeys. | The first paragraph contains good knowledge of penetration pricing. However, the second paragraph, although showing good knowledge of how dynamic pricing is used, cannot be rewarded. This is because the question clearly states the methods suggested must be 'other than dynamic pricing'.<br><br>There is good application to the case study throughout the answer, referencing taxis, for example. However, application can only be rewarded where it is used to correctly answer the question, which in this instance is only in paragraph one.<br><br>The first paragraph has a good chain of developed analysis showing what would happen if penetration pricing is used (attract customers from competitors, increasing the customer base). It is a shame that the second paragraph is based on an incorrect method of pricing strategy as this also contains a good chain of analysis, but this cannot be rewarded.<br><br>*5/8 marks* |

**d** Evaluate whether Ray should join Summus. [12]

*Adapted from Cambridge International AS & A Level Business (9609) Paper 21 Q1d, June 2021*

| Example student response | Examiner comments |
|---|---|
| One reason why Ray should join Summus is that it is the first company to offer a smartphone app that will connect passengers to taxi drivers. Ray has seen his demand fall for his own taxi service, alongside an increase in competition. In order to be able to survive in the market he needs to set himself apart from these competitors and the use of an app is a really good idea for this. People like using apps these days to run their lives and the case study says that passengers like the Summus app as it's quick and easy to use. This means that if a customer wants a taxi, instead of phoning for a taxi they may use the Summus app and then Ray can take the customers that come through the app. This would give him a way of earning revenue, which he seems to be struggling to do at the moment. However, we are told that Summus signs up too many taxi drivers, so if Ray is not quick when a taxi alert comes through, then he may not get to the app in time, which means one of his competitors will and so Ray will not get any revenue. Based on this, I think that Ray should not join Summus. | There is very clear knowledge and understanding shown throughout this answer. Relevant points are raised discussing factors that need to be considered when making a decision. |
| | The answer is very clearly discussing Ray and this particular case study. There is good reference to the evidence provided, which is used well within the answer. Words such as 'taxi' and 'fares' and case study quotes are evident throughout the answer. |
| Another reason why Ray should join Summus is that they use dynamic pricing to set the fare for a journey. This might mean that if Ray was to work during the busy periods, which is when fares are likely to be at their highest prices, then he might actually earn more revenue then he would in his own business (if that did not also use dynamic pricing). However, if Summus charges prices that are too high during these peak times, customers have the choice to go to one of the many other competitor taxi companies in the area if they are cheaper, meaning that Ray would lose out on this revenue. | The answer contains strong chains of analysis that explore the arguments both for and against Ray joining Summus and the impact of these on Ray. There are good arguments shown for each point that highlight benefits and drawbacks that are linked to each other. |
| A reason for Ray not to join Summus is that Ray would only get to keep 80% of the revenue he earns and Summus would keep the other 20%. This means that Ray would be taking home less of his own revenue than he would if he was a sole trader, where he would keep all of his revenues, meaning he would be financially worse off. However, his ability to bring in revenues from taxi fares is massively increased through this smartphone app so Ray may actually end up bringing in more revenue in total. | There is a small judgement at the end of the first paragraph where the student comes to a valid conclusion on whether Ray should join Summus that clearly answers the question. However, this is not developed beyond a basic assertion. There is further attempt at a judgement at the end of the answer. This has not been justified; however, the student has given a suggestion of an alternative that Ray could consider in this instance although this has not been justified. Both attempts at evaluation are in fact judgements with no evaluative comment. |
| I do not think that Ray should join Summus. There are lots of disadvantages and not many advantages. I think Ray should just lower his prices and try and be better than the competitors in the taxi market by himself. | *7/12 marks* |

Now that you have read the example student responses to the previous question, here is a similar question which you should attempt. Use the guidance in the commentary to help you as you answer the question.

7

### Market Solution (MS)

Market Solution is a public limited company in the tertiary sector. MS advises businesses on elements of the marketing mix. Most of its customers are small businesses who cannot afford their own marketing departments. MS designs marketing materials for these businesses to use. Although MS uses computer-aided design (CAD), the business is labour-intensive. MS employs specialist marketing workers as well as administrative support workers. Table 1 shows some data about employees of MS.

| | Specialist marketing workers | Administrative support workers |
|---|---|---|
| Average number of workers in 2019 | 40 | 88 |
| Payment method | Salary plus bonus | Performance-related pay plus bonus |
| Number of workers who left in 2019 | 2 | 11 |
| Average pay (compared to national average) | High | Low |
| Main need of the workers | Achievement | Affiliation |
| Main hygiene factors | • Pay<br>• Flexible hours of work | • Staff restaurant<br>• Holidays |
| Is a bonus expected in 2020? | Yes | No |

**Table 1:** MS employee data

**CONTINUED**

MS has recently employed Hetti as the new human resources manager. Hetti thinks that the ideas of the motivational theorists are important when managing employees. She is particularly worried about the labour turnover of the administrative support workers. MS has recently taken on a new customer, named Books Outlet (BO). BO has an objective to increase its revenue by targeting a younger market segment. BO has provided MS with the following information about its current marketing mix (see Table 2).

| Product | Price |
|---|---|
| • Books aimed at customers who are 30 years and older <br><br> • Specialist books on many topics – BO is often the only seller in the area | • Price skimming |
| **Promotion** | **Place** |
| • Window display <br> • Local newspaper advertising | • A retail shop on the main street <br> • Postal sales from a brochure |

**Table 2:** Current marketing mix for BO

a   i   Define the term 'tertiary sector'.                                                    [2]

    ii  Explain the term 'performance-related pay'.                                   [3]

b   i   Refer to Table 2. Calculate the **difference** between the labour turnover of the specialist marketing workers and the labour turnover of the administrative support workers.                         [4]

    ii  Analyse how Hetti could use the ideas of **two** motivational theorists to reduce the labour turnover of the administrative support workers.                                                          [8]

*Adapted from Cambridge International AS & A Level Business (9609) Paper 22 Q2a, b, June 2020*

c   Explain **one** possible advantage to MS of being labour-intensive.                                                                          [3]

d   BO has an objective to increase its revenue by targeting a younger market segment. Evaluate how BO should change its marketing mix to achieve this objective.                             [12]

# 26 Location and scale

## KNOWLEDGE FOCUS

You will answer questions on:

**26.1** Location decisions

**26.2** Scale of operations

## EXAM SKILLS FOCUS

In this chapter you will:

*   manage your test anxiety by considering what time of day is most effective for you to study

*   further practise marking a student response, focusing on how marks are awarded for different assessment objectives.

A good way of managing your test anxiety is learning when you study most effectively and preparing your revision schedule around this. Students often describe themselves as 'morning people' or 'night people'. Some students prefer to study in the morning, when they feel they can concentrate better. Alternatively, some students prefer to study later in the day, believing there are fewer distractions at that time.

Understanding how assessment objectives are demonstrated in exam answers will help you develop your own answers. It can help to see sample student answers to exam questions. The Exam practice sections include sample student responses to past paper questions. When reading through the responses, make a note of which areas the response has scored well in and where the student could improve their answer. Effective answers will demonstrate knowledge and understanding of the syllabus (AO1), clear links to the text provided (AO2), a study of the material to demonstrate an understanding of the information presented (AO3) and the subjective arrival at a conclusion (AO4).

# 26.1 Location decisions

**1**   Identify **three** factors that determine location.

Question 2 provides an opportunity to mark a sample student response. Copy the response, then mark it by writing either K (knowledge), AP (application), AN (analysis) or EV (evaluation) beside each of the sentences. When you have done this, compare it with the annotation for this question in the Answers section.

**UNDERSTAND TERMS**

- quantitative factors
- qualitative factors
- offshoring
- reshoring

**2**

### American Ice Cream (AIC)

Like other businesses in the industry, AIC finds that its sales are very seasonal. With this in mind, Michael, the new director of marketing, believes that the business would benefit from developing the brand internationally and establishing itself as a global brand. Michael believes that this would provide more even sales figures, with temperatures in Central America remaining warm during the USA winter period. The business is weighing up two options as a base for its Latin American operations.

| | Option 1 | Option 2 |
|---|---|---|
| Fixed yearly costs | $16 000 000 | $18 000 000 |
| Expected monthly sales, units | 2 000 000 | 2 100 000 |
| Expected selling price | $2.50 | $2.65 |
| Expected variable costs | $1.75 | $1.85 |

**Table 26.1:** Sales and revenue

Analyse **two** factors that might determine the choice of location for AIC.        [8]

One factor for AIC to consider is the cost of running its factory. If they were to select Option 2, this has an increased yearly fixed cost of $2 000 000. Due to the increased cost of running a factory in Option 2, AIC would possibly make lower profits than Option 1 as their fixed costs are higher. This could affect any further growth plans they have as they may take longer to be able to afford them.

Another factor for AIC to consider is the potential revenue they can make at the location. Option 1 has a potential monthly revenue of $5 000 000 (price x sales) and Option 2 has a potential monthly revenue of $5 565 000 which means that AIC would potentially make more revenue if they decided to locate at Option 2, which would lead to the business potentially being able to make more profits, if costs are not too high.

**REFLECTION**

Do you understand the difference between AO1 Knowledge and understanding, AO2 Application and AO3 Analysis?

« RECALL AND CONNECT 1 «

Explain how the culture of a business might change when it opens up in a new location.

## 26.2 Scale of operations

1   Copy and complete Figure 26.1, showing some of the factors influencing the scale of operations for AIC.

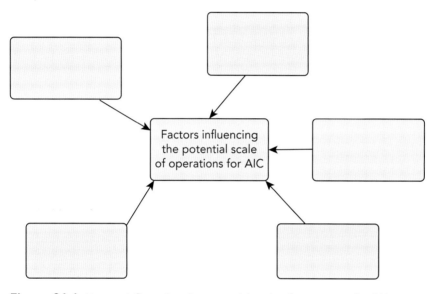

**Figure 26.1:** Factors influencing the potential scale of operations for AIC

**UNDERSTAND THESE TERMS**

- scale of operations
- internal economies of scale
- internal diseconomies of scale
- external economies of scale
- external diseconomies of scale

2   For each of the following methods of internal economies of scale, you should explain the term, give an example of how it could be achieved by a business and explain the effect the method can have on the average costs for a business:

a   purchasing economies

b   financial economies

c   technical economies

d   marketing economies

e   managerial economies.

REFLECTION

Have you managed to learn your most effective study times and plan your revision accordingly? Remember that there is much more to effective study planning than simply devising an effective revision schedule. Effective study also includes knowing when to study, so are you a 'morning person' or a 'night person'?

## ≪ RECALL AND CONNECT 2 ≪

a   How might the role of the human resources department be crucial to avoiding diseconomies of scale as a business grows?

b   How might the management/leadership of a business be crucial in minimising or limiting the internal diseconomies of scale of a business as it expands?

## SELF-ASSESSMENT CHECKLIST

Let's revisit the Knowledge focus and Exam skills focus for this chapter.
Decide how confident you are with each statement.

| Now I can | Show it | Needs more work | Almost there | Confident to move on |
|---|---|---|---|---|
| assess the importance of location decisions to the success of a business | Using Table 26.1 in the coursebook, make a list of some of the problems that a business might experience if it chooses the wrong location. | | | |
| evaluate the factors that influence location and relocation decisions | Investigate businesses in different industries in the secondary, service, retail and quaternary sectors. Consider some factors that might influence their choice of location. | | | |
| analyse why businesses may want to increase their scale of production | Make a list of your school's fixed and variable costs. Label whether each cost will (a) rise directly as output rises (unit cost remains unchanged), (b) rise as output rises but by a lower percentage (unit cost falls), or (c) will not rise as output rises (unit cost falls significantly). | | | |
| analyse the importance of economies and diseconomies of scale and the impact on unit costs | Choose two businesses within the same industry (but with different scales of operation), e.g., a large supermarket brand and a small food store. Make a list of advantages (economies of scale) and disadvantages (diseconomies of scale) of both. | | | |

**CONTINUED**

| | | | | |
|---|---|---|---|---|
| manage my test anxiety by considering what time of day is most effective for me to study | Consider what time of day you study best and then prepare a revision/study timetable that takes this into account to make effective use of your time. | | | |
| further practise marking a student response, focussing on how marks are awarded for different assessment objectives | Pay particular attention to the longer student sample responses in the Exam practice sections and make a note of the characteristics of each response. Make a note of the difference between responses with the command word 'evaluate' and those where the command word is 'analyse'. How do sample answers score marks in both AO3 and AO4? | | | |

# 27 Quality management

## KNOWLEDGE FOCUS

You will answer questions on:

**27.1** Quality control and quality assurance

**27.2** Benchmarking

## EXAM SKILLS FOCUS

In this chapter you will:

- learn to distinguish between different question types, with a focus on answering eight-mark questions

- practise writing answers to essay-style questions, focusing on using examples from the data provided.

Typically, eight-mark questions will require you to make two points. These could be two impacts or an advantage and a disadvantage, for example. An eight-mark question will require you to show the skills of AO1 Knowledge, AO2 Application and AO3 Analysis.

Looking at past paper questions is an excellent way of revising. When planning your answers identify the knowledge that may be required for AO1 Knowledge and understanding. When you read the case study, use a highlighter or pencil to underline relevant points that you may be able to use in your answer for AO2 Application. Finally, consider how you can develop each of the points in order to score marks for AO3 Analysis.

# 27.1 Quality control and quality assurance

| UNDERSTAND THESE TERMS |
|---|
| • quality product |
| • quality standards |
| • quality control |
| • quality assurance |
| • total quality management (TQM) |

1   a   What is meant by the term 'quality control'?

     b   What are the impacts of quality control on a business?

     c   What is meant by the term 'quality assurance'?

     d   What are the impacts of quality assurance on a business?

2   Explain how customers and producers may have different views of what is meant by the term 'quality'.

3   Copy and complete the diagram in Figure 27.1 in order to illustrate the three stages of quality control.

**Figure 27.1:** The three stages of quality control

Question 4 provides an opportunity to test yourself on the command word 'analyse'. You will need to show your AO1 Knowledge and understanding and AO2 Application skills, applying this knowledge to the example provided. For this reason, 'analyse' questions will generally be related to the text/data response provided. Finally, you will also need to apply AO3 Analysis. Note that you are not required to provide balance with this command word, distinguishing it from the command word 'evaluate'.

**4**

**Not Just Water (NJW)**

NJW produces a range of soft drinks which it sells in retail outlets across the USA. The organisation recently recruited a marketing manager, whose first task was to complete a survey of customers regarding their level of satisfaction for each of its drinks. She wants to use the results as the basis for improvement in both future products and for potential improvements to existing products. The results of the survey are included in Table 27.1.

| Product | Price | Customer satisfaction index (0–100) |
|---|---|---|
| $H_2O$ | $4.00 | 62 |
| Kola and Lime | $5.00 | 56 |
| King Raspberry | $7.50 | 98 |
| Luscious Lime | $6.75 | 84 |
| Double Strawberry | $5.75 | 90 |

**Table 27.1:** Survey results

Analyse **two** reasons why quality is important to NJW. [8]

**REFLECTION**

Are you able to define the word 'quality' and apply it to a service business? Do you understand the requirements of the command word, examining the importance of product quality methodically and in detail to explain and interpret it? How confident are you in tackling 'analyse' questions? How would your response have been different if the command word had been 'evaluate' rather than 'analyse'?

**≪ RECALL AND CONNECT 1 ≪**

Identify the role of employee motivation on product quality.

## 27.2 Benchmarking

1   Analyse advantages and disadvantages of benchmarking to NJW.                    [8]

UNDERSTAND THIS TERM

• benchmarking

### REFLECTION

Have you included a definition of benchmarking in your list of question cards for revision purposes? How confident are you in applying your knowledge of benchmarking to specific businesses? Practise applying your knowledge of benchmarking to a business that you know well. Think about how you could practise this skill during your revision.

### ≪ RECALL AND CONNECT 2 ≪

Explain the role of benchmarking in operational strategy.

### SELF-ASSESSMENT CHECKLIST

Let's revisit the Knowledge focus and Exam skills focus for this chapter.
Decide how confident you are with each statement.

| Now I can | Show it | Needs more work | Almost there | Confident to move on |
|---|---|---|---|---|
| analyse the concept of quality and the importance of quality | Post an online review for a product or service you have recently bought, explaining how you felt about its quality. Rate the quality in terms of 'fit for purpose' effectiveness, value for money and then perceived versus actual quality. | | | |
| analyse the difference between quality control and quality assurance | Understand the difference between the two terms, identify the role that quality control plays in the quality assurance process and write out a paragraph explaining this role. | | | |
| explain the importance of businesses establishing quality assurance systems | Identify and then write out some of the problems that a business would face if it failed to establish effective quality assurance systems. | | | |

| CONTINUED | | | | |
|---|---|---|---|---|
| evaluate the effectiveness of total quality management | Make revision cards for each of the aspects of total quality management. On the reverse side of the card, explain how each aspect makes a contribution to improved product quality. Now write a paragraph explaining what would happen to product quality without total quality management within the organisation. | | | |
| evaluate the importance of benchmarking in quality management | Write out a list of your own strengths and weaknesses as a student. For each weakness write a target that you can use as a benchmark for improvement. Consider how important benchmarking is to help working on each weaknesses. | | | |
| learn to distinguish between different question types, with a focus on answering eight-mark questions | Practise answering eight-mark questions in this chapter and the Exam practice sections. | | | |
| practise writing answers to essay-style questions, focusing on using examples from the data provided | Practise answering some past paper questions and make sure you use examples from the data provided. | | | |

# 28 Operations strategy

## EXAM SKILLS FOCUS

In this chapter you will:

- understand the different requirements of the command words 'analyse' and 'evaluate'.

A crucial part of doing well in your exam is understanding what is required by different command words. The command words 'analyse' and 'evaluate' are often used in longer-answer questions but have different requirements.

# 28.1 Operations decisions

**1** Explain how the human, marketing and finance resource availability of a business can affect the following operational decisions:

**a** to expand capacity

**b** to relocate operations.

**2** Describe some of the applications for AI in business operations.

## ≪ RECALL AND CONNECT 1 ≪

A business produces a single product and has variable costs of $20 per unit. The total fixed costs of the business are $400 000 per year. The business sells their products for $17 per unit. What is the contribution per unit?

# 28.2 Flexibility and innovation

**1** Explain the ways that operational flexibility can improve business efficiency.

The following Exam skills questions involve the command words 'analyse' and 'evaluate'. Both command words require different skills, and it is important that you understand the difference between both and what each command word requires. You should write down an explanation of what these terms mean before moving on to Questions 2 and 3.

**UNDERSTAND THESE TERMS**

- operational flexibility
- process innovation

**2**

> **Belgium Chocolates (BC)**
>
> BC is a well-established business operating in the Netherlands, Belgium and Luxembourg, and enjoying sales growth of 5% per year. Despite the business doing well, one of the business partners believes that any business must open new stores and has suggested accompanying the expansion plans with a significant rise in marketing spending to launch the expansion.
>
> In addition to BC's expansion plans, the firm is also reviewing its manufacturing processes, with Mark keen to maintain its current production facility, while Chris believes that the business should outsource production to a specialist manufacturer. Chris would like BC to design the product, and then leave production to the specialist manufacturer.

Analyse **two** possible advantages of process innovation to BC.          [8]

**3** Evaluate the importance of process innovation for a chocolate manufacturer in a competitive market. [12]

**« RECALL AND CONNECT 2 «**

What are the **four** competencies of emotional intelligence suggested by Goleman?

## 28.3 Enterprise resource planning

**UNDERSTAND THIS TERM**

- enterprise resource planning (ERP)

**1** Explain, using examples, how ERP can be used within a business.

**2** Evaluate whether BC should use an ERP programme. [12]

**« RECALL AND CONNECT 3 «**

Explain the disadvantages of government subsidies to support existing businesses in an economy.

## 28.4 Lean production

**1** Draw a diagram showing the impact of Kaizen on product quality.

**2** Analyse the likely impact on BC of adopting lean production techniques. [8]

**« RECALL AND CONNECT 4 «**

What role can Kaizen, simultaneous engineering and cell production play in improving product quality?

**UNDERSTAND THESE TERMS**

- kaizen
- cell production

# 28.5 Operations planning

Baking a cake involves the processes shown in Table 28.1.

| Step | Process | Duration | Proceeded by |
|---|---|---|---|
| A | Prepare the icing. | 12 minutes | - |
| B | Prepare the ingredients for the sponge. | 10 minutes | - |
| C | Prepare the filling ingredients for the fruit centre. | 8 minutes | - |
| D | Stir and then mix the filling fruit for the centre. | 26 minutes | C |
| E | Stir the icing so that it remains the correct consistency. | 9 minutes | A |
| F | Mix the butter and sugar. | 14 minutes | B |
| G | Take two eggs and combine with all the ingredients. Mix together to create the cake mixture. | 10 minutes | D, E, F |
| H | Add the cake mixture into the pan and bake. | 10 minutes | G |

**Table 28.1:** How to bake a cake

1   Using the information from Table 28.1, draw a critical path analysis on the process of baking a cake.

2   a   Identify the critical path for baking a cake.   [1]

   b   Identify the minimum time to bake a cake.   [1]

3   Evaluate the usefulness of critical path analysis to BC when making operational decisions.   [12]

## UNDERSTAND THESE TERMS

- critical path analysis (CPA)
- critical path
- earliest start time
- latest finish time
- total float
- free float
- dummy activities

## REFLECTION

How confident are you in answering 'evaluate' questions? Have you included a conclusion to finish off your response? It's important to include a conclusion in an answer to an 'evaluate' question. Have you used the WAGOLL approach to your revision? WAGOLL stands for 'What a good one looks like'.

## SELF-ASSESSMENT CHECKLIST

Let's revisit the Knowledge focus and Exam skills focus for this chapter.
Decide how confident you are with each statement.

| Now I can | Show it | Needs more work | Almost there | Confident to move on |
|---|---|---|---|---|
| understand the factors influencing operations decisions, including IT and AI | Write out some of the things that can go wrong for a company when making operations decisions without the use of IT and AI. | | | |
| analyse the need for flexibility and process innovation | In situations where demand for a good or service is different than expected, explain why businesses need operational flexibility. | | | |
| evaluate the impact of ERP | Make a list of some of the benefits and weaknesses of ERP. This should focus on the impact of ERP on productivity, reporting structures, efficiency and collaboration. | | | |
| evaluate the techniques of lean production | Investigate how lean production is used in the following: cable manufacture, printing, customer service and truck manufacturing. | | | |
| evaluate the key elements of operations planning | Make a list of some of the key elements of operations planning and then turn this list into revision cards for future learning. | | | |
| evaluate the usefulness of CPA and network diagrams in project management | List the steps involved in revising for your exams. Include timings and the order in which steps should be completed. Turn this revision list into a network diagram, including the critical path. Review your network diagram and explain its usefulness to the revision process. | | | |

## CONTINUED

| | | | | |
|---|---|---|---|---|
| understand the different requirements of the command words 'analyse' and 'evaluate' | Practise writing an explanation for each the command words 'analyse' and 'evaluate' on question and revision cards. | | | |

# Exam practice 8

This section contains both past paper questions from previous Cambridge exams and practice questions. These questions draw together your knowledge on a range of topics that you have covered up to this point and will help you prepare for your assessment.

For Question 1(a) read the question, example student response and commentary provided. Then, in Question 1(b), write an improved answer to the question, focusing on a large (online) computer manufacturer that sells directly to the consumer via its own delivery vehicles. Use the guidance in the commentary to help you as you answer the question.

**1    a**    Analyse factors that might determine the relocation of a business.          [8]

*Cambridge International AS & A Level Business (9609) Paper 12 Q7a, March 2022*

| Example student response | Examiner comments |
|---|---|
| Relocation is best described as when a business moves from one location to another. When a business makes the decision to relocate there are a range of factors that it may choose to consider. | Knowledge of factors of location is included in the answer, showing clear understanding of the issues. However, the student has included many more factors than are needed to gain the knowledge marks: there are never more than two marks for knowledge available on any question. This means that only two pieces of knowledge are needed, and will be rewarded. |
| One of the factors is geographic, for example, the climatic or physical conditions and a consideration of CSR/environmental effects. This is especially relevant for businesses operating outside or where there is a need for expansion. | |
| A second factor might be demographic, for example, a firm may relocate according to changing population structure, in which case the business may find that its target market no longer exists in the original location or consumer attitudes to the business may change. An example might be a café aimed at a younger target market and forced to move because of a rise in the age profile of the local population. | The answer contains limited application to a business context. This does not appear until the third paragraph with the discussion of a café. The rest of the answer is theoretical. More examples and application of the theory to business situations needs to be provided. |
| Legal factors might also cause a firm to move operations to a different country, such as changes in import and export laws or more restrictive planning laws. Political factors are another consideration forcing some businesses to relocate, for example, a change in attitudes of the prevailing government to a particular business. | The answer is, at best, a list of factors that might determine the relocation of a business. There is very limited application of these factors, nor any discussion of the relationship between the factor and how it could cause relocation. At the end of the third paragraph, there is at attempt to include some analysis between the factor and the impact it has on relocation. |
| Being closer to its raw materials inputs or labour might also encourage a business to relocate if there is a change in the available resources in its existing location. Finally, access to better infrastructure or improved communication links might also be a driving factor. | |
| | *3/8 marks* |

**b** Now write your own answer to Question 1(a), focusing on a large (online) computer manufacturer that sells directly to the consumer via its own delivery vehicles.

The following questions have example student responses and commentaries provided. For each question, work through the question first, then compare your answer to the example student response and commentary.

**2** Analyse **one** factor that could influence the scale of operations of a business. [5]

*Adapted from Cambridge International AS & A Level Business (9609) Paper 11 Q3, June 2019*

| Example student response | Examiner comments |
|---|---|
| Scale of business means the size of the operations of a business from small/limited sized business to a large/extensive one.<br><br>There are a number of factors that influence the size of any business. One of these is the amount of capital available, which may be limited and so growth will be restrained. This is especially the case for sole traders and partnerships that are unable to access share capital. | There is knowledge of a relevant factor that can influence the scale of operations of a business (amount of capital needed). This is not explained and is not applied to a business context.<br><br>The reference to the greater impact on sole traders and partnerships is a judgement, which is not a skill that is awarded on a question with the command word 'analyse'. For analysis, there should be a discussion on how/why the factor influences the scale of operations in a business, which is not evident in this answer. The analysis is implied, but not explicitly presented so cannot be rewarded.<br><br>*1/5 marks* |

**3**

**Rolling Wheels (RW)**

Kadeem is a keen cyclist and he had the idea that selling bicycles might be profitable. Without a business plan, he set up Rolling Wheels five years ago in the capital city of Country X. RW is now a private limited company and Kadeem owns 95% of the shares. RW sells bicycles, accessories, specialist clothing and replacement parts. Half of these products are imported. RW also offers bicycle repairs and servicing. RW is one of the largest independent bicycle businesses in the city and employs ten people. It offers customers a personal service and charges prices that are competitive compared to other specialist bicycle retailers. However, there are large general retailers that sell and repair bicycles at lower prices. These large retailers have over 80% of the bicycle supply and repair market in the city. RW's major competitive advantage is that it is the only business of its type located very close to a university.

## CONTINUED

The students and employees of the university are the main customer base and they value the convenience, reliability and personal attention.

### Human resource management issues

Kadeem employs Asif as the store manager. Asif has noticed an increase in the number of complaints from customers in the last year. He is worried that this will lead to loss of reputation, falling sales and reduced customer loyalty. Asif raised the following concerns with Kadeem. RW has not increased employee pay for over a year.

- Customer service training is given in-store while employees are working.

- New employees are slow at servicing and repairs.

- The store seems busy but many visitors do not buy anything.

- Employees feel that they are working as individuals and are not part of a team.

- Kadeem has been very busy for three months drawing up future plans.

- Half the employees are thinking of leaving because they do not feel involved in the business.

Kadeem gave some serious thought to these concerns. As a result, he is considering introducing management by objectives (MBO) and ways to improve communication within the business.

### Quality issues

The meeting between Kadeem and Asif highlighted customer complaints regarding quality. New bicycles arrive from manufacturers in several parts and are assembled in-store. The assembly of some bicycles has not been done well, with customers pointing out faults or returning bicycles for adjustment soon after purchase. Other complaints have also been made about the servicing and repair of bicycles. The workshop manager is responsible for this work. She checks some of the bicycles following assembly, service or repair. She then asks any available employee to correct the fault without investigating the cause of the problem. Kadeem knows that RW needs to improve quality, possibly by introducing total quality management (TQM).

Analyse the likely benefits to RW of introducing total quality management (TQM). [8]

| Example student response | Examiner comments |
|---|---|
| Total quality management (TQM) is a holistic approach to quality that involves all employees in ensuring best possible processes and outcomes and includes quality chains, quality circles, internal customers and Kaizen. Perhaps the most significant characteristic of TQM is the process of continuous checking for quality at every stage of the production process. More traditional quality control methods generally involved completing the quality checks at the end of the process.<br><br>Looking at the case study example of RW, the business may well benefit from introducing TQM. For example, the extract highlights that there are currently many faults in servicing and repair, with the workshop manager responsible and a lack of involvement by employees.<br><br>Some of the advantages that introducing TQM might bring include the problems identified from early saving costs of correction. Another benefit might be the lower need for final inspection, saving costs as the checking would be completed by employees throughout the process. Tracing reasons for faults will also be easier, because checks are made more often, and this could lead to lower costs. With employees themselves responsible for quality control, accountability may improve and there will be more opportunities for employee responsibility and so greater motivation levels. The text suggests that currently employee motivation is low. Other benefits include less wastage of materials and time, so saving costs. Better customer relations are also likely to be observed, thus more chance of repeat business. | The response demonstrates a good knowledge of TQM, including the characteristic that it involves continuous checking for quality at every stage of the production process.<br><br>A number of opportunities to include application to the business context/case study are seen throughout the answer, e.g. many faults in servicing and repair, workshop manager responsibility and a lack of involvement by employees.<br><br>There is some evidence throughout the response of basic analysis with some acknowledgment of the impact of any potential benefit on RW. However, these are not developed and provide little more than a list of points. Note that because the question asks the student to analyse the benefits, they will not be rewarded for including any disadvantages of TQM.<br><br>*6/8 marks* |

For Question 4(a) read the case study, question, example student response and commentary provided. Then, in Question 4(b), write an improved answer to the question, using the guidance in the commentary to help you.

4

**Allnatural Products (AP)**

AP is a public limited company with its head office and final processing and packaging factory in Country X. AP produces and sells a large range of skin creams and hair products made from natural ingredients. AP has expanded very quickly since becoming a PLC and sells its products through large retailers worldwide. However, the market is becoming increasingly competitive, with retailers offering more of their 'own brand' natural skin and hair products.

**CONTINUED**

| Area | 2015 | 2016 | 2017 |
|------|------|------|------|
| EU | 1% | (2%) | (3%) |
| USA | 4% | 3% | (1%) |
| Asia | 5% | 6% | 8% |

*Figures in brackets indicate negative change

**Table 1:** Percentage change in AP's sales by geographical area

### Finance

Dividends to shareholders had increased every year since the company went public eight years ago, but last year both profits and dividends decreased. At the recent annual general meeting (AGM) some shareholders expressed their dissatisfaction about the lower dividend and also commented that AP did not seem to be focused on increasing shareholder value. AP's CEO, Mary, announced her growth plans for AP at the end of the AGM. In order to make necessary investments in the company's future, she warned shareholders that it may be necessary to decrease dividends again next year. A summary of AP's accounting data and forecasts for 2017–2018 is shown in Table 2.

| | 2017 (actual) | 2018 (forecast) |
|---|---|---|
| Revenue | $550 000 000 | $580 000 000 |
| Operating profit | $56 000 000 | $60 000 000 |
| Share price | $4.00 per share | $3.80 per share |
| Dividend per share | $0.30 per share | $0.28 per share |
| Retained earnings ($m) | $10 000 000 | $12 000 000 |
| Gearing ratio | 35% | 35% |

**Table 2:** Summary of AP's accounting data and forecasts as at December 2017

### Operations

AP sources raw materials from many countries in Africa and Asia. The first stage of the production process is often completed in the country of origin, for example, shea butter made from shea nuts in Africa. AP ensures that producers are paid a fair price for the raw materials. AP's main factory in Africa is old and needs replacing. Production is labour-intensive. Recently there have been media reports of worker exploitation and even the use of child labour. Mary has asked the operations director to investigate the cost and feasibility of replacing the old factory with a new larger factory, with up-to-date computerised equipment. This would enable all stages of the production and packaging of products to be completed in the new African factory. AP would send a management team from head office to supervise this project, including the introduction of modernised processes. Nigel, the operations director, has calculated that the total cost of the project will be $15 500 000. He has also estimated the durations of the activities needed to complete the project. These are shown in Table 3. AP's board of directors has decided to go ahead with the project based on these estimates.

## CONTINUED

| Activity | | Duration (weeks) | Preceding activities |
|---|---|---|---|
| A | Plan new building and employ building contractor | 8 | None |
| B | Remove existing building | 2 | A |
| C | Clear and prepare the site | 1 | B |
| D | Deliver building materials to site | 1 | A |
| E | Complete building work | 4 | C, D |
| F | Connect water supply and electricity | 2 | E |
| G | Install machinery | 3 | E |
| H | Recruit new workforce | 4 | A |
| J | Train workforce on site | 1 | F, G, H |

**Table 3:** Estimated times for activities for building and equipping the new factory

### Human resource management for the new factory

Once the factory is functioning it will be managed and operated by some existing AP employees as well as by new recruits. The workforce in the new factory will be organised into product teams, each of which will be supervised by a team leader. Each team will be set production targets every month and all team members will receive a bonus if targets are met. All workers will be members of Kaizen groups which will meet monthly. Suggestions for new products will also be welcomed by factory managers, who will pass them on to the head office marketing team for consideration.

### Selling in new markets: A strategic choice

Mary would like to expand AP and she has been carrying out some research. She has identified two possible options for growth.

### *Option A*

Working together with a popular European holiday hotel group, AP would set up and operate small salons within each hotel. AP products would be used in services such as hairdressing and beauty treatments. The hotel would also buy AP products in bulk and provide them for guests to use in their rooms.

## CONTINUED

### Option B

AP would develop and launch a new range of products aimed at the market for men's skin and hair care. Market research has suggested that this is a high-growth market for products such as skin moisturiser.

Table 4 shows selected information for each option.

| | Option A: Salons in hotels | Option B: New range of products for men |
|---|---|---|
| Estimated cost of initial Investment | $10 000 000 | $12 000 000 |
| Forecast payback period | 4 years 6 months | 3 years |
| Greatest constraining factor | Lack of AP directors' experience in setting up and operating salons | Existing product development focus on products for women |
| Greatest driving factor | Increasing the market for AP hair and skin care products | Entry into the growing market for hair and skin care products aimed at men |
| Estimated chances of strategy success | 70% | 60% |
| Greatest risk factor | Seasonal demand for holiday hotels | Competitors already established in the market |

**Table 4:** Information for the two options

a    Evaluate the usefulness of critical path analysis (CPA) to AP when planning the new factory project.    [12]

**Adapted from Cambridge International AS & A Level Business (9609) Paper 32 Q4b, March 2018**

| Example student response | Examiner comments |
|---|---|
| Critical path analysis or network diagrams are a way of sequencing activities to identify those activities which cannot be delayed without delaying the whole project. These are generally created by specialist teams and can be time-consuming to carry out. Network analysis can be used to reduce the time frame to carry out a project by calculating the activities which can be carried out at the same time, allowing resources to be ordered when needed. One weakness, however, is that like any plan they could fail to account of unforeseen delays, which may then delay the whole project. | The response includes a lot of relevant knowledge. The response shows a good understanding of CPA analysis as well as how it can be used to save time when completing a project. |

| Example student response | Examiner comments |
|---|---|
| Referring to Table 3, the installation of services such as water might be an example of those tasks that might end up delaying the project due to unexpected problems, for example, bad weather might delay some of the building work. Equally, delays in the building project might also result from potential lack of expertise, due to a lack of knowledge of local conditions in Africa.<br><br>In situations where the project is delayed by unforeseen circumstances, the time and energy spent on completing the network analysis then becomes obsolete, reducing the effectiveness of the technique.<br><br>In conclusion, network diagrams would appear to have a role to AP when planning the new factory project, but are only as accurate as the information and expertise used to compile them. | The response also includes a number of references to the business in the text, for example, it refers to examples of factors that might lead to potential delays in the project.<br><br>The response highlights one limitation of network analysis in the first paragraph, which is developed.<br><br>The response includes a basic judgement at the end. The 'application' contained in the final sentence is made up from words used in the question, so cannot be regarded as an applied judgement. Additionally, there is no evaluation, or attempt to weigh up the key arguments in the answer to justify the judgement made. This needs to be provided before considering information that may affect the overall conclusion.<br><br>*7/12 marks* |

**b**   Now write an improved answer to Question 4(a).

Here is another practice question which you should attempt. Use the guidance in the commentaries in this section to help you as you answer the question.

**5**   Analyse **two** advantages for a business of a just-in-time (JIT) system
   of inventory management.                                                      [8]

   ***Adapted from Cambridge International AS & A Level Business (9609)***
   ***Paper 13 Q5a, November 2021***

For Question 6(a) read the case study, question, example student response and commentary provided. Then, in Question 6(b), write an improved answer to the question, adding in two different disadvantages of holding stock and providing more detail. Use the guidance in the commentary to help you as you answer the question.

**6**

### Quality Furniture (QF)

Quality Furniture is a public limited company in Country S. It manufactures furniture for cafés. The number of cafés in Country S has increased by more than 50% over the last five years. This has meant that QF has been able to expand and achieve internal economies of scale. However, the growth of the café market has attracted new firms supplying café furniture and increased competition for QF. An extract from QF's income statement is shown in Table 1.

| Revenue | $300 000 000 |
| Cost of sales | $120 000 000 |
| Gross profit | $180 000 000 |
| Expenses | $150 000 000 |

**Table 1:** Extract from QF's income statement for 2020

Although QF has been successful so far, Javid, the managing director, has identified two problem areas: inventory and human resources.

### Inventory

QF's inventory includes raw materials, work in progress and finished tables and chairs. QF buys 80% of its materials from Country T and there is a long delivery lead time. This means that QF holds a high level of buffer inventory which has a high value.

### Human resources

QF's production employees are unhappy that they have not received any benefit from the company's expansion. Profit has doubled over the past three years but employees have not received any pay increases or bonuses. The employees have all been trained by QF and have specialist skills which had ensured that customer expectations were met. However, customers are starting to complain about a fall in the quality of the furniture, which could be the result of the low morale of the employees. Some highly trained employees have left QF to work for competitor firms.

a    Analyse **two** disadvantages to QF of holding a high level of inventory.    [8]

*Cambridge International AS & A Level Business (9609) Paper 21 Q1c, November 2021*

| Example student response | Examiner comments |
|---|---|
| Businesses hold inventory in the form of raw materials, work in progress and finished goods.<br><br>One disadvantage of maintaining a high level of inventory might be the cost. Some of the inventory held by the business is valuable and higher costs then lead to lower profit levels.<br><br>A second disadvantage is the level of security required. Much of the stock has a high value and so would be worth stealing. This will require the business spending considerable sums on security, as well as expensive insurance premiums. | The response includes an explanation of inventory and demonstrates good knowledge of two disadvantages of holding a high level of inventory. The costs of wastage and damage and the costs of tying up storage space which could have been utilised for other purposes would also have been suitable disadvantages.<br><br>The response contains no application to the case study. Many opportunities to link to the business are ignored, e.g., the number of cafés increased by more than 50% over the last five years and with it the cost of sales has risen to $120,000,000 (40% of revenue). It could also have been mentioned that 80% of materials were delivered from country T, the long delivery lead times and the need to reduce costs.<br><br>While two relevant disadvantages of holding a high level of inventory are included, neither is developed. In the first paragraph, there is no analysis of why inventory has a cost (i.e. a storage cost), which could lead to a lower profit. In the second paragraph, the reference to security is a loose reference to cost. If we take the answer to mean the cost of employing a member of security staff, then the fact the business needs to spend 'considerable sums' on this, implies a cost impact. Clearer use of language would have helped here, as well as including a disadvantage of the spending on security, e.g. the potential opportunity cost of this.<br><br>*3/8 marks* |

b    Write out an improved answer to Question 6(a), adding in two different disadvantages of holding stock and providing more detail.

# 29 Business finance

## EXAM SKILLS FOCUS

In this chapter you will:

- practise answering exam questions that assess knowledge of key terminology

- revisit using a 'brain tip' to help manage test anxiety.

It is important to have a good working knowledge of key terms so that you can apply them to exam questions. In this chapter you will practise answering questions that are assessing your AO1 (Knowledge and understanding) skill. This is very important as the assessments for AS Level Business place a great deal of emphasis on this skill.

In Chapter 3 you were introduced to the concept of using a 'brain tip' to help you manage test anxiety. In this chapter you will revisit this technique to help you further increase your understanding of its use.

# 29.1 The need for business finance

## UNDERSTAND THESE TERMS

- start-up capital
- working capital
- liquidity

1   Why do businesses need finance?

2   What is the difference between short-term finance and long-term finance? Give examples of when a business might need to use each type of finance.

3   Explain what is meant by the terms 'administration', 'bankruptcy' and 'liquidation'.

## ≪ RECALL AND CONNECT 1 ≪

What are the differences between the public and private sectors of the economy?

# 29.2 Working capital

## UNDERSTAND THESE TERMS

- current assets
- current liabilities

1   What might happen if a business does not have enough working capital?

2   What is the disadvantage of having too much working capital?

3   Managing the level of working capital can be achieved by managing inventory, managing trade payables and managing trade receivables (debtors who owe the business money). Copy and complete Table 29.1, outlining how each method might be used to manage the level of working capital.

| Managing inventory | Managing trade payables | Managing trade receivables |
|---|---|---|
|  |  |  |

**Table 29.1:** Methods of managing the level of working capital

4   What is the difference between revenue expenditure and capital expenditure?

5

### Cruise Cuisine (CC)

CC is a large private limited company that provides frozen foods. Its customers are exclusively luxury cruise liners. It has found it challenging recently to manage its working capital as it has needed to offer longer trade credit periods to its customers to stop them taking their orders to a competitor in the frozen foods market.

| Non-current assets | $20 000 000 |
| --- | --- |
| Inventory | $6 000 000 |
| Trade receivables | $2 500 000 |
| Cash | $1 500 000 |
| Current liabilities | $8 000 000 |
| Non-current liabilities | $14 000 000 |
| Equity | $8 000 000 |

**Table 29.2:** Extract from CC's statement of financial position

a   Calculate CC's working capital.                                    [3]

b   Explain **one** way in which CC could increase its working capital.   [3]

## « RECALL AND CONNECT 2 «

Explain McGregor's Theory X and Theory Y.

# 29.3 Sources of finance

## UNDERSTAND THESE TERMS

- non-current assets
- overdraft
- hire purchase
- leasing
- long-term loans
- debentures

1   Explain how a public company can raise finance through the sale of shares. How is this different to how a private limited company can raise finance through the sale of shares?

2   What are the benefits of using crowdfunding as a source of finance for a new business?

3  What is the purpose of a mortgage as a source of business finance?

4  Do you think a business should always try to select a method of raising business finance that does not increase debt? Explain your answer.

5  Copy Table 29.3 and complete it by ticking the appropriate boxes alongside each source of finance. For each type of business finance, you should identify whether it is an internal or external source of finance.

| Source of finance | Where the finance is from | |
| --- | --- | --- |
| | Internal | External |
| Share capital (through sale of shares to the public) | | |
| Debentures | | |
| Owners' investment | | |
| Debt factoring | | |
| Sale of unwanted assets | | |
| Share capital (through rights issue of shares) | | |
| Bank overdraft | | |
| Mortgage | | |
| Crowdfunding | | |
| Microfinance | | |

**Table 29.3:** Sources of finance

The skill of knowledge and understanding (AO1) is worth 35% of the marks on AS Level Paper 1 and 30% of the marks on AS Level Paper 2. In this section you will practise developing your knowledge skills for short-answer questions related to business finance.

6  Define the term 'debt factoring'. [2]

7  Define the term 'sale and leaseback'. [2]

8  Define the term 'bank overdraft'. [2]

9  Define the term 'venture capital'. [2]

10  Define the term 'trade credit'. [2]

11  Define the term 'mortgage'. [2]

12  Define the term 'hire purchase'. [2]

**UNDERSTAND THESE TERMS**

- share (or equity) capital
- business mortgages
- venture capital
- collateral security
- rights issue
- microfinance
- crowdfunding

REFLECTION

REFLECTION

How confident did you feel when answering Questions 6–12? Did you feel that you had enough knowledge to answer these successfully? As a way of developing your knowledge, you should try to write a selection of 'define' questions on other topics that you have studied. It would be useful to place these onto flashcards to help your revision.

## 29.4 Factors affecting the source of finance

1   Selecting the most appropriate source of finance is essential for long-term business success. For each of the following factors, explain why the factor should be considered when determining the right source of finance to use.

   a   why finance is needed and the time period it is needed for

   b   cost

   c   amount needed

   d   form of business ownership and desire to retain control

   e   level of existing debt

   f   flexibility.

### ≪ RECALL AND CONNECT 3 ≪

What is meant by the term 'demographic market segmentation'?

## 29.5 Selecting the appropriate source of finance

1   Imagine you were starting up a new business as a sole trader. You want to create an app to help match A Level Business students to tutors in their local area. The students will pay a small fee for your service. What would be the most appropriate sources of finance for you to use to start this business venture? Explain your answer.

In Chapter 3 you were introduced to the concept of a 'brain tip'. Remember, a brain tip is a useful technique to use to help you identify the knowledge you have on a topic before you think about what to include in your answer and helps you reflect on your answer. Here is an opportunity to reflect on this technique and practise using it again.

Complete a brain tip for Question 2. The following is a reminder of the steps you need to go through.

- Step 1: select the area of business knowledge you are being assessed on (in this case, it is sources of finance).

- Step 2: allow yourself one minute and write down anything you can think of to do with this area of business knowledge.

- Step 3: from the points you have written down, select the one you think you know most about: use this as the basis of your answer.

Once you have done this, write an answer to Question 2.

2

> **Next Day Guarantee (NDG)**
>
> NDG is a private limited company that offers a parcel delivery and courier service. Its main customers are retail stores which use its services to send online orders to their customers. It is currently considering investing into a new fleet of delivery vans that will cost around $1.5 million.

Analyse **one** source of finance that NDG could use to purchase a new fleet of delivery vans. [5]

### REFLECTION

How did you feel using a brain tip for Question 2? Is this something you have used since it was introduced in Chapter 3? Are there any changes you could make to this technique to make it work better for you?

### SELF-ASSESSMENT CHECKLIST

Let's revisit the Knowledge focus and Exam skills focus for this chapter. Decide how confident you are with each statement.

| Now I can | Show it | Needs more work | Almost there | Confident to move on |
|---|---|---|---|---|
| analyse reasons why business activity requires finance | Create a history timeline of a business of your choice and identify key points where it may have required finance for different reasons. | | | |
| analyse the importance of working capital to a business and how it is managed | Look at your answer to Question 3 in Section 29.2 and use your coursebook to add any missing answers to your table. | | | |

**CONTINUED**

| | | | | |
|---|---|---|---|---|
| differentiate between capital expenditure and revenue expenditure | Write down the definitions for both these terms. | | | |
| analyse the different sources of long-term and short-term finance, both internal and external | Develop a revision mind map to show the advantages and disadvantages of at least six different sources of finance. | | | |
| evaluate the factors managers consider when taking a finance decision | Look at your answer to Question 1 in Section 29.4. Which option do you think is the most important factor? Explain your answer in no more than 100 words. | | | |
| recommend and justify appropriate sources of finance for different business needs | Look at a selection of case studies from this chapter and consider which source of finance might be most appropriate in each case and try to explain why. | | | |
| practise answering exam questions that assess knowledge of key terminology | Write three example exam questions that test your knowledge of microfinance. You should then answer these. | | | |
| revisit using a 'brain tip' to help manage test anxiety | Teach another student how to use the brain tip technique and explain the benefits of this to them. | | | |

# 30 Forecasting and managing cash flows

It is important to understand that a wide range of command words can be used to assess different skills. This also applies to some of the more 'numerical' concepts of this course. You need to be prepared to answer questions on a topic that requires skills and techniques. In this chapter you will be provided with exam questions related to cash flow and forecasting that use the command words 'explain', 'calculate' and 'analyse'. It is important that you understand what each command word is instructing you to do.

# 30.1 Cash flow forecasts: Meaning and purpose

1  Outline four causes of cash flow problems to a business.

2  There are two ways to improve net cash flow:

- increase cash inflows

- reduce cash outflows.

Copy and complete Table 30.1. For each item, you should state whether it is a method of increasing cash inflows or reducing cash outflows. You should then make notes on how the item works to improve net cash flows.

| Method | Reduces inflows or outflows? | How it works |
|---|---|---|
| **a** Sale of unwanted assets | | |
| **b** Managing trade receivables | | |
| **c** Overdraft | | |
| **d** Cutting overhead expenditure | | |
| **e** Managing trade payables | | |

**Table 30.1:** Reducing cash inflows and outflows

## ≪ RECALL AND CONNECT 1 ≪

Why can a lack of cash lead to business failure?

## UNDERSTAND THESE TERMS

- cash inflow

- cash outflow

- net cash flow

The following questions are based on cash flow forecasts that use different command words.

An 'explain' question requires you to set out purposes or reasons / make the relationships between things evident / provide the why and/or how of a matter and support with relevant evidence. You need to show some knowledge of the concept and then describe this in detail, in this instance by using case study evidence.

**3**

---

### Deep Blue Swimming Pools (DBSP)

Zachir has always enjoyed designing swimming pools, so he has recently decided to turn this passion into a business. Zachir studied A Level Business at school and remembers that it is a good idea for new businesses to complete a cash flow forecast. He can then show this to a bank if he decides DBSP needs to apply for a loan to help it through the first few months of trading.

| | Month 1 | Month 2 | Month 3 | Month 4 |
|---|---|---|---|---|
| **Cash in** | | | | |
| Owners' capital | $20 000 | $0 | $0 | $0 |
| Grant | $10 000 | $0 | $0 | $0 |
| Revenue | $0 | $15 000 | $23 000 | $29 000 |
| Total cash in | $30 000 | $15 000 | $23 000 | $29 000 |
| **Cash out** | | | | |
| Capital expenditure | $25 000 | $0 | $0 | $0 |
| Utilities (power, water, etc.) | $0 | $0 | $15 000 | $0 |
| Labour costs (wages and salaries) | $7000 | $7000 | $7000 | $7000 |
| Trade payables (materials) | $8000 | $9000 | $10 000 | ? |
| Total cash out | $40 000 | $16 000 | $32 000 | $18 000 |
| Net cash flow | $(10 000) | $(1000) | $(9000) | $11 000 |
| Opening cash balance | $0 | $(10 000) | $(11 000) | ? |
| Closing cash balance | $(10 000) | $(11 000) | $(20 000) | X |

**Table 30.2:** DBSP cash flow forecast

---

   **a**   Explain **one** limitation to Zachir of using cash flow forecasts.   [3]

An 'analyse' question requires you to examine in detail to show meaning and to identify elements and the relationship between them. This means that you need to show knowledge, explain how this applies to the case study and then develop an implication/impact of this element. In this question you are required to analyse one advantage and one disadvantage: you need to make sure these are specific points that could be felt by DBSP.

   **b**   Analyse **one** advantage and **one** disadvantage for DBSP of using a short-term loan to help manage its cash flow.   [8]

A 'calculate' question requires you to work out from given facts, figures or information. As part of this, you are always advised to show your working as this can be used to explain how you arrived at your answer. There may be some marks awarded for showing some correct stages of calculation. Additionally, it is very important on 'calculate' questions to give a clear final answer, with appropriate units.

    c    Refer to Table 30.2. Calculate DBSP's forecasted closing balance in month 4 (X). [3]

An 'evaluate' question requires you to evaluate evidence in order to make reasoned judgements, present substantiated conclusions and, where appropriate, make recommendations for action and implementation. This means that you need to provide a developed judgement or conclusion in the context of the business that draws together analytical and evaluative comments which weigh up key arguments.

    d    Evaluate the benefits to DBSP of producing a cash flow forecast. [12]

## REFLECTION

Questions 3(a)–(d) explored the concept of cash flow forecasting using a variety of different command words. How did your approach to answering questions change? Did you find some of the questions more challenging than the others?

## SELF-ASSESSMENT CHECKLIST

Let's revisit the Knowledge focus and Exam skills focus for this chapter. Decide how confident you are with each statement.

| Now I can | Show it | Needs more work | Almost there | Confident to move on |
|---|---|---|---|---|
| analyse the importance of cash to business | Explain what would happen if a business did not have enough cash. | | | |
| explain the difference between cash flow and profit | Explain the difference between cash flow and profit to a friend. | | | |
| analyse the purpose of cash flow forecasts | Check your answers to Question 3 – are there any more points you can add to these? | | | |

## CONTINUED

| | | | | |
|---|---|---|---|---|
| interpret and amend simple cash flow forecasts | Copy out Table 30.2 and amend it to reflect a 20% increase in revenues for months 2, 3 and 4 as well as a 50% increase in trade payables in months 1, 2 and 3. | | | |
| analyse the different causes of cash flow problems | Make notes on the different causes of cash flow problems and explain which one you think would cause the biggest problem for a business. | | | |
| evaluate different methods of improving cash flow | Create a revision card detailing at least five different methods of improving cash flow. | | | |
| practise using a range of command words that can be used in exam questions related to numerical concepts | Look through some past papers and find some other questions related to numerical concepts. | | | |

# 31 Costs

## EXAM SKILLS FOCUS

In this chapter you will:

- make links across the AS Level concepts using a topic grid

- further practise calculation skills.

In your exams, you will be given some questions that are focused on an individual topic and others that are more open and require you to reach across different areas of the syllabus to be able to answer them. As a result, you need to be able to make links between topic areas and understand how these can be used together. In this chapter you will be given a topic grid to support you in developing links between topics on your AS Level Business course.

Calculation skills are important to master as they are needed throughout your course. It is vital that you continue to practise and develop your calculation skills, just as much as you do with your extended writing skills, so that you can gain confidence when faced with numbers, data sets and questions that require you to show your numerical abilities in exams. This will help reduce any anxiety associated with these types of questions. Throughout this chapter you will be given many opportunities to practise your calculation skills in relation to business costs.

# 31.1 The need for accurate cost information

| UNDERSTAND THESE TERMS |
| --- |
| • direct costs |
| • indirect costs |
| • fixed costs |
| • variable costs |
| • total costs |

1 What are the uses of cost information for a business?

2 Why can it sometimes be difficult to classify costs into fixed and variable? Give an example in your answer.

## ≪ RECALL AND CONNECT 1 ≪

Explain what is meant by 'free-market economy', 'command economy' and 'mixed economy'. Which term do you think best describes the economy of the country where you live? Explain your answer.

# 31.2 Approaches to costing

| UNDERSTAND THESE TERMS |
| --- |
| • full costing |
| • contribution costing |
| • marginal cost |

1 a What is the formula to calculate average costs?

   b If a firm produces 50 000 units with a variable cost of $2.50 per unit and fixed costs of $2 000 000.00, what is the average cost per unit?

2 What are the limitations of using a full costing technique for a business that produces multiple products?

3

**Quality Cycles (QC)**

Quality Cycles is a small business that manufactures bicycles, but in a rather unique way. Customers enter the workshop, where they will select their ideal cycle frame, wheels and accessories from the range on offer to them and QC will put these all together to provide the customer with their very own custom-made bicycle. QC has found it very challenging to manage its costs, opting to charge a price that it thinks reflects its product, rather than one that considers the costs of production. The owners know that this is not suitable going forward and that they need to find a more appropriate method of using costing information to set prices.

a   Analyse **one** advantage and **one** disadvantage of QC using full costing to allocate its costs.   [8]

b   Analyse **one** advantage and **one** disadvantage of QC using contribution costing to allocate its costs.   [8]

**≪ RECALL AND CONNECT 2 ≪**

Explain the differences between the main four management styles: autocratic, democratic, paternalistic and laissez-faire.

# 31.3 Uses of cost information

1

**Sweet Dreams Bakery (SDB)**

Sweet Dreams Bakery produces cakes that are sold to a range of cake shops in the area and has overheads of $55 000. The business has not been trading for a long time but has already managed sales of 400 000 units. The bakery already sells a range of 12 different cupcakes but is keen to attract an order from a supermarket. The sales and cost data for SDB are given in Table 31.1.

| Cost item | Amount |
|---|---|
| Selling price of each cupcake | $0.30 |
| Total current sales volume, in units | 400 000 |
| Total available capacity of factory, in units | 520 000 |
| Overheads | $55 000.00 |
| Direct cost (per cup cake) | $0.10 |

**Table 31.1:** Sales and cost data for SDB

The supermarket wishes to place an order for 25 000 cupcakes but will only pay $0.15 per unit. Should SDB accept the order? Show evidence of calculations in your answer.

**2** What other factors should be considered when taking on such an order? You should use the topic grid to help you with this.

The topic grid (Table 31.2) displays a range of topics and concepts that are covered in this AS Level Business course. You need to select a letter and a number and try to apply that concept to help you answer Question 2. For example, for E3 (recruitment), SDB may need to recruit more staff to take on the new order from the bakery. How many of the topics can you link to your answer in Question 2?

| | A | B | C | D | E | F |
|---|---|---|---|---|---|---|
| 1 | Opportunity cost | Management styles | Productivity | Workforce planning | Sources of finance | Business plan |
| 2 | Marketing mix (price) | Profit | Factors of production | Marketing mix (product) | Stakeholders | Marketing mix (promotion) |
| 3 | Motivational theories | Business size | Working capital | Market segmentation | Recruitment | Market research |
| 4 | Inventory management | Marketing mix (place) | Business objectives | Business costs | McGregor's Theory X and Y | Marketing function |
| 5 | Business ownership | Demand and supply | Capacity utilisation | Business growth | Operations | Added value |
| 6 | Cash flow | Break-even analysis | Business activity | Human resources | Employee training | Finance function |

**Table 31.2:** Topic grid for AS Level Business

**REFLECTION**

Did you find some topics easier to link to your answer in Question 2 than others? Are there ways you could make each topic in the grid apply to the concept of break-even analysis and taking special orders? You might find it useful to speak to another student about areas in which you were unable to make a direct link between the topic and break-even analysis to see if they can help you.

# 31.4 Break-even analysis

**1**    A business has a break-even point of 420 units and currently produces 570 units. Calculate its margin of safety.

**2**    Explain **three** uses of break-even analysis for a business.

**3**

> ### Winston's Windows (WW)
>
> Winston Lee has always wanted to be his own boss. He has recently been made redundant from his job, so has decided to set up his own window cleaning business called Winston's Windows. He will specialise in cleaning windows on domestic properties, as he has some experience in doing this. He needs to work out what price to charge his customers for his service and has noted the following costs that will be involved.
>
> | Cost item | Amount |
> |---|---|
> | Variable costs per property (based on an average house size) | $12 |
> | Fixed costs per annum | $10 000 |
> | Maximum number of properties that could be serviced per year | 800 |
>
> **Table 31.3:** WW costs
>
> Winston needs to decide whether to charge $30 or $40 for each cleaning job as these were the prices most commonly suggested in his market research.

    **a**    Answer the following questions based on a price of $30.

        **i**    Calculate Winston's break-even level of output.    [3]

        **ii**    Calculate the margin of safety if Winston is currently cleaning 600 properties a year.    [3]

        **iii**    Calculate the total maximum profit Winston will make, assuming that he is working at maximum capacity.    [3]

    **b**    Answer the following questions based on a price of $40.

        **i**    Calculate Winston's break-even level of output.    [3]

        **ii**    Calculate the margin of safety if Winston is currently cleaning 600 properties a year.    [3]

        **iii**    Calculate the total maximum profit Winston will make, assuming that he is working at maximum capacity.    [3]

## « RECALL AND CONNECT 3 «

What is the difference between tangible and intangible attributes of a product?

# SELF-ASSESSMENT CHECKLIST

Let's revisit the Knowledge focus and Exam skills focus for this chapter.
Decide how confident you are with each statement.

| Now I can | Show it | Needs more work | Almost there | Confident to move on |
|---|---|---|---|---|
| analyse the need for cost information | List five reasons why a business needs to know cost information. | | | |
| analyse types of costs: fixed, variable, direct and indirect | Give an example of each type of cost. | | | |
| analyse the differences between full costing and contribution costing | Look at the definitions for these two terms and select two differences that might exist between them as costing methods. | | | |
| apply and evaluate the technique of contribution costing | Create a small revision card outlining the benefits and limitations of contribution costing. | | | |
| apply contribution costing to accept/reject special order decisions | Look back at your answers to the questions in Section 31.2. Can you add any more points to this list? | | | |
| draw and interpret break-even charts and calculate the break-even point | Create a break-even chart for Winston's Windows in Section 31.4 based on each price being explored. | | | |
| apply and evaluate break-even analysis in simple business decision-making situations | Look at your answers for WW in Section 31.4. What price do you think Winston should charge to clean a property's windows? Write a short paragraph explaining your answer. | | | |
| make links across the AS Level concepts using a topic grid | Create a mind map to show links between all of the topics in the topic grid. | | | |
| further practise calculation skills | Looking back at the case study in Section 31.4, calculate how many properties WW would need to clean to break even if he charged $50 per job. | | | |

# 32 Budgets

## KNOWLEDGE FOCUS

You will answer questions on:

**32.1** The meaning and purpose of budgets

**32.2** Variance analysis

## EXAM SKILLS FOCUS

In this chapter you will:

- show that you understand a selection of command words that can be used to assess the skills of the same concept in different ways

- find out what to do next in order to improve your preparation for taking your AS Level Business exam.

An important exam skill is recognising the different ways you can be assessed on the same topic. It is important that you are prepared to be assessed on your skills of knowledge, application, analysis and evaluation for all topics and that you practise questions using a variety of different command words to support you with this skill development. This chapter presents you with a variety of different command words that you have been introduced to throughout this book.

As this is the final chapter in the AS Level section of this guide, you should now be in a position to be able to consider what you need to do next in order to help you prepare for your exams. By preparing yourself thoroughly, you should be able to move forward with a good level of confidence.

# 32.1 The meaning and purpose of budgets

1 Explain **three** impacts for a business if it does not complete any financial planning such as budgeting.

2 Explain how each of these different types of budgeting works.

   a incremental budgeting

   b zero budgeting

   c flexible budgeting.

3

> **Café Delight (CD)**
>
> Nadia founded CD three years ago when she was made redundant by her employer. CD provides catering for small events including corporate meetings, weddings and dinner parties. Nadia has built up a loyal clientele as she has developed a reputation for excellent customer service, as well as a wide range of menu choices for her customers. Nadia has never really understood the financial side of her business, so she has recently taken a college course to learn how to manage her finances and has now started to prepare a budget for CD for the next year.

Evaluate the benefits for Nadia of using a budget. [12]

## ≪ RECALL AND CONNECT 1 ≪

Outline the purpose of a quality circle.

## REFLECTION

Think about the skills and techniques you have learnt throughout the AS Level chapters of this resource. Which exam skills do you feel most confident with? Which ones do you feel need more development? Can you explain the assessment objectives to a friend?

## UNDERSTAND THIS TERM

- variance analysis

## 32.2 Variance analysis

1   Table 32.1 contains a budget for a new business. Using this information, copy the table and complete the actual figures for month 1. Calculate the variance and determine whether the variance is adverse or favourable.

| | Budgeted figures | Actual figures | Variance | Adverse or favourable? |
|---|---|---|---|---|
| Revenue | $9000 | $ | $ | |
| Cost of materials | $1200 | $ | $ | |
| Labour costs | $1500 | $ | $ | |
| Gross profit | $6300 | $ | $ | |
| Overheads | $2700 | $ | $ | |
| Operating profit | $3600 | $ | $ | |

**Table 32.1:** Budget for month 1

Actual figures for month 1 are as follows.

- Revenue is $1000 more than budgeted.
- Cost of materials is 30% more than budgeted.
- Labour costs are 12% higher than budgeted.

Knowledge is an important skill to master in order to support you in answering exam questions. A selection of questions that are assessing your knowledge of budgets follows. Table 32.2 shows the budgeted and actual figures for a business.

| | Budgeted figures | Actual figures | Variance |
|---|---|---|---|
| Revenue | $8500 | $6250 | $2250 |
| Cost of materials | $1750 | $1275 | −$475 |
| Labour costs | $1200 | $1344 | $144 |
| Gross profit | $5550 | | −$1919 |
| Overheads | $3200 | $3200 | $0 |
| Operating profit | $2350 | | |

**Table 32.2:** Budget for exam skills questions

2   a   Identify **one** disadvantage of setting budgets.   [1]

   b   Explain the term 'favourable variance'.   [3]

   c   Calculate the operating profit variance figure.   [3]

3   Copy out Table 32.3 and fill in the missing information. You need to decide whether each issue would cause a favourable or adverse variance, and explain why this might happen, and then explain the impact of this on a business.

| Issue faced by the business | Favourable or adverse variance? | Why might this happen? | Impact on the business |
|---|---|---|---|
| Revenue is lower than budgeted. | | | |
| Raw material costs are higher than budgeted. | | | |
| Labour costs are lower than budgeted. | | | |
| Overheads are higher than budgeted. | | | |
| Gross profit is lower than budgeted. | | | |

**Table 32.3:** Variance situations

## ≪ RECALL AND CONNECT 2 ≪

What is the difference between cash flow forecasts and budgets?

## REFLECTION

Thinking about the exam day, do you know how much time you have to complete each exam? Do you know what equipment you need to take with you? Make sure to look at the *Cambridge International AS & A Level Business Coursebook* and at the resources available from Cambridge Assessment International Education, including past papers for further advice and support.

## SELF-ASSESSMENT CHECKLIST

Let's revisit the Knowledge focus and Exam skills focus for this chapter.
Decide how confident you are with each statement.

| Now I can | Show it | Needs more work | Almost there | Confident to move on |
|-----------|---------|-----------------|--------------|----------------------|
| understand why financial planning is important | State two reasons why financial planning is important to a business. | | | |
| analyse the benefits of setting budgets | Create a revision card detailing the benefits of setting budgets on one side of the card. | | | |
| examine the importance of types of budgeting: incremental, zero and flexible | Why would a firm choose to use each of these types of budgets? Explain your answer to this question. | | | |
| analyse the potential limitations of budgeting | Using the revision card you created to detail the benefits of setting budgets, on the other side write down some of the limitations of setting budgets. | | | |
| use variance analysis to assess adverse and favourable variances from budgets | Go back to Table 32.3. Try to add three different situations to the table and assess the impact of these variances to a business. You may want to use the coursebook chapter to help you identify these. | | | |
| show that I understand a selection of command words that can be used to assess the skills of the same concept in different ways | Look through some past exam papers and find some alternative command words to those in this chapter that have been used to assess the concept of budgets. How would you answer these? | | | |
| find out what to do next in order to improve my preparation for taking my AS Level Business exam | Create a revision planner to support you in preparation for your AS Level Business exams. | | | |

# Exam practice 9

This section contains both past paper questions from previous Cambridge exams and practice questions. These questions draw together your knowledge on a range of topics that you have covered up to this point and will help you prepare for your assessment.

For Question 1(a) and (b) read the question, example student response and commentary provided. Then, in Question 1(c), write an improved answer to Question 1(b) but using a different way from the one in the example student response. Use the guidance in the commentary to help you as you answer the question.

1    a    Define the term 'marketing mix'.                                                      [2]

*Cambridge International AS & A Level Business (9609) Paper 13 Q1a, November 2021*

| Example student response | Examiner comments |
|---|---|
| This is another name for the four Ps, which are the components of effective marketing. | This answer provides not only a basic understanding of what the marketing mix is, but also then develops this for a second rewardable point to explain what the four Ps actually are. Awarded **two** marks. |

    b    Explain **one** way that a business can use the place element of the marketing mix.                                                      [3]

| Example student response | Examiner comments |
|---|---|
| One way a business can use place is to make sure that customers can access its product. | This student understands that place, as part of the marketing mix, is how the customers can access the product, recognising the distribution element involved. However, there is no example of the place element being used in a business context (application). Awarded **one** mark. |

    c    Think of another way that a business can use the place element of the marketing mix and write your own answer to Question 1(b).

Question 2 has example student responses and commentaries provided. For each part of the question, work through the question first, then compare your answer to the example student response and commentary.

2 a Define the term 'business stakeholders'. [2]

*Cambridge International AS & A Level Business (9609) Paper 13 Q2a, November 2021*

| Example student response | Examiner comments |
|---|---|
| Stakeholders are people who own shares in a business. | Very often the term 'shareholder' and 'stakeholder' are confused by students, and this can be seen within this answer. The answer needs to show a clear understanding of stakeholders being 'any individuals or groups who are interested in a business and are affected by their activities'. Awarded **zero** marks. |

b Explain **one** reason why conflict might arise between different stakeholders. [3]

| Example student response | Examiner comments |
|---|---|
| Different stakeholders have different objectives, and it is challenging for all of these objectives to be met at the same time. For example, workers might want to be paid higher wages, but owners might want to make more profits. | In this answer a reason why conflicts might arise is stated, then explained, and a good example is given to further show the students' understanding. Awarded **three** marks. |

For Question 3(a) read the question, example student response and commentary provided. Then, in part (b), write your own answer to the question but using a different reason from the one in the example student response. Use the guidance in the commentary to help you as you answer the question.

3 a Explain **one** reason why it is important for a business to have effective human resource management (HRM). [3]

| Example student response | Examiner comments |
|---|---|
| HRM involves the selection and recruitment of employees. If a firm does not have workers, it cannot operate. | This is a good answer. The student understands the function of human resource management, and why this is important to a business. However, this is not as in-depth an answer as it should be at this level. Awarded **two** marks. To improve this answer, there needs to be more focus on what 'effective' human resource management is and **why** this is important, not just a general impact on the business. |

b Think of another reason why it is important for a business to have effective HRM and write your own answer to Question 3(a).

The following question has an example student response and commentary provided. Work through the question first, then compare your answer to the example student response and commentary.

4 Analyse **two** advantages for a business of a just-in-time (JIT) system of inventory management. [8]

| Example student response | Examiner comments |
|---|---|
| One advantage of a just-in-time (JIT) system of inventory management is that it can keep costs low for a business. This is because by buying inventory only when it is needed, the costs of holding inventory are reduced. This should lead to the business making more profits. However, by using a just-in-time system of inventory, it could be more expensive. Smaller inventory orders are likely to mean the firm is unable to gain significant economies of scale, so its average unit costs might be higher using JIT.

Another advantage of a just-in-time system of inventory management is that it can minimise waste and encourage efficiency. JIT only works if the culture of the organisation is structured and organised. There need to be excellent employee–employer relationships. JIT means there is more flexibility within production. JIT can mean that delivery costs will be high if there are lots of little orders arriving. It can also be a problem if there is an issue with traffic and the business doesn't get its order on time so it can't produce anything. If inventory only arrives when it's needed, then there is less risk of it being damaged than if inventory was being stored for a long period of time. | This answer contains lots of knowledge and understanding about the just-in-time system of inventory management. There is probably too much knowledge shown in this answer. If we look at the second paragraph, this provides a list of benefits and drawbacks relating to just-in-time, which is not an appropriate way to approach questions.

The first paragraph does not provide any specific application to any type of business. The points made are quite generic and not focused on a specific type of business. The second paragraph attempts to apply the points, which it does slightly more successfully through the use of the term 'traffic', which provides an example of a relevant business scenario.

The benefit of using a just-in-time system (low cost) is clearly identified in the first paragraph and the impact on the business is mentioned. The student develops this well by analysing how much the advantage will be felt by the business. The second paragraph contains minimal development of the points that have been made. This is a shame, as the points raised are all valid, but are not linked to each other in a chain or structured argument.

*6/8 marks* |

Here is another practice question which you should attempt. Use the guidance in the commentaries in this section to help you as you answer the question.

5 a Analyse **two** ways business might use break-even analysis when planning to launch a new product. [8]

b Evaluate the factors that directors of a large pharmaceutical company should consider when choosing how to finance growth. [12]

Question 6 has example student responses and commentaries provided. For each part of the question, work through the question first, then compare your answer to the example student response and commentary.

6

## Jim's Farm (JF)

JF is a private limited company which owns a farm. It produces crops including maize and sunflower seeds. The crops are sold to manufacturers that produce cooking oils for supermarkets. Jim is worried, as the price JF receives for its crops is falling. JF is only paid four times a year when the crops are ready, so cash flow is poor. Sam, Jim's son, has recently completed a management degree at university. He is worried that the farm will not reach its break-even point if the price continues to fall. He has researched ways his father could increase the value added to the crops. Sam has identified that healthy eating is a growing trend. He has created a plan for the business which considers two options, shown in Table 1. Sam has identified that supermarkets would buy most of the new products and he could also sell them to independent retailers.

| | Option 1 | Option 2 |
|---|---|---|
| Product | Healthy snacks | Healthy cooking oil |
| Market type | Mass | Niche |
| Start-up capital | $100 000 | $75 000 |
| Annual expenses | $50 000 | $35 000 |
| Annual cost of goods sold | $60 000 | $75 000 |
| Forecast annual market growth | 10% | 15% |
| Forecast annual sales | 300 000 units | 100 000 units |
| Proposed price per unit | $0.50 | $2.00 |

**Table 1:** Options for the future of JF

Figures 1 and 2 show extracts from articles about the two options.

Healthy eating campaigns in schools are changing the way that young people snack and the sales of 'healthy snacks' made from nuts and seeds are growing. Healthy eating is rapidly becoming an important social issue and, for some consumers, quality is more important than price.

**Figure 1:** The rise of the healthy eating campaign

Business analysts are excited about the potential profitability of premium cooking oils, which offer a healthy alternative to traditional products. High-income consumers are prepared to pay high prices for healthy oils made by small independent producers.

**Figure 2:** Future demand for healthy cooking oil

a   i   Define the term 'break-even'. [2]

   *Cambridge International AS & A Level Business (9609) Paper 22
   Q1a i, March 2019*

| Example student response | Examiner comments |
|---|---|
| When a business does not make a profit or a loss. | This answer shows a basic understanding of the term 'break-even'. There needs to be specific reference to the output level. Awarded **one** mark. |

   ii   Explain the term 'value added'. [3]

   *Adapted from Cambridge International AS & A Level Business
   (9609) Paper 22 Q1a ii, March 2019*

| Example student response | Examiner comments |
|---|---|
| The difference between the cost to make a product and the price it is sold for. | This is a good answer to this question. There is clear knowledge of what value added is, with the two main features (cost to make and prices) identified. Awarded **three** marks. |

b   Evaluate which option Jim should choose using the information
    in the case study. [12]

| Example student response | Examiner comments |
|---|---|
| If Jim decides to go with healthy snacks, this provides a new market opportunity for him. Table 1 states that the market is a mass market, which means that there is potential for large amounts of sales, which should lead to positive revenues for Jim. This could also be useful as these revenues are likely to be received all year round, rather than only the four times a year that he is currently receiving. This should provide Jim with a more constant cash flow and more certainty, allowing him to feel more confident in the future of JF. The possibility for success is also backed up with the information in the extract that tells us that healthy eating campaigns in schools are meaning the demand for healthy made snacks is growing. However, this option has incredibly high start-up capital and annual expenses. Jim's son is worried that the farm isn't going to reach its current break-even point, which suggests that it might already be in financial difficulties so it may not actually have the finance available to be able to invest in this new market opportunity and it may need to source finance, which could increase its overall costs. I think that entering the healthy snacks market would be a good business move for Jim. | The student displays an excellent level of knowledge and understanding of the relevant points that need to be considered in decision-making.

Throughout this answer, there are very clear and detailed references to the case study, including the use of data. This information is all used as evidence to strengthen knowledge. Data from the case study has not been added in unnecessarily and all additions have a purpose. The student assesses the impact of their points on JF, exploring relevant consequences, both positive and negative. |

| Example student response | Examiner comments |
|---|---|
| Although he has little experience within this market, he is experienced at running a business in the food industry and the revenue potential from entering this market would be important given the current failure of JF. Jim would probably need to do a little bit more research into the market, assessing what existing competitors there are, how much can be charged for the healthy snacks and how he would make the healthy snacks in order to help him gain success, which I think he will be able to do.<br><br>Option 2 is related to healthy cooking oil. This is a very niche market and has lower forecast annual sales then the healthy snacks (100 000 units compared to 300 000 units). However, because of the higher price that can be charged per unit, the total overall expected revenue is actually higher than the healthy snacks and, given that the annual expenses and start-up capital are also lower, this market may generate more profit for Jim. There is also evidence in the case study that the market is due to grow, and people might be prepared to pay an even higher price for good-quality cooking oils, making this an even more attractive option for Jim. If Jim decides to sell healthy cooking oil, then this links with what he is already doing, so he has got experience in doing this, which should mean that it is more successful. | This answer contains some developed evaluation at the end of the first paragraph, where a good two-sided argument is given with an overall judgement that is contextual, providing a piece of developed evaluation. However, the answer fails to provide an actual answer to the question to specify which option Jim should actually take, which would have improved the answer.<br><br>*10/12 marks* |

c   Analyse **two** suitable sources of finance JF could use for the option
    you have chosen in Question 6(b).                                    [8]
    *Adapted from Cambridge International AS & A Level Business (9609)
        Paper 22 Q1d, March 2019*

| Example student response | Examiner comments |
|---|---|
| One suitable source of finance for JF is to sell shares. Jim could turn his farm into a PLC and put it on the stock market so he could sell his shares and raise the money needed to invest in developing his farm.<br><br>Another suitable source of finance would be an overdraft. He could use his overdraft to pay for any costs involved in running his business and as he is already an Ltd, the bank will definitely give him an overdraft to use. | The student shows some knowledge of two sources of finance: shares and an overdraft.<br><br>There is reference to the business context provided through a reference to what the finance will be used for (developing the farm) and the fact the business is already running as an LTD.<br><br>The answer does not provide any implications of the sources of finance being selected on JF, for example, turning into a PLC would mean Jim would lose control, or it would be expensive for JF to do and an overdraft is likely to have high interest rates and need to be repaid quite quickly, affecting the cash flow of JF.<br><br>*4/8 marks* |

Question 7 parts (a) and (b) have example student responses and commentaries provided. For each part of the question, work through the question first, then compare your answer to the example student response and commentary.

**7**

> ### Umpire Umbrellas (UU)
>
> UU is a private limited company that sells umbrellas with pictures it prints on them. All of the pictures on the umbrellas are printed using batch production. The umbrellas can be used to shelter from the rain or as a shade from the sun. The company has two main markets: consumer and business. UU sells individual umbrellas to consumers. These have pictures of famous people or places on them. They are mainly sold through UU's website. UU produces 20 000 of each design. The business market for UU is made up of businesses that want their logo printed on a large number of umbrellas. UU guarantees all business orders are delivered within ten days. Recently, UU received an order from a large bank for 10 000 umbrellas with the bank's logo printed on them.
>
> The bank gave an umbrella to any customer who opened a new account. The fixed cost for the order was $2000 and the variable costs were $0.75 per unit. UU made $3000 profit on the order. UU's board of directors has been considering two different options to grow the business.
>
> #### Option 1
>
> UU would sell franchise opportunities to entrepreneurs who can print and sell UU branded umbrellas to the consumer market in the entrepreneur's local area. These entrepreneurs would pay a fee to UU as well as 10% royalties on the profits. In return UU would provide the machinery needed to print the umbrellas. The franchisee would be required to purchase all of their inventory from UU.
>
> #### Option 2
>
> UU would increase its product portfolio by selling other goods to the business market, such as pens, USB sticks and clothing. This would require external finance to purchase the machinery needed to be able to print on these products. The market for these is growing but very competitive.

a    i    Define the term 'consumer'.    [2]

**Cambridge International AS & A Level Business (9609) Paper 22 Q2a i, June 2018**

| Example student response | Examiner comments |
|---|---|
| Somebody who buys a product. | This student has confused the term consumer with customer and provided a definition of what a customer is. Awarded **zero** marks. A consumer is somebody who uses a product, but not necessarily the person who buys the product. |

ii Explain the term 'variable costs'. [3]

*Adapted from Cambridge International AS & A Level Business (9609) Paper 22 Q2a ii, June 2018*

| Example student response | Examiner comments |
|---|---|
| This is a cost that changes. | This answer attempts to show some understanding that the variable cost is one that does change; however, all costs are likely to change at some point. It must be referenced that changes are related to levels of production to gain any knowledge and understanding marks. Awarded **zero** marks. An example of a variable cost would also help to improve this answer further. |

**b** i Calculate the total revenue of the order from the large bank. [3]

*Adapted from Cambridge International AS & A Level Business (9609) Paper 22 Q2b i, June 2018*

| Example student response | Examiner comments |
|---|---|
| Total revenue – total costs = profit<br><br>Total costs = FC + VC<br><br>$2000 + ($0.75 × 10000) = $9500<br><br>$9500 + $3000 = $12500 | The student has realised that the case study does not have the revenue figure and that is what they need to work out, which they do by reordering the formula. Very clear workings are shown, allowing the thought processes behind the answer to be seen. Awarded **three** marks. |

ii Explain **one** reason why UU needs accurate cost data. [3]

*Cambridge International AS & A Level Business (9609) Paper 22 Q2b ii, June 2018*

| Example student response | Examiner comments |
|---|---|
| Accurate cost data is important so it can calculate how much profit it has made. | This is a relatively straightforward answer that provides a reason why a business might need accurate cost data. There is no application to UU so only knowledge is demonstrated. Awarded **one** mark. |

Now you should attempt parts (c) and (d). Use the guidance in the commentaries in this section to help you as you answer the questions.

c   Analyse **two** advantages to UU of using batch production.          [8]

   *Cambridge International AS & A Level Business (9609) Paper 22 Q2c, June 2018*

d   Evaluate which of the two options for growth UU should use.          [12]

# 33 Financial statements

## KNOWLEDGE FOCUS

You will answer questions on:

**33.1** Statement of profit or loss

**33.2** The statement of financial position: Meaning and purpose

**33.3** Inventory valuation

**33.4** Depreciation

## EXAM SKILLS FOCUS

In this chapter you will:

- practise your calculation skills in relation to statements of profit or loss and of financial position

- further practise managing your time on Paper 4 questions.

In this chapter you will practise your understanding of how to calculate statements of profit or loss and statements of financial position for a business given a set of data. Both statements require several calculations, and practising these will help increase your confidence.

Paper 4 consists of two compulsory essay questions, each worth 20 marks. You will need to allow time to read the case material as well as plan your answers before you write them. For each question, plan to spend about half of your planning/writing time on each side of the argument. Also remember to leave time to write a conclusion and to check your answer.

## 33.1 Statement of profit or loss

1   Identify some of the uses of the statement of profit or loss.

2

| | Million rupees | | | | | |
|---|---|---|---|---|---|---|
| | 2014 | 2015 | 2016 | 2017 | 2018 | 2019 |
| Revenue | 3332 | 3363 | 5011 | 7369 | 12154 | 14850 |
| Cost of sales | 2819 | 2802 | 4039 | 6304 | 10542 | 12820 |
| Gross profit | | | | | | |
| Expenses | 254 | 267 | 369 | 364 | 725 | 871 |
| Profit from operations (operating profit) | | | | | | |
| Taxation (25%) | | | | | | |
| Profit for the year | | | | | | |
| Dividends (30%) | | | | | | |
| Retained earnings | | | | | | |

**Table 33.1:** Nimir Industrial accounting data

Referring to Table 33.1, calculate the gross profit, operating profit, taxation paid, profit for the year, size of dividends and retained earnings for Nimir Industrial for each year between 2014 and 2019.

3   Calculate the statement of profit and loss for Nimir Industrial for the years 2020 and 2021 assuming a 20% rise in sales revenue (each year), a 20% rise in cost of sales (each year) and a 10% rise (each year) in expenses.

**REFLECTION**

Do you feel confident that you are able to calculate both gross and net profit from a given set of data? Would you be able to show your working? You will need to identify how you calculated gross profit (revenue – cost of sales) and net profit (gross profit – overheads/expenses). You can still score marks for incorrect answers if you have shown the correct working.

4   Evaluate Nimir's financial performance between 2014 and 2019.          [20]

**REFLECTION**

You should now reflect on the timing you allowed yourself to answer Question 4. How did you decide how long you would allocate for this? Did you run out of time and not complete your answer, or did you have time to spare? What have you learnt from doing this timing activity?

**《 RECALL AND CONNECT 1 《**

How will businesses use profit or loss and other financial statements from previous years to support their future planning and strategy?

## 33.2 The statement of financial position: Meaning and purpose

**1** Explain the difference between current and non-current liabilities.

**2** Explain the difference between current and non-current assets.

**3** Explain **one** purpose of a statement of financial position. [3]

When completing Question 4 be careful not to state that the published accounts could be 'wrong' because this is not the same as a limitation. Limitations should be focused only on limitations of the accounts process to investors. Also note that because the question asks you to analyse two limitations, you will not be rewarded for including advantages in your response.

**4** Analyse **two** limitations to investors of using published accounts to decide whether to invest in Nimir Industrial. [8]

**REFLECTION**

Have you studied the definition of the historical nature of published accounts, for example, how much performance from previous years can tell us about the current state of the business?

**《 RECALL AND CONNECT 2 《**

What business tools do organisations use to compare predicted financial and income statements with the actual ones once they are published?

## 33.3 Inventory valuation

**1** How is NRV calculated?

**《 RECALL AND CONNECT 3 《**

**a** Which types of private business structures are required by law to publish accounts? Which are not required by law?

**b** What are the **two** methods of inventory management system that organisations employ to calculate inventory values?

**UNDERSTAND THESE TERMS**

- shareholders' equity
- trade receivables (debtors)
- trade payables (creditors)
- non-current liabilities
- net assets
- net current assets
- reserves

**UNDERSTAND THIS TERM**

- net realisable value (NRV)

# 33.4 Depreciation

1   State **two** reasons why assets decline in value.

2   Explain the impact of depreciation on the statement of financial position and the statement of profit and loss.

3

|  | 2020 | 2021 |
|---|---|---|
| **Non-current assets** |  |  |
| Property (factory and office) | $11 000 000 | b |
| Machinery | $14 600 000 | c |
| Intangible assets | $2 000 000 | d |
|  | a | e |
| **Current assets** |  |  |
| Value of inventory | $3 000 000 | $3 500 000 |
| Cash | $330 000 | $300 000 |
| Trade receivables | $4 600 000 | $4 200 000 |
|  | f | g |
| **Total assets** | h | i |
| **Equity and liabilities** |  |  |
| **Current liabilities** |  |  |
| Trade payables | $3 400 000 | $3 600 000 |
| Overdraft | $325 000 | $330 000 |
| Tax owed | $250 000 | $250 000 |
|  | j | k |
| **Non-current liabilities** |  |  |
| Bank loans | $8 000 000 | $6 800 000 |
| **Total liabilities** | l | m |
| **Shareholders' equity** |  |  |
| Share capital | $22 000 000 | $23 000 000 |
| Retained earnings | $1 000 000 | $20 000 |
| Other reserves | $455 000 | $200 000 |
| **Total equity and liabilities** | n | o |

**Table 33.2:** Current value of a company's total assets in 2020 and 2021

Calculate each of the missing values in Table 33.2 (a–o), if the firm depreciates its fixed assets by 5%.

## REFLECTION

How can you remember the difference between assets and liabilities, and the difference between shareholders' equity and long-term liabilities? You could make revision cards to remember the terms 'current assets', 'non-current assets', 'current liabilities', 'non-current liabilities', 'shareholders' equity' and 'liabilities'.

## « RECALL AND CONNECT 4 «

How are different sources of finance illustrated on a financial statement such as the one in Table 33.2?

## SELF-ASSESSMENT CHECKLIST

Let's revisit the Knowledge focus and Exam skills focus for this chapter.
Decide how confident you are with each statement.

| Now I can | Show it | Needs more work | Almost there | Confident to move on |
|---|---|---|---|---|
| analyse the need for businesses to keep accounts | Make a list of all of the stakeholders for either Nimir Industrial or another business. For each one, explain why they are interested in reading the organisation's financial accounts. | | | |
| analyse the main components of a statement of profit or loss (income statement) | Write the nine components of a statement of profit or loss (income statement) and then test yourself, by writing out a statement using your own figures. Extend your knowledge by changing one or more of the variables and then rewriting the income statement to reflect those changes. | | | |

## CONTINUED

| | | | | |
|---|---|---|---|---|
| analyse the main components of a statement of financial position | Write the following components of a statement of financial position on revision cards: non-current assets, current assets, current liabilities, non-current liabilities, shareholders' equity, share capital. On the reverse, identify different examples of each. Then test yourself on the contents of the revision card. | | | |
| evaluate the importance of inventory valuation | Imagine you work in a factory storeroom and are in charge of ensuring that the inventory under your control is valued correctly. Write a short personal specification for your position explaining the importance of your role and identify some of the problems that might emerge if inventory was overvalued or undervalued. | | | |
| evaluate the importance of depreciation | Write a short letter to the directors of a company explaining the impact on both the organisation's profit or loss and financial statement if depreciation was not used to revalue fixed assets annually. | | | |
| practise calculation skills in relation to statements of profit or loss and of financial position | Practise completing gross and net profit as well as calculating the value of assets and liabilities from a given set of data. | | | |
| further practise managing time on Paper 4 questions | Practise exam responses for different Paper 4 questions using the allocated time available. | | | |

# 34 Analysis of published accounts

Understanding what is required to achieve certain marks is important for students but it can be a challenge. This chapter includes an opportunity to learn about mark scheme awareness, by annotating a sample student response.

It is important to focus on establishing a consistent pre-exam routine to help you manage test anxiety. Everyone will use a different routine, but make sure that you get plenty of sleep the night before (you should not stay up all night revising) and eat a good meal before the exam.

# 34.1 Liquidity ratios

## UNDERSTAND THESE TERMS

- current ratio
- acid test ratio

**1**

| | Coca-Cola ($ millions) | PepsiCo ($ millions) |
|---|---|---|
| Revenue (all sales on credit) | 37 266 | 67 161 |
| Gross profit | 22 647 | 37 029 |
| Operating profit | 10 086 | 10 291 |
| Current assets | 20 411 | 17 645 |
| Current liabilities | 26 973 | 20 461 |
| Average inventory | 3225 | 3233 |
| Trade receivable | 3971 | 7822 |
| Average cash balance | 13 215 | 6590 |
| Capital employed | 59 408 | 59 086 |

**Table 34.1:** Comparing the accounts of the cola giants (2019)

Calculate the current ratio and acid test ratio for both Coca-Cola and PepsiCo. using the figures from Table 34.1.

Copy the sample student answer for Question 2 and then write either knowledge (K), application (Ap), analysis (An) or evaluation (E) to indicate where each assessment objective is demonstrated.

**2** Evaluate the usefulness of liquidity ratios to potential investors in a business. [12]

Liquidity ratios are an important class of financial metrics used to determine a debtor's ability to pay off current debt obligations without raising external capital. Common liquidity ratios include the acid test and current ratio. An investor is any person or other entity (such as a firm or mutual fund) which commits capital with the expectation of receiving financial returns.

Potential investors in a business need to know that the business they invest in has the ability to survive and be profitable in the longer term. A business that is unable to meet its current liabilities in unlikely to survive, even if it is profitable. A business that cannot meet its current liabilities will find that banks might recall overdrafts or that suppliers will refuse to supply the business due to a lack of payment for goods supplied or fear of lack of payment.

An unsatisfactory liquidity ratio could indicate poor management or poor decision-making, which might deter potential investors. Alternatively, poor liquidity might be a consequence of a fast-growing business, where the business overextends itself in terms of spending to facilitate that growth. This could be highlighted by the liquidity ratio. Has the business arranged a large overdraft? Is it taking on more employees?

For most businesses, the current ratio is an adequate measure of liquidity and so can be used by investors to measure the success of a business but there will be exceptions to this rule – when it does not provide an accurate metric for investors. An example of this might be when a business holds a high level of inventory, which may not be easy to turn into cash. In such a case, the acid test ratio is a better measure as it excludes stock levels from its value of current assets. This may be typical of many retail businesses, for example.

In conclusion, potential investors would consider a firm's liquidity ratios when making an investment decision but must consider other factors as well, e.g., profit trends, while any analysis must compare any financial information with other businesses in the same industry.

## ≪ RECALL AND CONNECT 1 ≪

Explain the difference between a firm's cash flow and its liquidity.

## 34.2 Profitability ratios

### UNDERSTAND THESE TERMS

- profitability
- gross profit margin ratio
- operating profit margin
- return on capital employed (RoCE) ratio
- capital employed

1   Using Table 34.1 as a reference, calculate the gross profit and profit margin for both Coca-Cola and PepsiCo, as well as the return on capital employed.

2   Evaluate how Coca-Cola might improve its profitability.                          [12]

### REFLECTION

How well do you understand the concept of profitability that you needed to successfully answer this Exam skills question? How will you learn the difference between profitability and the related concept of liquidity? Do you understand the importance of providing a suitable conclusion in an 'evaluate' question?

## ≪ RECALL AND CONNECT 2 ≪

Explain the link between profitability and the size of an organisation.

# 34.3 Financial efficiency ratios

## UNDERSTAND THESE TERMS

- rate of inventory turnover
- trade receivables turnover (days)
- trade payables turnover (days)
- credit purchases

1

|  | Coca-Cola ($ millions) | PepsiCo ($ millions) |
|---|---|---|
| Revenue (all sales on credit) | 37 266 | 67 161 |
| Cost of sales | 8100 | 30 132 |
| Average inventory | 3225 | 3233 |
| Trade receivable | 3971 | 7822 |
| Trade payable | 2856 | 6490 |

**Table 34.2:** Supplementary information on the accounts of the cola giants

Referring to Table 34.2, calculate the inventory turnover ratio and trade receivables (days).

Question 2 assesses your ability to use the command word 'analyse'. In this example, this means that you should provide two ways that PepsiCo could improve their financial efficiency and support each way with evidence or argument.

Use the following checklist to write out a response for Question 2; then compare your response to the answer provided in the Chapter 34 Answers section.

- Comment on improving financial efficiency only. You should not comment on methods that might increase profitability, liquidity or shareholder ratios.

- Identify that financial efficiency or activity ratios measure how efficiently the resources/assets of a business are being used.

- Include the asset turnover ratio, trade payables (creditor) days ratio and trade receivables ratio.

- Include ways that each of the above might be improved, e.g., reducing inventory levels, reducing the time for debtors to pay by offering discounts, increasing the time to pay creditors just-in-time inventory management.

- Include a recognition that some of these measures, while improving efficiency, may affect other factors adversely, e.g., discounts for prompt or early payment, reduction in the gross/operating profit margin.

- Include two different ways that PepsiCo can improve its financial efficiency.

- Write in full sentences and use separate paragraphs to highlight each separate point that you make.

2   Using Table 34.2, analyse **two** ways in which PepsiCo could improve their financial efficiency.   [8]

<< RECALL AND CONNECT 3 <<

Explain the link between efficiency and the size of an organisation.

## 34.4 Gearing ratio

1   Identify the meaning and importance of a firm's gearing ratio.

2

| | Coca-Cola ($ millions) | PepsiCo ($ millions) |
| --- | --- | --- |
| Current liabilities | 26 973 | 20 461 |
| Non-current liabilities | 27 516 | 9979 |
| Capital employed | 59 408 | 59 086 |

**Table 34.3:** Additional financial information of the cola giants

a   Using Table 34.3, calculate the gearing ratio for Coca-Cola.   [3]
b   Using Table 34.3, calculate the gearing ratio for PepsiCo.   [3]

<< RECALL AND CONNECT 4 <<

Explain the strengths and weaknesses of loan and equity-based sources of finance.

## 34.5 Investment ratios

1   Explain **two** possible effects of a board of directors' decision to take a high level of retained earnings.

Use the following checklist to write out a response for Question 2 before comparing your response to the one provided in the Chapter 34 Answers section.

- Demonstrate your knowledge of accounting ratios in your response.

- Make sure you include two of the following ratios: RoCE, dividend yield, gross/operating profit margins.

- Make sure you spend roughly half the time on each of the two ways.

- As the command word is 'evaluate', make sure you balance your response, including both strengths and weaknesses for each of the two ways you include.

- Make sure you write in full sentences and use separate paragraphs to highlight each separate point that you make.

- Include a conclusion in which you make an overall judgement on your response.

**UNDERSTAND THIS TERM**

- gearing ratio

**UNDERSTAND THESE TERMS**

- share price
- dividend
- dividend yield ratio
- dividend per share
- dividend cover ratio
- price/earnings ratio
- earnings per share

2   Evaluate **two** ways in which a business could improve its investment
    ratio results in future.

## ≪ RECALL AND CONNECT 5 ≪

a   Is it possible for a business to grow quickly without high levels
    of borrowing?

b   Does franchising provide a way of enabling a business to grow without
    the organisation running a dangerous level of gearing?

## SELF-ASSESSMENT CHECKLIST

Let's revisit the Knowledge focus and Exam skills focus for this chapter.
Decide how confident you are with each statement.

| Now I can | Show it | Needs more work | Almost there | Confident to move on |
|---|---|---|---|---|
| calculate liquidity ratios and evaluate methods of improving liquidity | Investigate a series of financial tables from an organisation's statements of profit or loss and financial statements. Calculate the current ratio and acid test ratio. Consider ways that the business might be able to improve its liquidity. | | | |
| calculate profitability ratios and evaluate methods of improving profitability | Using the figures identified earlier, calculate the gross and operating profit margin. Consider ways that the business might be able to improve its profitability. | | | |
| calculate financial efficiency ratios and evaluate methods of improving financial efficiency | Using the same figures, calculate the following financial efficiency ratios: rate of inventory turnover, trade receivables turnover (days), trade payables turnover (days). Then list some ways the business could improve each ratio. Compare with the methods you identified to improve liquidity. | | | |
| calculate gearing ratios and evaluate methods of improving gearing | Calculate the gearing ratio for different businesses. Describe some disadvantages of having a high gearing ratio and explain ways a firm can reduce its gearing level. | | | |

| CONTINUED | | | | |
|---|---|---|---|---|
| calculate investor ratios and evaluate methods of improving returns to investors | Using earlier figures, calculate the following investor ratios: dividend yield ratio, dividend per share, dividend cover ratio, price/earnings ratio (P/E ratio), earnings per share. Explain how the business might improve the returns to its investors. | | | |
| learn mark scheme awareness | As part of your study plan, read through the Exam practice sections. Make a note of how each example student response is completed. Try to recognise the difference between responses to questions with different command words and different mark allocations. Practise annotating responses using AO1–AO4. | | | |
| manage test anxiety | As part of your revision/study preparation, learn the importance of relaxation, exercise, regular sleep patterns and, finally, controlling the way you breathe. A focus on taking deep breaths can reduce your test anxiety and improve your preparation for the exam. | | | |

# 35 Investment appraisal

## KNOWLEDGE FOCUS

You will answer questions on:

**35.1** What is meant by investment appraisal?

**35.2** Quantitative techniques: Payback and accounting rate of return

**35.3** Quantitative techniques: Discounted cash flow

**35.4** Investment appraisal decisions

## EXAM SKILLS FOCUS

In this chapter you will:

- develop your metacognitive practice by trying out a range of metacognition strategies

- practise using diagrams to make connections between different concepts within and between chapters.

When studying for your course it is useful for you to understand metacognitive practice. There are various metacognition strategies you can try when you revise. Do not keep your studies to yourself; verbalising your thoughts can help you make more sense of the material so talk through your material with other students, friends and teachers. Brainstorm your own questions and consider: does this answer make sense and how can I solve this? Take notes when you read something; the process of writing out a concept is more effective at helping you to remember it than simply reading alone.

To help you understand connections between concepts, use a concept map, a mind map or a spider diagram to visualise material and recognise the connections between the various concepts you are learning.

## 35.1 What is meant by investment appraisal?

### UNDERSTAND THESE TERMS

- net present value (NPV)
- investment appraisal
- forecasted net cash flow

1   What quantitative information must a business collect before making an accurate investment exercise of any project under consideration?

2   Describe some of the disadvantages of using quantitative appraisal techniques when making an investment decision.

In Question 3, make sure you demonstrate your knowledge and apply it to the information in Table 35.1 so that it supports or justifies the conclusions that you have made.

3

### Jill's Snacks (JS)

JS is a large and well-established company making healthy snacks for children. The company is considering investing in a wind power project at its main factory to reduce costs. It has identified the following three projects for consideration.

| | Initial cost of the investment ($) | Year 1 return ($) | Year 2 return ($) | Year 3 return ($) | Year 4 return ($) | Year 5 return ($) | Scrap value (year 6) ($) |
|---|---|---|---|---|---|---|---|
| Project A | 100 000 000 | 20 000 000 | 20 000 000 | 25 000 000 | 25 000 000 | 25 000 000 | 10 000 000 |
| Project B | 95 000 000 | 40 000 000 | 30 000,000 | 20 000 000 | 10 000 000 | 10 000 000 | 0 |
| Project C | 135 000 000 | 30 000 000 | 35 000 000 | 35 000 000 | 35 000 000 | 35 000 000 | 25 000 000 |

**Table 35.1:** Summary of the cost and expected return on each project

Advise JS on which project it should invest in.          [12]

### REFLECTION

Have you practised calculating payback period, ARR and NPV for a range of different projects? Remember that calculating different methods of investment appraisal is best mastered by practice.

### ≪ RECALL AND CONNECT 1 ≪

Explain the role of investment appraisal in the budgeting process.

## 35.2 Quantitative techniques: Payback and accounting rate of return

### UNDERSTAND THESE TERMS

- payback period
- accounting rate of return (ARR)

**1** Which of the two methods, payback period or ARR, is the most important for JS to consider when deciding which project to invest in?

**2** **a** Analyse **two** benefits to a business of using the payback period. [8]

   **b** Analyse **two** benefits to a business of using ARR. [8]

### REFLECTION

Are you able to describe two benefits of payback period and two benefits of the ARR as methods of investment? Which of the metacognitive techniques mentioned earlier could you use to improve your recall of benefits of different methods?

### ≪ RECALL AND CONNECT 2 ≪

Explain the role of cash flow and organisational liquidity when choosing which investment appraisal technique to prioritise when deciding on a suitable investment project.

## 35.3 Quantitative techniques: Discounted cash flow

### UNDERSTAND THIS TERM

- discounted cash flows

**1** Explain the advantages and disadvantages of using the net present value (NPV) method of investment appraisal.

**2** Which of the following describes an advantage of the use of the NPV appraisal technique, rather than payback or ARR?

Option A. Unlike the payback period and ARR, NPV considers both the size of the net cash flows as well as the timing of them.

Option B. Unlike the payback period and ARR, NPV considers the minimum (required) criteria of any investment.

Option C. Unlike the payback period and ARR, NPV considers the amount of money borrowed/invested in calculating any business decision.

Option D. Unlike the payback period and ARR, NPV also considers the time the rate of inflation in any calculation.

| Year | 1 | 2 | 3 | 4 | 5 | 6 |
|---|---|---|---|---|---|---|
| | 0.93 | 0.86 | 0.79 | 0.74 | 0.68 | 0.63 |

**Table 35.2:** Discount factors (for an interest rate of 8%)

3   Using the discounted factors figures in Table 35.2, calculate the net present value of the three projects identified by JS in Table 35.1. Write your answers in a copy of Table 35.3.

| Value of the investment | Project A | Project B | Project C |
|---|---|---|---|
| Initial cost | $100 000 000 | $95 000 000 | $135 000 000 |
| Year 1 | | | |
| Year 2 | | | |
| Year 3 | | | |
| Year 4 | | | |
| Year 5 | | | |
| Year 6 | | | |
| Net present value of the investment | | | |

**Table 35.3:** Estimated returns

REFLECTION

How will you learn the different methods of investment appraisal: payback period, ARR and discounted cashflow?

« RECALL AND CONNECT 3 «

Explain the difference between a firm's cash flow and the discounted cash flow investment appraisal technique? Why is it important for organisations to 'discount' the value of cash receipts coming into the business when deciding on the viability of a specific project?

# 35.4 Investment appraisal decisions

1 Compile a list of **five** qualitative factors that might have an impact on any business decision.

2 Copy Table 35.4. Use it to explain the strengths and weakness of the three investment appraisal techniques identified in this chapter.

| | Payback | ARR | NPV |
|---|---|---|---|
| What is being measured? | | | |
| When is it most useful? | | | |
| Major limitations | | | |

**Table 35.4:** Investment appraisal methods

3 Refer to Tables 35.1, 35.2 and 35.3. Evaluate the project in which JS should invest. [12]

## SELF-ASSESSMENT CHECKLIST

Let's revisit the Knowledge focus and Exam skills focus for this chapter.
Decide how confident you are with each statement.

| Now I can | Show it | Needs more work | Almost there | Confident to move on |
|---|---|---|---|---|
| explain what investment means and the need for appraising investment projects | Make a list of all of the things that might go wrong if a firm commits to an investment project without first completing an appraisal of the likely return from the investment. | | | |
| analyse the meaning, calculation and interpretation of the payback method of investment appraisal | Write out expected returns for a range of different projects and then calculate the payback period for each of the projects. Remember to calculate the payback period to the nearest month or day. | | | |
| analyse the meaning, calculation and interpretation of the ARR method of investment appraisal | Use the figures you created for the previous task to complete the ARR for each project. Compare the two sets of figures. Which offers the best investment from a payback perspective and which offers the best ARR? Which do you believe is the more important for businesses to consider when considering which investment project to complete? | | | |
| analyse the meaning, calculation and interpretation of the NPV method of investment appraisal | Using the figures you created for the last two tasks, use the discounted cash flow method to calculate the net present value of each project and explain why this method of appraisal presents a more relevant method than either ARR or payback periods. | | | |

## CONTINUED

| | | | | |
|---|---|---|---|---|
| evaluate quantitative results and their impact on investment decisions | Using the results that you created in the payback period, ARR and NPV tasks, consider which of the investment projects offers the best return based on the calculations that you have made. | | | |
| evaluate qualitative factors and their impact on investment decisions | For the results that you created in the payback period, ARR and NPV tasks, consider some of the non-quantitative factors that might mean that the figures presented are not necessarily an accurate prediction. | | | |
| compare investment appraisal methods, including their limitations | Review the strengths and weaknesses table you completed for Question 2 in Section 35.4. Write out revision/flash cards for each of the appraisal methods from this chapter and on the reverse of each card write out the strengths and limitations for each. | | | |
| develop my metacognitive practice by trying out a range of metacognition strategies | Brainstorm your own questions and use concept maps or graphic organisers to visualise material and see the connections between the various concepts you are learning. | | | |
| practise using diagrams to make connections between different concepts within and between chapters | Complete a mind map showing connections between each of the sections of this chapter, as well as where each links to other chapters in the coursebook. You may find that the Recall and connect questions act as a guide in this task. | | | |

# 36 Finance and accounting strategy

Do not underestimate the importance of unfocused time because this allows your brain to learn new things. Try the Pomodoro Technique, which involves working for 25 minutes and then taking a break for five minutes.

There are relaxation techniques that you can use to manage test anxiety. Focus on staying calm and confident right before and during your exam. Meditation or listening to relaxing music can help to calm your mind. Some students find that closing their eyes and imagining a positive outcome can also help. Relax tight muscles by stretching, standing or walking around. In addition, you can slow down a racing heart or help reduce anxious feelings with deep breathing.

# 36.1 The use of accounting data in strategic decision-making

1   Describe the contents of an annual report.

2   Copy and complete the stakeholder diagram provided in Figure 36.1, explaining how each of the stakeholders would make use of the annual report.

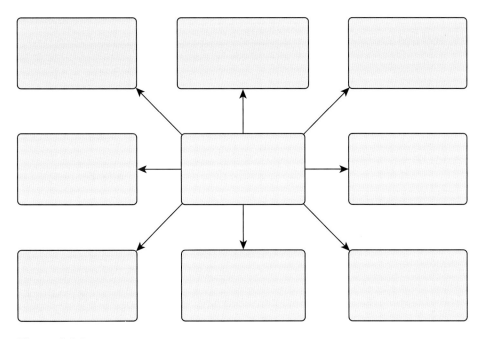

**Figure 36.1:** Stakeholder diagram

3   Explain the main uses of information in annual reports for five different business stakeholder groups.

<< RECALL AND CONNECT 1 <<

Explain why public limited companies are required to publish their annual report each year while other forms of business are not.

# 36.2 The use of accounting data and ratio analysis

| Rupees (m) | 2016 | 2017 | 2018 | 2019 | 2020 | 2021 |
|---|---|---|---|---|---|---|
| Revenue | 5011 | 7369 | 12154 | 14850 | 16355 | 17990.5 |
| Cost of sales (50% of sales revenue) | 2505 | 3684 | 6077 | 7425 | 8167.5 | 8995.25 |
| Gross profit | 2505 | 3684 | 6077 | 7425 | 8167.5 | 8995.25 |
| Overheads/expenses | 1000 | 1100 | 1400 | 1800 | 1470 | 1890 |
| Profit | 1505 | 2584 | 4677 | 5625 | 6697.5 | 7105.25 |
| Tax (25%) | 376.25 | 646 | 1169.25 | 1406.25 | 1674.38 | 1776.31 |
| Profit after tax | 1881.25 | 1938 | 3507.75 | 4218.75 | 5023.13 | 5328.94 |
| Dividends to shareholders (30%) | 564.38 | 581.4 | 1052.33 | 1265.63 | 1506.94 | 1598.68 |
| Retained earnings | **1316.88** | **1356.6** | **2455.43** | **2953.13** | **3516.19** | **37230** |
| Current assets | 2300 | 2060 | 4590 | 6700 | 7250 | 7350 |
| Current liabilities | 2100 | 1950 | 4100 | 6250 | 6950 | 7100 |

**Table 36.1:** Nimir Industrial accounting data

1 Explain some of the factors that determine the level of annual dividend paid to shareholders.

2 Explain the likely impact of the following business strategies on the ratio results of Nimir Industrial.

- rationalisation
- new product development
- market development
- low price strategy.

Question 3 provides an opportunity to understand 'what a good one looks like'. When the command word is 'evaluate', you will need to include all AO1–AO4 objectives. A sample answer has been provided for you, but it is not an example of a 'good' answer. Using your knowledge of exam skills, you should create an improved answer to Question 3.

3 Evaluate the impact of ratio results on Nimir's future business strategy. [20]

Accountants will use ratio analysis to measure the financial performance of a business. By comparing different accounting ratios with comparable businesses, Nimir will be able to compare its performance with other businesses in the same field.

There are a number of different methods of ratio analysis but the two that can be derived from the table are liquidity and profitability ratios. Liquidity ratios include the current ratio, calculated by current assets divided by current liabilities. This assesses whether Nimir has sufficient assets to cover its liabilities. A ratio of two shows there are twice as many current assets as current liabilities. A ratio in excess of one shows liquidity levels are sufficient because there are sufficient current assets (cash or liquid assets) to cover the firm's current liabilities. Encouragingly, the current ratio of Nimir exceeds this figure in every year of the table.

A second ratio that can be derived from the table is the profitability ratio. Both the gross and net operating profit margins can be derived from the table and this ratio is of particular significance when it is compared with comparable businesses. By dividing net profit before tax by the total value of capital employed we can learn the RoCE (return on capital employed) to see how good the business is at turning capital into profit. This ratio is of particular interest to shareholders when they decide how to invest their capital.

Efficiency ratios can also be derived from the table, for example, the debtors' turnover, which measures the average number of days it takes Nimir to collect payments from its customers. Creditors' turnover, by contrast, measures the number of days it takes Nimir to pay suppliers, while finally the stock turnover ratio measures the number of days for which the business holds stock.

In conclusion, accounting ratios are useful for potential investors and interested parties for the information included. However, the limitations of accounting ratios are also obvious and therefore any stakeholders using them should be aware of those limitations.

## ≪ RECALL AND CONNECT 2 ≪

Explain how the economic performance of a business has an impact on its overall strategic plan.

## REFLECTION

How could you incorporate relaxation techniques into your revision time? You could try the following technique. Close your eyes and breathe deeply, taking long, deep breaths. Ensure that your muscles are relaxed and your body position is correct. For example, ensure that your shoulders are pushed back. Hold them in this position for a few seconds and then relax. Repeat this every 40–50 minutes. Does this help reduce any anxiety you may have?

## SELF-ASSESSMENT CHECKLIST

Let's revisit the Knowledge focus and Exam skills focus for this chapter.
Decide how confident you are with each statement.

| Now I can | Show it | Needs more work | Almost there | Confident to move on |
|---|---|---|---|---|
| apply accounting data to strategic decision-making | Use the accounting data in Table 36.1 to devise a strategic plan for Nimir Industrial for the years 2022–2026. Include some of the following elements of a strategic plan: vision, mission, SWOT analysis, core values, goals, objectives and action plans. | | | |
| evaluate business performance using accounting data and ratio analysis | Use the accounting data in Table 36.1 to evaluate the business performance of Nimir Industrial, using accounting data and ratio analysis for the period 2016–2021. | | | |
| assess the impact of accounting data and ratio analysis on business strategy | Assess how the accounting data in Table 36.1 might impact on the following areas of business strategy: vision statements, mission and value statements, long-term goals for the business, financial and operational objectives, SWOT and Nimir's action plans. | | | |
| evaluate the impact of strategic decisions on ratio results | Explain how the strategic decisions made to satisfy the goals and mission of Nimir Industrial might impact on the ratios of the company. Refer to Table 36.1 in your response. | | | |
| evaluate the usefulness of published accounts and ratio analysis | Identify how each of the stakeholders of Nimir Industrial might use the published accounts and ratio analysis from Table 36.1. | | | |

## CONTINUED

| | | | | |
|---|---|---|---|---|
| understand the importance of focused and unfocused time while I am learning | Review the revision schedule you prepared and ensure that it includes both focused and unfocused time. To do this, you will need to experiment with how long you are able to concentrate for without losing your focus and then build this into your schedule. | | | |
| manage test anxiety by using relaxation techniques | Ensure your revision schedule includes a note to remind yourself to relax and keep your muscles loose. | | | |

# Exam practice 10

This section contains both past paper questions from previous Cambridge exams and practice questions. These questions draw together your knowledge on a range of topics that you have covered up to this point and will help you prepare for your assessment.

Question 1 has example student responses and commentaries provided. For each part of the question, work through the question first, then compare your answer to the example student response and commentary.

**1  a**  Analyse **two** benefits for a new business of producing a cash flow forecast.  [8]

> *Adapted from Cambridge International AS & A Level Business (9609)*
> *Paper 12 Q7a, March 2019*

| Example student response | Examiner comments |
|---|---|
| Cash flow forecasts are an estimate of the amount of money expected to flow in and out of a business and includes all projected income and expenses. This is generally calculated monthly. | The first paragraph illustrates that the student understands cash flow forecasts and what role they play in a business. However the answer asks for the benefits of producing a cash flow forecast. These are not seen until the next paragraph. It should be noted that the question asks for two benefits of producing a cash flow forecast. The answer provides more than this (four benefits are provided). Only the first two benefits provided in the answer will be accepted. |
| The benefits for a new business of producing a cash flow forecast include being able to identify potential shortfalls in cash balances in advance, effectively an 'early warning system'. For example, if the completed forecast shows a negative cash balance (for a period) then the business needs to ensure it has a sufficient bank overdraft facility. Alternatively, the business could reschedule some of its payments to cover this period. | |
| A second benefit of producing the cash flow forecast is by highlighting whether the trading performance of the business (revenues, costs and profits) will actually turn into cash and, if not, again it can make corrective action to convert more of its sales into cash inflows. This might, for example, mean the business requests payment immediately, rather than providing credit terms as it had originally planned. The survival of any business is particularly precarious within the first year and the measures outlined may prevent early business failure. | Examples of situations that may arise as well as some application to a new business are included in the response.

Some analysis of the benefits for a small new business of producing a cash flow forecast are included. The second benefit provides an example of developed analysis where the impact is expanded to include a consequence. |
| Completing a cash flow forecast also highlights when payments are due to a business's suppliers and may help the business identify when it can afford to pay suppliers and employees. Suppliers which don't get paid will soon stop supplying the business and disputes will arise if employees are not paid on time, so it is imperative that the fledging business is able to plan when payments are due. | |

| Example student response | Examiner comments |
|---|---|
| Another benefit of the forecast might be enabling the new business to spot problems with customer payments, where the issues are, etc. Equally, by preparing the forecast the business is encouraged to look at how quickly customers are paying their debts. The cash flow forecast does not, of course, ensure that any of these problems can be resolved easily but it will highlight where the issues are so that it can address the challenges.<br><br>Finally, in addition to the internal uses of a cash flow forecast, there may also be external uses for any new business. For example, external stakeholders such as banks may require a cash flow forecast if the business wants a bank loan. | While this is a very good answer, it is far too long for an eight-mark question. Spending time writing unnecessarily lengthy responses to some questions will reduce the time available to answer questions that do require more focus and longer responses.<br><br>*7/8 marks* |

**b** Evaluate how a large food retailer might best improve its profitability ratios. [12]

*Adapted from Cambridge International AS & A Level Business (9609) Paper 12 Q7b, March 2019*

| Example student response | Examiner comments |
|---|---|
| Profitability is illustrated by the gross profit margin and operating profit margin, calculated from the income statement using revenue, cost of sales and expenses. In short, therefore, a business can improve its profitability ratios by either raising prices or reducing the cost of sales and/or expenses.<br><br>Gross profit margin measures the cost of goods sold as a percentage of sales and is calculated by gross profit × 100 / sales revenue. This ratio shows how well a company controls the cost of its inventory and the manufacturing of its products and subsequently passes on the costs to its customers. The larger the gross profit margin, the better for the company. Operating profit margin is calculated by operating profit before interest and tax as a percentage of sales. This is a measure of overall operating efficiency, incorporating all the expenses of ordinary, daily business activity, calculated by operating profit / sales revenue × 100. This ratio shows how much of each sales in dollars shows up as net income after all expenses are paid, e.g., if net profit margin = 5%, then 5 cents of every dollar are profit.<br><br>Both ratios can be improved when a business maximises earnings and minimises expenses. Raising revenue can be done by more effective brand building, reducing the PED of a good, so that the firm can raise prices without a significant drop in sales. Other methods might include a more effective sales process, staff training, updated procedures etc. The business may also be able to raise revenue levels with the use of extension strategies for existing products and improved communications with customers. | This response shows excellent knowledge, beginning with a clear and accurate definition of both profit margins, and there is clear understanding of both demonstrated throughout the beginning of the response.<br><br>The student attempts to apply their findings but it is not obvious from the responses that the question relates to a large food retailer, meaning there is no application shown in the answer.<br><br>There is analysis of the ways to improve profitability ratios in a business, e.g., by raising revenue, which can be done by more effective brand building or reducing the PED of a good. |

| Example student response | Examiner comments |
|---|---|
| Alternatively, a business might improve its profitability ratios by reducing its cost levels. A business may achieve this by finding cheaper resource suppliers to cut its cost of sales, while the business may be able to reduce overheads by adopting cheaper production processes, for example, moving to more capital-intensive methods and so enjoying greater savings from economies of scale, reducing wastage and improving staff training and adopting a JIT inventory management system. The firm could also find ways to reduce overheads, internal staffing and admin costs, utility bills, storage costs and rent etc, while some businesses have found cheaper ways of producing using outsourcing.<br><br>However, businesses will also need to be aware that measures aimed at either increasing sales revenue and/or reducing costs may be expensive in the short term through higher marketing costs, the costs of training and of updating and buying new machinery etc. In addition to the financial costs, there is the loss of time and the impact on quality and potential staff disruption caused by change. | The response is divided in two: methods that a business might use to increase sales revenue and measures that a business might use to reduce costs. There are a range of different measures identified and a reasonable attempt to prioritise the importance of each in raising profitability levels. There is a clear judgement and evaluative comment related to how best to improve profitability ratios, but again there is no application to a large food retailer, impacting this answer's ability to access the top marks it may have achieved with application.<br><br>*7/12 marks* |

For Question 2(a) read the question, the example student response and the commentary provided. Then, in Question 2(b), write an improved answer to the question, using the guidance in the commentary to help you.

2 a Analyse **two** disadvantages to a business of using debt factoring to improve its cash flow. [8]

*Adapted from Cambridge International AS & A Level Business (9609) Paper 12 Q5a, June 2020*

| Example student response | Examiner comments |
|---|---|
| Debt factoring is when a business sells its debts to a third party, and firms will sell some or all of their debts to relieve short-term liquidity issues. The company selling the debt to a third party is then paid a proportion of the full debt. Debt factoring has a number of disadvantages. The first of these is that the full value of the debt is not paid by the debt factor (usually about 80% of the value of the debt is received). This would have a significant impact on a firm's cash flow if a sizeable proportion of a firm's payments were sold in this way and the 20% would have to be written out of company profitability.<br><br>A second disadvantage is that debt factors usually refuse to take the long-term bad debts so the business still has debts that it might struggle to recover, while debts that are easy to recover are easy to sell to debt factors. An additional disadvantage is that some customers might not like having their debt sold to a third party because they will now have to deal with someone outside of the original business they dealt with and in such cases those customers might not want to deal with the business again. | The response demonstrates a good understanding of the term 'debt factoring' and more importantly, the disadvantages of debt factoring, which is what the question is asking for. The response also includes two clear and developed disadvantages of debt factoring.<br><br>There is no reference to a business context in the answer, so it is not applied.<br><br>The first paragraph contains some analysis of the disadvantage, with the impact on cash flow highlighted. This is then developed to consider the consequence of this for (any) business that it would need to write off some of this payment, and this would have an impact on the calculation of profitability. There is no development of analysis shown in the second paragraph. |

| Example student response | Examiner comments |
|---|---|
|  | Basic analysis can be seen in the impact that 'customers may no longer wish to deal with them again', but no consequence of this is provided.<br><br>*5/8 marks* |

**b** Now write an improved answer to Question 2(a).

Work through Question 2(c), then compare your answer to the example student response and commentary.

**c** Evaluate the limitations of using accounting ratios to compare the performance of different businesses. [12]

*Adapted from Cambridge International AS & A Level Business (9609) Paper 12 Q5b, June 2020*

| Example student response | Examiner comments |
|---|---|
| Accounting ratios are calculated from the financial and income statement of a firm using revenue, cost of sales, expenses, assets and liabilities. Ratios provide a record of a firm's profitability, liquidity, efficiency and gearing.<br><br>Financial ratios can provide a great deal of information that a company may find useful, while it is also the case that the use of ratios also has limitations and these can depend on why the ratios are being compared and by whom – if it is a potential investor then they will need a lot more information.<br><br>One obvious limitation is that comparisons can only be reasonably made between businesses in the same industry and of the same size. For example, a large business is likely to have more purchasing power than a small one and is likely to receive discounts, which reduces costs. This will be reflected in ratio analysis and so any comparison between large and small businesses is unfair. Equally, while ratios can show trends over time and between businesses, they need to be used with a degree of caution because, for instance, the accounting techniques used differ between businesses and different methods of depreciation can affect the profitability ratios, making like-for-like comparison difficult.<br><br>A second limitation of their use is that all ratios are calculated from financial statements, which are by definition results based on past information. While this may not present a weakness of ratio analysis, it could do so if the present situations in different businesses are now different. This can happen suddenly if, for instance, one business might be researching and introducing a new product soon which could alter its ratios significantly in the future, while the other is not. This means that while ratios may tell us quite a bit about an organisation's past performance, they tell us less of what is happening now or in the future. | This response demonstrates excellent knowledge of financial ratios, beginning with a definition of all the key ratios and brief explanation of their uses.<br><br>There is good evidence of application to the context of different businesses throughout the answer, such as the differences in comparisons between small and large businesses and reference to businesses who are considering the launch of a new product.<br><br>The response clearly identifies the limitations of the use of financial ratios as a way of measuring business performance. A good example of developed analysis can be found in the third paragraph where there is a discussion about the limitation of using ratios to compare firms that are not the same size, as well as making sure the method of depreciation they use is also the same as this can impact on comparisons. |

| Example student response | Examiner comments |
|---|---|
| Another limitation is that ratios only provide fairly crude quantitative data, which has its use but does not give any qualitative information such as the level of motivation of the employees or company reputation – all factors that are not included on current financial documents but may well have an impact on the financial performance of the business moving forward.<br><br>In conclusion, it is probably most accurate to say that while ratios can provide useful trends and comparisons for comparing the performance of a company over time and with comparable businesses within the same industry, they should be treated with caution and will need to be used in conjunction with other qualitative data to be really useful. | The response could have been improved in its approach to evaluation. High level evaluation requires a developed judgement (in context) and a developed comment (in context). While the response provides lots of well-explained and developed information about the weaknesses of their use, there is only brief coverage on what ratios are used for. The response did, however, end with an evaluative comment. However, this is not related to a business context and adds nothing more than a repetition of points already made. There is no attempt to make a judgement on the greatest limitation or directly answer the question.<br><br>*8/12 marks* |

Question 3(a) has an example student response and commentary provided. Work through the question first, then compare your answer to the example student response and commentary. Then use the guidance in the commentaries in this section to help you answer Question 3 (b).

3  a  Analyse how cost information can be used to monitor and improve the performance of a business. [8]

***Cambridge International AS & A Level Business (9609) Paper 12 Q7a, November 2020***

| Example student response | Examiner comments |
|---|---|
| Information about business costs is critical to management decisions, with different types of cost used to monitor the businesses performance as well as plan strategies to improve business performance. Businesses will rely on cost information to provide information relating to pricing, budgets, targets, profitability and competitors and this is essential for managers. One use of cost information is to allow comparisons to be made, both internally and externally. Based on costing information a business can then change strategy if considered appropriate and necessary, e.g. cost reduction strategies. | The response demonstrates a good understanding of most of the key terms in the question – cost information and business performance. |

| An example of this change in strategy might be when cost information suggests the need for a different production method or pricing strategy to be implemented. Cost information can also be used to control present activities, evaluate past activities and plan for the future. Similarly, cost variances can be analysed to identify significant factors that need attention, while costs may be benchmark indicators of internal and external performance. Cost information can also help with break-even analysis. | There is reference to the concept of cost information to the performance of a business through clear, well-developed examples of how accurate cost information can be used by a business. However, this is not sufficient for application as the points raised could be applied to any business context and there is no real world application shown. Opportunities to provide this have been missed. For example, in paragraph 2 this could have been applied to a business that is looking to launch a new product and needs to work out how much this will cost to identify the effect on pricing and the overall impact on the business's future following a launch. |
|---|---|
| | The response provides basic analysis by identifying some simple impacts on the business from using cost information, such as they can change their strategy. However, none of the points are developed. The answer provides a list of uses of cost information with no explanation of the consequences of these and how business performance will be improved. |
| | The answer provides an unnecessary conclusion. The command word 'analyse' does not require the answer to show skills of evaluation (which includes any judgement comments). This wastes time and shows a lack of understanding of the assessment objectives and command words. |
| | *4/8 marks* |

Try the following question for yourself.

**b** Evaluate the most appropriate source of finance for a private limited company to purchase an additional factory. [12]

**Adapted from Cambridge International AS & A Level Business (9609) Paper 11 Q7b, June 2022**

For Question 4(a) read the question, example student response and commentary provided. Then, in Question 4(b), write your own answer to the question but in the context of an established business in the same field. Use the guidance in the commentary to help you as you answer the question.

**4** **a** Evaluate the importance of cash flow forecasting to a new car hire business. [12]

*Adapted from Cambridge International AS & A Level Business (9609) Paper 12 Q7b, November 2020*

| Example student response | Examiner comments |
|---|---|
| Cash flow forecasting (CFF), also known as cash forecasting, estimates the expected flow of cash coming in and out of a business, across all areas, over a given period of time. A cash forecast may cover the next 6 to 12 months and can be used to identify any funding needs or excess cash in the immediate term.<br><br>A new car hire business can expect a number of challenges when starting up: competition from well-established business, lack of experienced staff, lack of experience among the management as well as the difficulty of establishing itself and winning the trust of customers.<br><br>Given the challenges highlighted above, a cash flow forecast might provide a range of potential benefits to the business. For example, if a business runs out of cash, it may face insolvency, so one obvious benefit of CFF is that it identifies potential shortfalls in cash balances in advance, providing an early warning system. A cash flow forecast will also highlight periods when finances are forecast to be particularly low, allowing the company to take corrective action, ensuring that it can pay employees and suppliers and helping with cash flow management and planning by identifying specific periods of cash deficiency. When a new car hire business sets up it will very often require financing from external stakeholders and the cash flow forecast will help provide, for instance, banks and potential investors with vital information which they may use as evidence before deciding whether to release funds to the business or not.<br><br>When this is applied to a new car hire business, a cash flow forecast might indicate, for example, the need to lease rather than purchase new cars, how to deal with maintenance and renewal costs, as well as how to deal with seasonal cash flow issues.<br><br>In the long term, of course, providing the business survives, other factors may grow in importance. Factors such as customer relationships, cost structures, revenue streams and profitability may be as important as CFF, while factors such as the quality of management/leadership, systems, the quality of the product offer, pricing strategy and marketing, will ultimately determine whether the business succeeds long term or not. | The response begins with a clear definition of cash flow forecasting, illustrating knowledge and understanding of the term.<br><br>There is clear application of the concept of cash flow forecasting in terms of relating the importance of it to a new car hire business, providing relevant examples such as the trade-off between leasing and purchasing stock.<br><br>Analysis is provided by highlighting the specific role of cash flow forecasting in reducing some of the risks associated with a new business, but these stop short of being clearly developed. For example, at the end of the third paragraph development could have been shown by outlining the consequence to the new car hire business of not being able to get funds from banks and potential investors.<br><br>The answer provides a good example of how to approach evaluation. A distinction is made between the short term (where CFF plays a key role in terms of survival) and the long term success of the business. |

| Example student response | Examiner comments |
|---|---|
| In conclusion, however, an accurate cash flow forecast may be the most important factor in the first 12 months of the business. A new car hire business is likely to experience significant financial stress during the first 12 months of operation, with liquidity particularly important to maintain. Completing an accurate and up-to-date cash flow forecast will certainly not alleviate all the difficulties the business is likely to face as it struggles to establish itself in this competitive marketplace. It will, however, allow the businesses to foresee time periods when liquidity might be difficult and make appropriate actions to counter them as much as possible. | It also highlights other factors that might be of equal importance for the firm's long-term survival. The only thing missing is a clear evaluative comment.<br><br>*10/12 marks* |

    **b**    Now write your own answer to Question 4(a), evaluating the importance of cash flow forecasting to an established business in the same field.

The following question has an example student response and commentary provided. Work through the question first, then compare your answer to the example student response and commentary.

**5**

**Planet Internet (PI)**

PI is a public limited company. It is an internet service provider. The business provides fast internet connections to households within Country X. Customers pay an average of $10 per month for the service. More than 80% of the households in the country can access PI's services. The business offers new customers three free months of internet service if they sign a contract for a minimum of 12 months. Very few of PI's customers switch to a competitor's service after the minimum 12-month contract has finished. The internet service market is very competitive. PI has an objective to become the largest internet service provider in Country X. The marketing director, Alisha, believes that if PI is going to achieve its objective, then the company needs new customers. She thinks that the key to gaining more new customers is to focus on promotion. Alisha has prepared some secondary market research comparing PI with its main competitors in Country X (see Table 1). Some of the directors are disappointed with the financial performance of PI compared to its competitors.

| | Planet Internet (PI) | Totally Broadband (TB) | W Solutions (WS) |
|---|---|---|---|
| Market share | 31% | 32% | 15% |
| Value of sales | $12.4 billion | $12.8 billion | $6 billion |
| Gross profit margin | 74% | 70% | 70% |
| Net profit margin | 8% | 12% | 16% |
| Working capital | ($45 000) | $300 000 | $0 |
| Current ratio | 0.9:1 | 3:1 | 1.1 |

**Table 1:** Research about the internet service providers in Country X, 2018

Refer to Table 1. Evaluate the financial performance of PI compared to its competitors. [12]

| Example student response | Examiner comments |
|---|---|
| When evaluating the performance of PI compared to its competitors it is clear that no one indicator is sufficient and more information is required to properly compare its performance with TB and WS. What little information is contained in the table means some assumptions can be made. For example, the gross profit margin of PI is higher that the competitors, suggesting that PI is efficient in terms of controlling its direct costs and one suggestion might be that it has been able to take advantage of economies of scale effectively. That said, its net profit margin is lower than all of the other competitors', suggesting that PI is inefficient in terms of indirect costs (diseconomies of scale).<br><br>One very worrying aspect of the business is that its working capital is negative, suggesting that PI could struggle to pay short-term debts. For example, does the business have enough cash to pay for any promotion, will PI be able to survive the short term and will PI need a short-term source of finance? The current ratio shows that PI does not have enough current assets to cover its current liabilities. By contrast, one of its competitors (TB) is perhaps too liquid – it seems to be holding too many CA and this questions whether or not this is efficient.<br><br>Web solutions also enjoys a much better (twice) net profit margin than PI, which raises the question, how can this business be so much more efficient? Can PI copy any of its techniques? Interestingly, though, PI enjoys twice the market share of WS and so it could be argued that this is of greater importance (in the long term) than short-term liquidity measures.<br><br>Overall, PI is clearly doing better than its competitors. | The answer shows a clear knowledge and understanding of both liquidity and profitability. There is good use of terminology related to this topic.<br><br>Application is shown throughout the answer. This can be seen through the identification that PI's GP was the highest among the three business in the table, as well as the comment that it was the only one of the three that has a negative working capital, making very good use of the provided data.<br><br>The response also contains sufficient analysis by the recognition that PI's GP was an indicator that it has low direct costs, while the poor liquidity ratio suggests that it may struggle to pay its debts. However, there are far too many questions presented in the answer. This is not a suitable approach to take: the answer should not be asking more questions. If there are any areas of information that are lacking, these need to be addressed within the points made and explanation given to why that information would be useful.<br><br>The answer concludes with a simple statement that PI is doing better than its competitors. There is no justification of this statement, so evaluation is basic and undeveloped. There is also no attempt to apply the judgement to PI, other than by name, which is not sufficient.<br><br>*7/12 marks* |